FORGOTTEN VOICES
DUNKIRK

Also available in the Forgotten Voices series:

Forgotten Voices of the Great War
Forgotten Voices of the Great War (illustrated)
Forgotten Voices of the Somme

Lest We Forget: Forgotten Voices from 1914–1945

Forgotten Voices of the Second World War
Forgotten Voices of the Second World War (illustrated)
Forgotten Voices of the Blitz and the Battle for Britain
Forgotten Voices of the Holocaust
Forgotten Voices of the Secret War
Forgotten Voices of D-Day
Forgotten Voices of Burma
Forgotten Voices: Desert Victory

Forgotten Voices of the Falklands

Forgotten Voices of the Victoria Cross

FORGOTTEN VOICES
DUNKIRK

IN ASSOCIATION WITH THE
IMPERIAL WAR MUSEUM

JOSHUA LEVINE

EBURY
PRESS

5 7 9 10 8 6 4

This edition published 2011
First published in 2010 by Ebury Press, an imprint of Ebury Publishing
A Random House Group company

Introduction © Peter Snow 2010
Text © Joshua Levine and Imperial War Museum 2010
Photographs © Imperial War Museum 2010

Joshua Levine has asserted his right to be identified as the author of this work
in accordance with the Copyright, Designs and Patents Act 1988

The Random House Group Limited Reg. No. 954009

Addresses for companies within the Random House Group can be found at
www.randomhouse.co.uk

A CIP catalogue record for this book is available from the British Library

The Random House Group Limited supports The Forest Stewardship Council®
(FSC®), the leading international forest-certification organisation. Our books
carrying the FSC label are printed on FSC®-certified paper. FSC is the only
forest-certification scheme supported by the leading environmental organisations,
including Greenpeace. Our paper procurement policy can be found at
www.randomhouse.co.uk/environment

Printed and bound by CPI Group (UK) Ltd, Croydon, CR0 4YY

ISBN 9780091932213

To buy books by your favourite authors and register for offers visit
www.randomhouse.co.uk

Contents

Acknowledgements   vi

Introduction by Peter Snow   vii

Phoney War   1

The March to War   39

A Fighting Retreat   55

The Trap Tightens   115

Massacres   143

Nearing Dunkirk   159

Evacuation   177

Coming Home   237

The Fight Goes On   255

Back in Blighty   281

Index of Contributors   301

General Index   304

Acknowledgements

I would like to thank the wonderful team in the Sound Archive at the Imperial War Museum. I am hugely indebted to Margaret Brooks, Peter Hart, Richard McDonough, Richard Hughes and James Atkinson for their enthusiasm, knowledge and generosity of spirit. They continue to inspire me. I would like to thank Liz Bowers, Abigail Ratcliffe and Madeleine James in the Museum publishing department. I am grateful to historians Terry Charman and Nick Hewitt who took the time and effort to check the text for accuracy – although any errors or omissions are solely my responsibility. My thanks to Josephine Garnier, Rosanna Wilkinson and Mariusz Gasior in the photographic archive. I would like to acknowledge Liz Marvin, Charlotte Cole and Jake Lingwood at Ebury Publishing, as well as Jim Gill at United Agents. I am grateful to Vicky Thomas, a woman who knows her way around the archive blindfolded. I wish her every success with her biography of Ursula Betts, the 'Naga Queen'. My most profound thanks to Claire Price, who worked on the book and gave me so much support. Finally, I would like to pay tribute to the individuals quoted in this book. As the events of 1940 drift beyond living memory, we must acknowledge our debt to them for the liberties that we enjoy today. Without their sacrifices, our world might have been a very different place.

Joshua Levine, January 2010

Introduction by
Peter Snow

This is the spellbinding story of the greatest rescue operation in British history – told by the men and women who were there. At the end of May 1940 Britain was about to lose its army. Rolled back by Hitler's overwhelming blitzkrieg, more than a quarter of a million men were trapped in a tightening stranglehold with their backs to the beaches of Dunkirk. One veteran soldier, who said he had tears in his eyes, summed up his feelings with the words: 'I never thought I'd see the British Army like this.' Winston Churchill's government hoped the massive seaborne armada it launched would save 45,000. Miraculously no fewer than 338,000 Allied troops were landed safely on Britain's south coast between 26 May and 5 June, 1940.

Forgotten Voices of Dunkirk brings alive for us, as never before, the physical and mental agony of those struggling to survive and the risks taken by their rescuers. Thanks to the invaluable resource of the Sound Archives in the Imperial War Museum, we can read first-hand memories of the desperate fighting withdrawal from Belgium and northern France. Sergeant Knight tells how he drove back through heavy enemy fire to retrieve some wounded men left behind in the rush for the beaches. Trooper Cheeseman recalls how his truck picked up a fleeing husband with a heavily pregnant wife. When she went into labour with the enemy closing in on all sides, the sergeant in charge took the huge risk of stopping the vehicle while she gave birth to a baby girl in the back of the lorry. There are many stories of courage and, yes, of cowardice too, and harsh tales of summary justice dispensed to those on the beaches who tried to jump the queue to board the ships.

Amid all this human suffering there is touching testament to the sense of humour of those facing the direst adversity. A fatally wounded friend falls into a trench beside Lance Corporal Lawrence Greggain with the words: 'Sorry to drop in on you like this, Corporal.' Captain Humphrey Bredin is delighted to find a steward aboard the Isle Of Man paddle steamer that takes him off the beach. Hoping to be served a beer, he's told he'll have to wait till the ship reaches the statutory three-mile limit.

This book, magnificently edited by Joshua Levine, is a great tribute to the extraordinary spirit of an army shattered in battle but determined not to surrender. More than a thousand vessels – 222 Royal Navy craft and some 800 civilian boats of all sorts of sizes and descriptions crossed the Channel in seas that were mercifully and unusually calm to bring the hard-pressed troops home. We hear how the Germans brought every available weapon to bear on them, right up to their last moments in France. One young second lieutenant, Peter Martin, had got his whole platoon into a whaler which made for a Royal Navy destroyer. Before they could reach it, it suddenly upped its anchor and started off for England: 'The padre leapt to his feet and shouted, "Lord, Lord, why hast thou forsaken us?" The boat rocked and water poured in. With one accord everyone yelled, "SIT DOWN!" ' – and the sound was so loud that the destroyer turned round and came back for them.

An essential ingredient in any compelling military history is evidence from eyewitnesses of the harrowing events they experience. I am currently collecting first-hand accounts of soldiers who fought in the campaigns against Napoleon Bonaparte 200 years ago. That was the first major war in which large numbers of men of all ranks had the wit, courage and literacy to write their very frank accounts of what they went through. Today we have the resources to record the voices of even greater numbers of those who are prepared to speak. And this book is the fullest and most colourful compendium of voices from Dunkirk that I have yet heard or read.

From this great treasure house of accounts of individual experiences we get a deep insight into the feelings of the men and women who were astonished at being welcomed home as 'heroes' after what most of them regarded as a crushing reverse in Britain's first confrontation with Nazi Germany. We now know, and this book helps us to understand, how these events gave rise to the 'Dunkirk Spirit' that was to inspire the country as the war got worse, becoming a phrase that is still used to signify the strength of the British in adversity. Their determination to get home and the tenacity of their rescuers allowed the British Army to survive and fight another battle. In JB Priestley's words, they 'snatched glory from defeat and then swept on to victory...the little holiday steamers made an excursion to hell and came back glorious.'

Peter Snow, January 2010

Phoney War

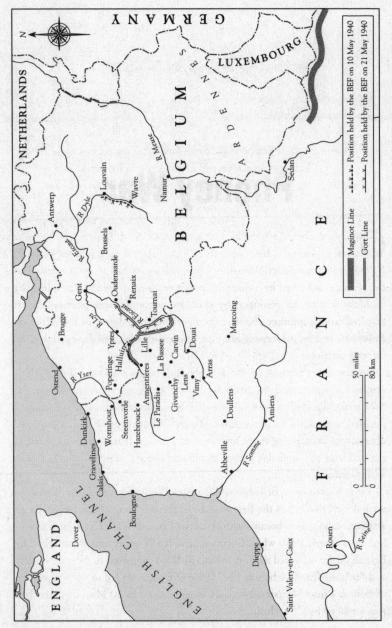

North France and Belgium

When we got to France, it had been like a holiday at the beginning.
It wasn't until the German breakthrough came and we started getting
shelled and bombed and shot at that we realised we might lose our lives.

Operation Dynamo – the evacuation of the British Expeditionary Force from Dunkirk – has come to be remembered as a great episode in British military history. Winston Churchill described it as 'a miracle of deliverance, achieved by valour, by perseverance, by perfect discipline, by faultless service, by resource, by skill, by unconquerable fidelity'. Yet it resulted from a military disaster: the overwhelming defeat of the Allies on European soil by a German army of fewer divisions and tanks and often inferior artillery.

In the years leading to the British declaration of war, Adolf Hitler's armies had reoccupied the Rhineland and taken possession of Austria, the Sudetenland and Czechoslovakia. On 1 September, 1939, the Wehrmacht invaded Poland. Two days later, Great Britain and France delivered ultimatums demanding the withdrawal of German troops. The ultimatums expired later the same day – and Britain and France were once again at war with Germany.

On 9 September a British Expeditionary Force of four infantry divisions set sail for France, but the first months of the war were characterised by an artificial calm which became known as the Phoney War. The calm was broken on 9 April, 1940 when Germany invaded Norway and Denmark. The British Army mounted a disorganised, ill-fated campaign to defend Norway and the consequent debate in the House of Commons led to the resignation of British Prime Minister, Neville Chamberlain. On 10 May, Chamberlain was replaced by Churchill.

On the same day, Germany invaded Holland, Belgium and Luxembourg. The Allies had long been anticipating a German offensive – but they expected it to come through Belgium, and they expected it to lead to an attritional struggle similar to the Great War. This thinking was encouraged by the existence of the mighty Maginot Line – a complex system of fortifications constructed by the French along their border with Germany. However, Hitler was thinking less conventionally. Following the advice of General Erich von Manstein, he planned an attack led by panzer tank divisions whose main thrust would be through the hilly, wooded area of the Ardennes, an area that was not protected by the Maginot Line, but by relatively weak French divisions. Marshal Pétain had described the Ardennes as 'impenetrable [to an invader] so long as we make special provisions in them'. But no special provisions were made. Once the panzer divisions had thundered through the region and crossed the River Meuse, it was planned that they sweep round in a 'sickle' motion which would cut the Allied armies in two.

The attack began with air raids and parachute drops on neutral Belgium and Holland. Belgium's proud Eben-Emael fortress was swiftly taken by German glider troops. The Allies responded with their longstanding plan of sending divisions to the Belgian River Dyle to block the expected German advance. The British Expeditionary Force – commanded by Lord Gort, a Great War Victoria Cross winner – moved up from the 'Gort Line' on the Franco–Belgian border to take its position on the Dyle between the Belgian and French armies. It was duly confronted by the divisions of German Army Group B, commanded by General von Bock, unaware that it was falling into a German trap, or that the course of the campaign – and almost that of the entire war – was to be dictated by events further to the south.

Sapper Frederick Carter
Artisans Works Company and 135 Excavator Company, Royal Engineers
When I heard war had broken out, I didn't really worry. It was rough in England at the time; unemployment was very bad, and I thought, maybe, if we had a war, something might happen. I was out of work, and I thought I'd join the Royal Engineers and work as I was used to working – as a concreter. Nobody seemed upset about the war starting. The way old Hitler was taking

General Ironside, Winston Churchill, General Gamelin, Lord Gort

over the world, we thought we should finish him off. I thought it would be over quick.

2nd Lieutenant Richard Annand
2nd Battalion, Durham Light Infantry

At the outbreak of war, I was very enthusiastic. It justified all the training that one had done, and it gave the chance to make some little contribution towards the task of defeating the enemy.

Sergeant John Williams
6th Battalion, Durham Light Infantry

We felt sorry for people who weren't in the army. We were having such a good time! We were being soldiers, and all the girls thought we were smart and handsome, and these poor sods were still working in the pit and the office. But I noticed that various of my contemporaries suddenly developed asthma and ailments we'd never known them to have before. One or two said, 'I wish I was fit enough to join up.' They were as fit as I was! It's human nature… but who would want men like that in the battalion?

Sapper Percy Beaton
218 Army Troops Company, Royal Engineers

I used to be called 'bolshie' in the army because I tended to question everything. And I often said, 'That's stupid!' which didn't go down well with the senior NCOs – especially the old hardened ones. I thought lots of things were stupid. You know – sloping arms, presenting arms, saluting people. As a civilian, you had your own life, and you were never dictated to. But when you went into the army, you were dictated to by a load of people who, in many cases, were completely ignorant. And the rules of the army at the time! Such as 'dumb insolence' – if you looked at somebody with a scowl on your face, you could be put on a charge and get seven days confined to barracks. *For looking at somebody!*

Lance Corporal Lawrence Greggain
5th Battalion, Border Regiment

We were on the move, and this time it was overseas. The usual rumours went round the companies. Some said we were to be fitted out with tropical kit and were bound for Burma or India. In contrast, others said they had seen cold-weather clothing arriving, and that we were bound for Arctic conditions, possibly Norway. We in the stores knew that they were both wrong.

Sergeant John Williams
6th Battalion, Durham Light Infantry
Before we went out to France, my mother said, 'Don't shoot any of those poor German boys, will you?' 'No, mum,' I said, 'not unless they shoot me first.'

Lance Bombardier William Harding
6th Battery, 2nd Regiment, Royal Artillery
We entrained for France at Lichfield Station. There was military police on the platform organising everything. It was like going on an outing. We were in a very happy, jolly mood.

Sapper Frederick Carter
Artisans Works Company and 135 Excavator Company, Royal Engineers
We left for France by train from Clacton, and it went all round the stations – Cambridge, Oxford, Sutton, down to Southampton. When we got on the boat, we were held up for 24 hours, because there was a submarine in the Channel.

Sapper Percy Beaton
218 Army Troops Company, Royal Engineers
The mood on the ship going out was quite cheerful. There were one or two people who'd just been married prior to being called up, and they weren't very happy. But most of the single lads were fine. Of course, there was so much unemployment about at that time that it was something for people to do – and there was about 14 shillings a week coming into their pockets.

Lance Bombardier William Harding
6th Battery, 2nd Regiment, Royal Artillery
We reached Cherbourg and we disembarked and lined up. After a lot of manoeuvring about, it was decided that the Scots would parade through the town. The Scots had their band with them, their pipes and drums. We were formed up behind them, and behind us was the Royal Air Force units. And we

marched through the town. It's a wonderful memory, people nearly falling out of the windows, and throwing flowers at us. Wonderful!

Private Thomas Russ
6th Battalion, Durham Light Infantry
As we left for France, one lad was telling me he could speak French. For a couple of days he was rehearsing all this French, and what was the first thing he said when he got off the boat? 'Where's the NAAFI, mate?'

Sapper Percy Beaton
218 Army Troops Company, Royal Engineers
My very first punishment was on the boat going across to France. All the tall chaps who were over five foot ten were issued with rifles because there were only 30 rifles between about 300 of us, and I was one of the unfortunate ones to get a rifle handed to me. I didn't want a rifle; it didn't interest me. But unbeknownst to me, everybody had been told to clean these rifles – and believe you me, they wanted some cleaning because they were thick packed with grease. They were told to be on top deck at a certain time with the rifles clean. And of course, I turned up with the rifle just as it was issued, and I got seven days' sanitary duties which I carried out when I got to France, in this school, and it was absolutely filthy. The French army had been sleeping in it, and there was about two foot of straw in every room. And there was excreta all over the place. The French had obviously wiped their backsides with their hands and wiped it down the wall. You can imagine as a young lad of 20, it didn't go down very well with me.

Sergeant John Williams
6th Battalion, Durham Light Infantry
The morale of the battalion was high – we were going to the magic place of France where a lot of our parents and uncles had been. We landed at Cherbourg, and my contemporaries were saying, 'You can talk French, can't you?' 'Yeah,' I said. So we went down, and there was a stall selling oranges under flickering gas lamps. I said, '*Combien des oranges, madame?*' But I was surprised to see all these blaring lights, because we had the blackout in England. All these bars and brothels with lights on. We saw some kids who said, '*Ici France! Vous Anglais! Allez!*' Cheeky little buggers…

A British labour contingent arrives in France in February 1940

Reverend Cyril Scarborough
4th Battalion, Royal Sussex Regiment

We landed at one of the ports, and this chap I knew was in the bar. He was a secret service sort of chap. After all the talks we'd been given about security, my first words to him were, 'What are you doing here?' Of all the silly remarks to have made.

Lance Bombardier William Harding
6th Battery, 2nd Regiment, Royal Artillery

We were taken to a French convent. We were told by our officer commanding that we were being granted an empty wing in this convent, on condition that we respected the privacy of the nuns, and we never interfered in any shape or form with noise. We were not even to approach them in conversation, not even to say good morning.

Sergeant John Williams
6th Battalion, Durham Light Infantry

Once we were in France, we were issued with battledress. Away went our regimentals. There was no longer any sign of the Durham Light Infantry, and no buttons to polish. We felt as though we'd slipped down the social scale.

Sapper Frederick Carter
Artisans Works Company and 135 Excavator Company, Royal Engineers

My battledress was very dodgy. You went to the quartermaster's stores, and he issued you with a uniform, and you had to do the best you could. Mine was three or four sizes too big. I had to shorten the trousers myself.

2nd Lieutenant Richard Annand
2nd Battalion, Durham Light Infantry

After arriving in France, we spent a week in some really lovely country in the Le Mans area, which was nothing but peach trees – and we nearly made ourselves ill eating peaches.

Lance Bombardier William Harding
6th Battery, 2nd Regiment, Royal Artillery

We were like a battery split in two. Half our battery had been sent to Singapore several weeks earlier, and the numbers were made up with reservists. Us young soldiers were all 20 to 25, but the reservists were older men and they were totally different to us. We didn't get on with them, and they didn't want to get on with us. They looked upon us as a lot of boys, and we were a little wary of them because they were such boasters. They kept talking of places all over the world we'd only heard of. And their main topic – any time of day – was women. They were like a lot of sex maniacs. We didn't believe half what they said.

Sergeant John Williams
6th Battalion, Durham Light Infantry

Down in Normandy, at a place called Fresnay-sur-Sarthe, we didn't think there was a war on. Everybody was nice. Normandy peasants. There was a widow there who was running a restaurant. We used to go in and ask for *oeufs sur le plat* – fried eggs. But she couldn't fry an egg! So I went into the kitchen, one day, and asked whether I could show her how to fry an egg. So I started getting my eggs for free and I used to sit drinking wine with her when the customers weren't there. And eventually, I had to fight this widow off. She became amorous. I wasn't interested in her – and she must have been slightly myopic if she was interested in me. But the food was very cheap and ample. Apples and eggs and bread. There was no rationing. It was like a holiday really.

Major Donald Wilson-Haffenden
HQ, 1st Division

We had gone to France thinking we should be in a war like the 1914 affair, but after a while we bedded down and got used to the idea that we were going to wait until the Germans moved. While we were there, on one occasion, I went to see the French Maginot Line. It was a wonderful thing, but it was completely designed for static warfare. The intention was that they would stop the Germans in front of the Maginot Line but you had this enormous gap on the left, which wouldn't protect us against the Germans coming through Belgium.

THE MAGINOT LINE

Private Harry Dennis
1st Battalion, East Surrey Regiment
We did a spell in the Maginot Line. Two weeks. We were billeted in old dis-
used houses in the village in front of the line, and we did our foot patrols into
no-man's-land, as it were, towards the German positions on the Siegfried
Line. The Maginot Line looked enormous. It was a huge concrete structure
and from the front it looked impregnable. We were impressed with the building of it, and the French treated it with great pomp and circumstance. They
gave us all big round badges that said, *'Ils ne passeront pas'* – 'They will not
pass.' It was propaganda. And while we were there, we saw the famous French
80-ton tanks. They looked more impressive than they turned out to be. They
showed us tank demonstrations – pulling a tree out by its roots. And we, naturally, thought, 'Well, this is it! The Germans are not going to get past here,
so if we keep behind this line, we're going to be all right!' We thought that the
line was impregnable. It wasn't until afterwards that you realised it was a
white elephant.

Private Ernest Leggett
2nd Battalion, Royal Norfolk Regiment
I remember thinking what a monstrous thing this Maginot Line was. With all
these guns, it was impregnable: there was no doubt about that. So long as
the enemy came from the front. But we wondered what would happen if the
enemy didn't come from the front. If they came from the right flank, or
the left flank. We were wondering that a long while before 10 May.

Captain Peter Barclay
2nd Battalion, Royal Norfolk Regiment
We had our chance of going up to the Maginot Line. It was absolutely unbelievable. It was controlled like the hub of a battleship. There was an enormous
control room with buttons and switches all over the place, deep down in the
bowels of the fort. When a mortar, for example, was called upon to fire, a but-
ton was pressed and a cupola on the top of a tower rose up. This mortar fired,
and having fired, it was lowered down again. All these guns that the Maginot
Line was equipped with had specific areas to fire on to. The territory in front

of the Maginot Line, including the ditches and the barbed wire entanglements, were chequered out in squares, and certain weapons were designated to bring fire to bear on particular squares. So, depending on what the observation posts reported, the sector commander in the control room would bring fire to bear on any particular area. It was the most complicated and fascinating arrangement. And there were little railway lines running all over the place. The heavy shells weren't manhandled at all. They were run in on pulleys and fed into the breeches of the guns. It was all mechanised to the nth degree – and I believe it had a very adverse affect on the mentality of the French forces as a whole. They just sat pretty in their positions. They seemed dead set against any form of patrolling, and they just sat in their trenches all through the night and waited for anything to happen that might happen. They were totally un-offensive minded.

Private Ernest Leggett
2nd Battalion, Royal Norfolk Regiment
In the mornings when we went for our ablutions we could see Germans on the other side of the Maginot Line. In the distance, we would wave at them and they would wave back. Where was the war? It was like waving at somebody across the street. We weren't feeling bloodthirsty. We knew the Germans' reputation, and what they'd done to Poland, but I had no great animosity to them at that point. And I don't think the others did either.

Captain Peter Barclay
2nd Battalion, Royal Norfolk Regiment
We went on patrols from our position in the Ligne de Contact, which was forward of the Maginot Line, and from which we were in contact with the German forward element for a week in early 1940. It was important for higher authority to know who was confronting us. So my commanding officer wanted me to go out – because it's jolly important to be offensive in this situation. And one wanted to know a bit about what sort of set-up there was on the other side of the enormously elaborate barbed wire entanglement that the Germans had in front of their positions. Also, a prisoner was wanted for identification purposes. So I went out on patrol with five – one other officer and three chaps. We went a long way into the German positions and discovered a great deal of information. The German positions were mostly breastworks – because the

British troops march into Fort de Sainghain on the Belgian frontier

An underground passage in a British sector of the Maginot Line

ground was so hard and it gave them a better field of fire. We didn't get a pris-oner, but we found a house that they'd been using until very shortly previously. When we came out of this house, we were spotted and we came under very heavy fire, and we had a very tricky time getting back home. A grenade landed between my legs – and it damaged my boots, but it didn't damage me.

Captain Anthony Rhodes
253 Field Company, Royal Engineers
We were stationed at the village of Veckring, and about a mile in front of it was the front line, in a wood occupied by a company of the Norfolk Regiment. They were all in dugouts, overlooking the German lines. Across the valley you could see the German outposts. To give some idea of how quiet everything was, we saw through our glasses a German soldier on the other side come out of the wood with a broom and start sweeping in front of the fence. The major I was with, who was fairly belligerent and felt that war was war, said to the Norfolks' major, 'Look, there's a German! Shoot him!' He was told, 'No, no. We mustn't shoot him because if we shoot at him, they may shoot back.' That was the only form of infantry war going on. Every now and then a shell landed, but they were always delivered in open territory. The reason being that we didn't want to destroy anything or kill anybody in case it started the war – which seemed rather strange. This was the 'Phoney War'.

During those nine months in France we had at least four 'flaps'. In November, at the end of December, again in February and March, when the Germans had suddenly concentrated on the Belgian frontier. Our intelligence must have got wind of it and it seemed as if they were going to invade at any moment. We thought the attack was coming, and we were going to have to go in. I had to go and look at the bridges in Belgium and report back on what state they were in for demolition.

THE GORT LINE

2nd Lieutenant Peter Vaux
4th Battalion, Royal Tank Regiment
When we arrived in France, we were told that there was the main Maginot Line, and from there to the sea was the Petit Maginot Line. And that we were

to be behind the Petit Maginot Line as a counter-attack force. But when we went to the Petit Maginot Line, it didn't exist at all. It was just a few pillboxes at perhaps a mile or two apart. Our infantry went up there and they started digging like mad. Digging trenches and putting up barbed wire, and sticking railway lines along the edges of ditches in the ground as tank obstacles. But this Petit Maginot Line was nothing more than a line on the map.

Colonel William Morgan
General Staff Officer, Grade 1, 1 Division

The first Gort Line was an anti-tank ditch which was not concreted. It was practically on the frontier, and it was supported by a series of manned concrete pillboxes that were being built when I arrived in January 1940. The position was rather flimsily wired. The country was flat and there was no observation at all. There were still many civilians in the area, going backwards and forwards across the frontier, and there was no security at all. I don't remember having any confidence in the strength of the line. It might have been a useful stopgap – but no more.

Lieutenant D'Arcy McCloughin
9 Field Company, Royal Engineers

My men had to set up concrete pillboxes, but the day of the bulldozer had not yet arrived, and for a long time the BEF didn't have any units which operated earth-moving machinery. Compared with the pillboxes that were put up in a hurry in England in June 1940, the pillboxes were big – about 20 to 30 feet across and 10 feet high, roughly circular with narrow slits and windows for guns or machine guns. Ours were located in somebody's garden, some way out from the town, and there was a great deal of upset on the part of the family when they heard their garden was going to get a pillbox – but I was kept away from the recriminations and arguments.

Captain Henry Faure Walker
HQ, 7th Guards Brigade

The men were occupied entirely with improving the position, and they used to work as navvies for seven or eight hours a day – which at least kept them fit and occupied. The sector consisted of a few anti-tank pillboxes – and nothing else. The so-called anti-tank obstacle was the River Marque, which was a shallow stream about five yards wide, and three feet deep, which would not have stopped a motor car, let alone a tank. The ground was mostly flat fenland and the water table was a few inches under the surface, so that it was quite impossible to dig trenches. We made the best of a bad job by erecting breastworks. These consisted of peat, and were revetted by the kind of basketwork fascines of which one saw drawings from the Crimean War. They would not have stopped a bullet, or a shell, and would probably have been washed away by heavy rain.

2nd Lieutenant Richard Annand
2nd Battalion, Durham Light Infantry
We remained on the Franco–Belgian frontier for the entire eight or nine months of the Phoney War. We were engaged in digging the Gort Line, which involved building breastworks upwards rather than trenches downwards. We had to try to get rid of the water as best we could. I found that if I did a bit of digging myself, I got more work out of the men. But an order came round from the brigadier that no officers were allowed to dig; they had to supervise the men. I think it was dictated by the theory that familiarity breeds contempt. But I'm afraid I didn't take much notice of the brigadier's orders, and one day – unbeknownst to me – the brigadier arrived at the top of the trench. He saw me digging, but I was in battledress, and I looked much the same as any other man. The brigadier was rather a sarcastic man, and after he left the trench, he turned to the colonel and said, 'I notice you have some very well-spoken private soldiers in your battalion…'

Major Donald Wilson-Haffenden
HQ, 1st Division
We always knew that we were going to try and stop the Germans on the Belgian frontier and it always struck us that it was very stupid, pouring all these tons and tons of cement into pillboxes along the French border, that we were going to leave before the war started.

Captain Henry Faure Walker
HQ, 7th Guards Brigade
At our defensive position on the outskirts of Lille, we had no facilities for any kind of tactical training, as we were not allowed to go on to the agricultural

A party of the Border Regiment prepares defences, February 1940

land, and there was no training area within 50 miles. So beyond a short period of spring drills on the roads and in the village squares, the Guards received no training whatsoever. The guardsmen were fairly comfortably billeted but they were extremely bored. They were in the houses of the industrial workers – but other than the pursuit of their hosts' daughters, there was no amusement or sport available. I must say, they behaved extremely well. Morale was high in spite of their boredom, and they were a real credit to the Brigade of Guards.

Sergeant John Williams
6th Battalion, Durham Light Infantry

We were all conscious of the fact that we weren't there just for fun – but we had no indication of anything that we could expect. If anything, there was a slight drop-off in discipline in France. Up until October, November, we'd been polishing our brass buttons and wearing our service dress. Then we got into this battledress which had no buttons to clean. Our gaiters had to be blancoed and our boots polished, but discipline's a strange thing. We weren't the smart, button-shining people we'd been a month before, but we still knew how to march and conduct ourselves in a proper fashion.

Sapper Percy Beaton
218 Army Troops Company, Royal Engineers

People were underestimating the Germans. There was a story running round that all the German tanks were cardboard, made of papier mâché, that holidaymakers had been going along in Germany, and these papier mâché tanks had come out of the trees, and the car had gone straight through them. These were the sorts of rumours running around.

Sergeant John Williams
6th Battalion, Durham Light Infantry

The thing is, if a German soldier had walked through our village, I probably wouldn't have recognised him. I'd have thought he was a member of the Belgian army. We knew roughly that the Germans wore grey-green uniforms, that they had different-shaped helmets, but we didn't know very much else. There was a lot of singing of that unfortunate song, 'We're going to hang out the washing on the Siegfried Line', which later became an ironic tune.

Major Donald Wilson-Haffenden
HQ, 1st Division

Among my own contemporaries, we were pretty sure that the Germans wouldn't have entered into a war unless they were far better equipped than we were told they were.

Private Harry Dennis
1st Battalion, East Surrey Regiment

We were billeted in an old carbon factory at a place called Halluin on the French–Belgian border, south of Lille. I don't know how long work had stopped there, but the place was absolutely filthy. You can imagine carbon being manufactured... it was black, and it was everywhere. We had to make ourselves comfortable, so naturally we shifted stuff around, we swept and scrubbed, we moved boxes and crates, planks of wood, bits of old machinery, bundles of wire, and eventually we did get the place reasonably clean. And then we had a shock when we went to read our daily orders one morning. We were told that we would be charged for barrack damages out of our pay. For moving stuff and changing things! It's the first time I have seen the British soldier near to mutiny. The chaps were really up in arms.

Of course, they always look for a ringleader, and if they can find him, they accuse him of mutiny. That shuts the others up. But very wisely, nobody became the ringleader. We all objected en bloc. We made so many verbal representations to our officers that they could see that everybody was objecting, and they couldn't get one particular individual to say that he was representing the others. We were saying that we had improved the place, not damaged it. And the charge of barrack room damage was stopped.

Sergeant John Williams
6th Battalion, Durham Light Infantry

In February we moved just a few miles west of Amiens. We were billeted in a parish hall. I found myself talking a little more to the locals. I remember one old man pointing towards a ravine, and saying, 'We killed a German down there with sickles!' I said, 'Were the Germans after you when they discovered you killed one of their men? I believe in the last war, the Germans were rather oppressive!' 'Oh no,' he said, 'this was in 1870.'

Sapper Percy Beaton
218 Army Troops Company, Royal Engineers

We went to Le Tréport where we were given a very large hotel called the Trianon which had to be converted into a hospital. And the French used it disgustingly. We had to clear out all this straw out of the rooms and wash all the walls down. And there was an instance where I put my foot in it good and proper. There was a big marble staircase, and as I was washing it down with water, down the staircase came Lord Gort, Hore-Belisha and a load of dignitaries. I said to them, 'Mind out where you're going! You're making my bloody stairs dirty! I've just cleaned them!' They looked most surprised that somebody had spoken to them like that. And I was severely reprimanded by a young captain who said, 'Do you know who you're talking to?' I said, 'I haven't a bloody clue and I couldn't care less. Look at my stairs!'

2nd Lieutenant Peter Vaux
4th Battalion, Royal Tank Regiment

A tank regiment is a very close-knit affair. I had four light tanks, and we would exercise together, we would cook together, we would sleep together. In our time off, I would take them swimming, and we would play games together. We were very close indeed. And the more we lived in the way we were living in France, the closer we became. There was no question, for example, of the troop sergeant going off to his wife and sleeping at home as we would do in England. Or the soldiers going out to the pictures with their girlfriends – because it wasn't like that.

Captain Henry Faure Walker
HQ, 7th Guards Brigade

The owners of the big ostentatious houses and villas in the area had somehow arranged it that they were immune from billeting, and our guardsmen were living in not-very-great-comfort in the houses of the industrial workers, and were not allowed to occupy these spacious mansions that dotted the countryside. Finally, my brigadier told me to arrange with the French billeting officer to take a census of the accommodation that was available, and to get the guardsmen into less crowded and more comfortable accommodation. This would ease the strain on both the guardsmen and their somewhat unwilling hosts. This was difficult because the owners of the smart houses were friendly with the local politicians, but I discovered that the mayor of Roubaix was an ardent communist, and that the billeting officer had been either an ardent right-winger or – more likely – heavily bribed by the owners of the big houses. I found out when the billeting officer was going on leave for a few days, and I invited the mayor and the second-in-command in the billeting office (who was also a communist) to come round with me to take the census. And, of course, the first properties we visited were the large houses belonging to the factory owners and managers.

From my point of view, it was a most amusing expedition, as my staff car would arrive at the front door of some magnificent house and we'd ring the bell, to be greeted by a servant. I announced that the billeting commission had arrived. In no time, the agitated proprietor would arrive to say that his property was exempt. The mayor, kitted out in his tricolour sash and chain of office, was armed with the relevant law, which had been in existence since Napoleonic times, which said that nobody was exempt from billeting soldiers when they were defending the country. We would say that we must inspect the house to see if there was room for British soldiers. With horror on his face, the proprietor would take us round the house.

In one case, we went into a lovely room full of billiard tables and ping-pong tables. The mayor asked, 'What is the purpose of this room, monsieur?' 'Ah, it's the children's games room,' said the owner. 'Not necessary in wartime!' said the mayor. 'Fifteen soldiers in this room!' This went on throughout the area, and I soon had sufficient comfortable accommodation for the soldiers. And we were soon inundated by anxious telephone calls from GHQ at Arras, from the liaison mission to the French army, saying that they had received a multitude of urgent messages from the highest quarters in Paris. We had caused a great deal of consternation – which caused much amusement amongst the British officers on the liaison mission. There were threatened visits from ministers but we stood our ground. When the French major in charge of billeting returned from leave, he was tearing his hair out, saying that he would get the sack and be sent to the front. 'In the name of God,' he said, 'can't you alter this disastrous decision?' 'I'm sorry, major,' said my brigadier, 'but the decision has been taken, and there's nothing more to be said.'

A number of cunning and luxury-loving British staff officers had already managed to get themselves into various of these luxurious houses, and had become members of the family, living off the fat of the land, and they were absolutely horrified that their peaceful high-living was about to be interrupted by an influx of common soldiers. They applied to the brigadier, and got no change whatsoever from him. He suggested that if they felt that way, they ought to go and see Montgomery. A few of them were foolish enough to do so – and immediately got posted to the most unpleasant quarters Monty could find.

Sergeant John Williams
6th Battalion, Durham Light Infantry

At Fresnay-sur-Sarthe, we were billeted in houses which appeared to have been emptied for us. They were unfurnished; we had paliasses and blankets. No complaints. It was January, but we had a roof, and we didn't have any snow. When we were across there, we weren't allowed to draw our full pay. As a sergeant, I was allowed to draw about a pound a week. This could be increased by application to your officer, if you wanted to buy something expensive. But we were surprised by the cheapness of everything, and the exchange rate was well in our favour. I remember I could go down on an evening, and get a chunk of bread and Normandy butter, a fried egg and chips, and coffee for about eightpence. All good quality and very, very cheap.

From there, we were sent to the French coalfields. I was billeted with two old ladies who had a post office and tobacco shop. I was taken there by our billeting officer, and the old ladies asked me whether I drank; I said yes. They asked whether I got drunk; I said no. I gained a certain amount of fame by being able to say to people I was living in a house with two mademoiselles – and then explaining that one was 70 and the other was 73. They were two dear old ladies. God bless them. I was billeted in a room that had been occupied by a German officer in the '14–'18 war. It was the same bed, and I had the same washbasin on the same washstand. One of the old ladies told me how during the previous war, the German officer who was billeted there was always drinking and staggering upstairs and being sick on the stairs. She had called him a 'drunken pig,' and she was hauled in front of the commandant, who said, 'How dare you call an officer of his Imperial German Majesty a drunken pig?' Whereupon she said, 'But it is simple, monsieur, he is a drunken pig.' And she got three weeks in the local lock-up. 'Mademoiselle,' I said, 'how terrible!' 'It was nothing, John,' she said, 'my sister used to throw bread to me through the bars. It was all right.'

Lance Bombardier William Harding
6th Battery, 2nd Regiment, Royal Artillery

The French civilians were absolutely marvellous. Absolutely fantastic. They went out of their way. They used to nod to you in the street, and if you went into a café, they would never keep you waiting. They'd count your change out, all the little coins, and make sure you understood what you'd paid for. They were very kind.

Sergeant John Williams
6th Battalion, Durham Light Infantry

On one occasion, one of our lads, a tough lad, a boxer, was challenged by a big tall Frenchman. The Frenchman said, 'Eh, Tommy! You box!' The lad of ours said, 'Sarge, let's have a go at him!' 'No,' I said, 'we're not supposed to.' But in the finish, I explained to the Frenchman and his followers about a circle, and that nobody else must fight. And our lad hit the Frenchman so hard, he knocked him down several times, clattering on the cobbles. Eventually the Frenchman got up, put his hand out, and said, *'Finis! Bon box Anglais!'* And they all went away good natured.

Captain Henry Faure Walker
HQ, 7th Guards Brigade

Relations between our troops and the French civilians in whose villages they lived were not good. The French resented the presence and discomfort caused by foreign troops in their villages and their houses. And the British disliked the French food and the French beer, and they thought that the French were grasping and charging them outrageous prices. Above all, there was no common language. This distressed me because I am a lover of France, and I could see the mutual dislike.

Lance Corporal Lawrence Greggain
5th Battalion, Border Regiment

I was extremely interested in the French way of life, and was determined to take the opportunity of investigating it as best I could. I have never forgotten how shocked I was when I was using what I thought to be a gents' toilet, and whilst I was standing there having a pee, a Frenchman walked in with his girl on his arm, and as he proceeded to pee, she squatted down and did likewise.

Sergeant John Williams
6th Battalion, Durham Light Infantry

There was never any trouble in the town. You could go into an *estaminet* just to drink, but there was a preference on the part of the troops – they were not wine drinkers. There were two sorts of beer – *bier brun* and *bier blond*, dark beer and light beer. The troops mostly stuck to the dark beer. In those days, it was almost effeminate to drink light ale or lager. You had to drink bitter beer. And wine was a foreign thing to us. Nowadays, I see Marks and Spencer full of wines, and it makes me laugh when I think of the days when wine was something rather strange that the French liked. If we did try any of the local stuff, it was the spirits. We tried that Calvados – very strong. There was a little bit of cider drinking. But in the main, everybody stuck to beer.

Lance Corporal Lawrence Greggain
5th Battalion, Border Regiment

I discovered a drink I enjoyed very much; it cost only one franc a glass, and from memory was called '*vin blanc citron*'. A friend of mine bet me that I could not drink off ten of these in as many seconds. As the glasses were very small, I took him on. The result of this was that I finished the last few steps of the stairs up to my billet on my hands and knees.

Lieutenant D'Arcy McCloughin
9 Field Company, Royal Engineers

In those early days we didn't get a great deal of leisure because there was so much to do but I have very happy recollections of small parties based in one area going to the same town on a Saturday or Sunday afternoon. Many of us were old friends from school, or Woolwich or our Cambridge days. The market place in the town would be a great meeting place and we'd go off for a cheap dinner in a small bistro. We learned a lot about French food and wine. I was very lucky and always had friends with me who knew a lot about wine.

2nd Lieutenant Richard Annand
2nd Battalion, Durham Light Infantry

I was attached to the Buffs mess in the Douai area. Whilst we were up in Nomain, we were able to buy champagne very cheaply. One could get a reasonable bottle of champagne for three and six, and if you paid five shillings, it wasn't bad at all. So while we were messing with four of us in the mess, we tackled a bottle every night. But the Buffs didn't go in for it, so every Saturday evening, I would allow myself a whole bottle.

Captain Henry Faure Walker
HQ, 7th Guards Brigade

The officers were extremely bored. There was no facility for entertainment. The regimental officers were billeted in the same villages as their troops and the only form of entertainment was to visit the one good restaurant. Otherwise there was absolutely nothing to do in Lille.

Sergeant John Williams
6th Battalion, Durham Light Infantry

Lille was a big city, and there was lots of opportunity for drinking. One of my functions as sergeant was to close the *estaminets* down at half-past nine. I would go into the first one, slap on the counter, and say, 'Madame! Finis!' and there'd be catcalls from the assembled troops. Then I'd go to the next one, and the next one... When I came back, there'd still be a few people there, and I'd say, 'Out!' and I'd get some more abuse. I'd go down the road again and when I came back, there'd still be some hardcore there, and one of the things you were taught was never to put a man into the position where he might strike a sergeant, because he would come out badly in a court martial. So I had to call a couple of my strong men in, private soldiers, who would bustle about, and chuck them out.

Private David Elliott
141st Field Ambulance, Royal Army Medical Corps

We'd heard about the brothel area in Lille. Few of us had any experience of sex, and we were keen to go and see. It was called Rue ABC, and it was a narrow street with cobbles. The only lights came from the houses each side, and the whole street was brothels. The doorways were cut in half like barn doors, and the bottoms were shut unless you wanted to go in. The infantry soldiers were very blatantly paying their money, choosing their girl, and going upstairs. Inside was a dance hall and a bar, and the scantily clad girls who were only interested in getting you to have a drink, and to take you upstairs. We visited the street once or twice, and walked the length of it before we had the courage to go into any of these establishments. I, being very tall, was the centre of a lot of attention, and my friends would say that my member was as long as I was… there was a lot of fun and games. None of us took advantage of it. We were all too naïve, and we just wanted to see what it was like. We'd make the excuse that we'd just been next door, and that we were 'trop fatigués' and we'd get a lot of abuse when we came to leave because we hadn't spent much money. But it was a revelation to me – and to see two women together. Because even though I was nearly 21, I don't think I'd ever heard the word lesbianism. It was an eye-opener.

Lance Bombardier William Harding
6th Battery, 2nd Regiment, Royal Artillery

I wasn't quite sure what to expect – and I think my eyes must have popped out like organ stops. I'd never seen anything like this in my life. There were girls going around with long black hair down their back. They only looked about 16 or 17. And they had a G-string – that's all – because I remember their bottoms. 'Christ!' I thought. Human nature being what it is, you just couldn't help yourself really. I mean, what could you do? You gave ten francs to a rather plumpish lady at the bottom of the stairs, and you went up to a girl, and it was all over in a couple of minutes. When I came downstairs, I said, 'I didn't think much of that…' The human touch wasn't there.

Lance Corporal Lawrence Greggain
5th Battalion, Border Regiment

Two quite attractive little girls who looked no more than 16 decided we were possible customers, and approached us. They were wearing quite decorative little knickers, and nothing else. Even in my state of celibacy, I must confess they looked rather eye-catching. I was watching my lay-preacher friend out of the corner of my eye, and he was obviously getting very excited. When the usual touching-up process produced only a limited response, they decided on somewhat stronger action. They pulled down their knickers, backed on to us, and rubbed their not-unattractive bottoms against the front of our trousers. I managed to push mine away, but by this time, my friend was out of control. He grabbed his girl, and departed upstairs at the double. Some half-hour later, he reappeared, looking as white as a sheet. His first question was 'Do you think I've caught something?'

Sergeant Alexander 'Sandy' Frederick
1st Fife and Forfar Yeomanry

The VD warnings used to frighten the life out of you. I'd already been warned by my father and various other older men – 1914–18 boys – about 'using the facilities'.

But the army showed us pictures of men whose genitals had become infected with VD and gonorrhrea – and they used to turn you off. Turn you off your food, actually.

Sergeant John Williams
6th Battalion, Durham Light Infantry

Captain Wood asked for my advice. We had this rapscallion in the battalion – a horrible type actually – who picked VD up. He'd been to the army hospital at Netley, and he was allegedly cured, and he'd come back to the battalion just before we'd left for France. Captain Wood said to me, 'How do you feel about him, Sergeant? Do you feel this man is fit enough? Should we accept him into the battalion when he's been bloody fool enough to get VD?' I said, 'Yes, sir. Why the hell should he escape foreign service just because he's a bloody fool and undisciplined in his sex life?' He said, 'I think you're probably right, sergeant…'

When we arrived at Cherbourg, we were allowed to have ten shillings of our pay in French money. We went down the road, and saw some brothels. One of the blokes said, 'Is that one of them places you can talk to the lasses?' We went in, and there was a big wench with a short blue dress on. It was a miniskirt! I'd never seen one before. She came and sat on my knee, and said, 'English soldier! You like nice girl?' I bought her a drink, and she asked me to go upstairs with her. There was a long line of soldiers coming down the stairs. Someone said, 'Hey, they're all right these, aren't they?' This girl was still on my knee, playing with my hat, patting my face, and I thought to myself, 'I wonder what it's like…' She wanted an absinthe, so I bought her one, and I said, 'Absinthe n'est pas bon pour demoiselle!' and she said, 'No, but it is good for making love!' And then, coming down the stairs, who did I see but this character who had VD. I looked at this lad, and I thought to myself that I'd nearly gone upstairs with this wench. This lad might still have VD, and I don't know any of these other characters, so I said, 'Allez! Finis!' And I remember her saying – if you'll excuse me – 'You fuck off! You no fucking bon!' She went away, and I remained moral for the rest of my army life!

2nd Lieutenant Peter Vaux
4th Battalion, Royal Tank Regiment

I remember German pamphlets which were circulated. We all saw them. The general theme was that while the Frenchmen were away in La Ligne Maginot, the British soldiers were sleeping with their wives. I don't think they believed it. We always hoped they didn't, anyway, because it wasn't happening.

Sapper Percy Beaton
218 Army Troops Company, Royal Engineers

I had my first girlfriend in Le Tréport. A French girl. Her father was a French army officer. She was a decent girl, had to have a chaperone everywhere. We were in a hotel on the corner, and she used to go past on her way to school every day. She used to look shyly up and smile at me, and we had the 10th Hussars staying in the same hotel, and one of them was a French interpreter. One Sunday morning, he came to look for me, and said, 'There's a young lady downstairs and she wants you to go to church with her.' I said, 'Young lady? I don't know any young lady.' I went down and it was this young girl, and she was Catholic, and I wasn't, and I told her I couldn't go to church – I didn't know the Catholic carry-ons. But we walked out for quite a while, and then, of course, when we got pushed back, we just lost touch with each other.

Lance Bombardier William Harding
6th Battery, 2nd Regiment, Royal Artillery

I became infatuated with a French girl, Anniek. She was really a very beautiful girl, with that nice dark, flushed, rosy-cheeked face. And she had a wonderful way with her. She was a really honest, hard-working, decent girl. I would never go to her house without taking chocolate for the little ones. Anniek's mother had quite a large family. Anniek cried one night, and made me understand that she had to give all her money up to her mother. I'd been in the same position at her age, so this was a common bond. I took her down the town and bought her a coat. I loved that girl, I really went for her, hook, line and sinker. I'm sure we would have got married. It was genuine love.

But then the battery – typical army, no warning – just upped and moved to the other side of Nantes. My mind was on Anniek all the time, but I had no way of letting her know. One day, the sergeant came out shouting, 'Who's Guillaume? Who's Guillaume with Anniek?' I thought Anniek had come, so I went over to the entrance, and it was the mum! A lot of the battery was standing here gawking at us, and in a typical French manner, she slung her arms round me and made such a fuss of me with tears running down her face. Of course, there was an uproar with all the blokes. She was jabbering in French, and I only understood the odd word, but she was saying that Anniek was crying every night, and why hadn't I let them know? So when I had time off, I caught a tram across Nantes to see Anniek, and we carried on as usual. But I had a terrible time from the chaps in the battery. They were saying that I was getting into bed between the mother and the daughter. Oh, the terrible things they were coming out with. I never lived it down!

Sergeant John Williams
6th Battalion, Durham Light Infantry

While I was in France I went home on leave and I went back to the Consett Iron Company, where I'd been working, to see some of my old friends, and I was talking to a chap called Philip, a great lad, who was a conscientious objector. One of the managers said to me, 'Don't talk to him. He's a bloody disgrace to his country.' I never liked this manager, and he wasn't my boss any longer, so I said to him, 'Mr so-and-so, one of the things we're fighting for is freedom of conscience! And I'll bloody well talk to him if I feel like it!' Phil later served as an ambulanceman.

Sapper Percy Beaton
218 Army Troops Company, Royal Engineers

In Le Tréport, we came into contact with a Liverpool company of Pioneers, and by God, they were a tough crowd. They became our labourers, you could say. A lot of them had been in prison, and released on the understanding that they went to France. They had a sergeant major with them, a huge man, 73 years old, and he used to carry a stick with a big ball on the end, and he used to whack them with it when they got out of hand. One of their sergeants thought he was clever, and he used to try and embarrass them, and make them look small. And one night, they found him in a restaurant on his own, having a drink. They took him outside, and they used him as a wheelbarrow – they dragged him down the cobbled streets face downwards. His head was

A lance corporal of the Royal Fusiliers washes in a petrol tin, early May 1940

British soldiers billeted in a barn

in bandages for weeks. You wouldn't have known it was him – only two slits and a little bit of mouth. They caught a fellow for it, and they put him into a French prison just off the seafront, and at high tide, there was six inches of water in his cell. It was absolutely terrible in there. He said, 'All the prisons I've been in in England, I've never had my heart broken… but this broke my heart.' Still, they might be a tough crowd, but they used to look after us. They looked on us as young and inexperienced soldiers, and they used to father us.

2nd Lieutenant Peter Vaux
4th Battalion, Royal Tank Regiment

As an officer, I was censoring the soldiers' mail. That was a job one disliked doing because one knew the soldiers too well. Every evening, we used to do it in the little room where we would have the squadron mess. It made it awfully difficult when you came to talk to a chap. When he was having some frightful bust-up with his wife or something like that, and he hadn't told one about it. And yet you knew about it – and he knew you knew. So if the chap really wanted, he could put the letter in to the base censor, so I would never see the contents. But the letter would be delayed a week or more if he did that. So the chap had to weigh it up. Most of them trusted us.

Sergeant John Williams
6th Battalion, Durham Light Infantry

We had one officer who was too familiar with the men: slapping them on the back and asking them if they'd enjoyed their visit to the brothel. Things of that nature. Perhaps my spirit was a bit puritanical, but I felt he should joke with them, but not get to the 'Hello, boys' stage.

2nd Lieutenant Philip Pardoe
2nd Battalion, King's Royal Rifle Corps

I remember once saying to my father, 'How does one adjust one's relationships to one's soldiers?' My family lived in Gloucestershire, and we had a small staff of a chauffeur, a groom and a gardener. My father said, 'Just carry on as you've done up to now. Talk to your soldiers just like you've done to Alec.' Alec was the name of the chauffeur.

2nd Lieutenant Darby Houlton-Hart
2nd Battalion, Lincolnshire Regiment
My commanding officer would march at the head of the company, and all the little French children would stand to attention and salute as we went by, and the commanding officer would always return the salute to these little kids.

Sergeant John Williams
6th Battalion, Durham Light Infantry
There were a lot of children hanging around sentries and headquarters. And a lot of them started interspersing their French with a popular English swear word that begins with 'F'. I once heard a young French boy use the word to his mother.

Captain Henry Faure Walker
HQ, 7th Guards Brigade
In 1939, I had taken part in manoeuvres in the east of France. I had found the French to be extremely likeable, but I was absolutely horrified by their state of discipline and training. I will never forget how the commanding officer of the battalion suggested that we should go down and see the arrival of reservists. In the barrack room, the adjutant-chef called the room to attention. To my utter amazement, this was the signal for an outburst of fury on the part of the newly arrived reservists. They rushed up to the commanding officer, shook their fists in his face, and called him the most obscene names. The commanding officer merely turned to me, shrugged his shoulders, and said, 'Ah, *c'est la politique…*'
Now, a year later, the spirit of the French army was – if anything – worse. Being French speaking, I got to know a number of French officers quite well, whom I used to meet in the local restaurant, and I heard from them the most alarming reports of the state of morale of their soldiers. I had one particular friend who was the medical officer of an infantry battalion, stationed not far from our left-hand boundary. He told me that the morale of the men was so low that he didn't think they would fight. He said they would have fought when they were first mobilised – but they'd been mobilised for six months, they'd been unoccupied, hanging about their billets with nothing to do, paid tuppence a day, they were very badly led, nothing was done for their welfare, they were fed up, saw no necessity for the war, and they thought of nothing but going home. He was of the opinion that they were militarily useless.

Sergeant John Williams
6th Battalion, Durham Light Infantry

The French soldiers all seemed so sloppy. Baggy, unkempt clothes, hands in their pockets, necks open sometimes, cigarettes hanging from their mouths. They seemed like caricatures. But they were really French soldiers, and we thought, 'Good God!' I certainly still had memories of the Great War when the French had put up such a good show at Verdun and places like that, and I was thinking to myself, 'I hope they're better soldiers than they look!' Listen to the arrogance of the British soldier who thought if they didn't look smart, they couldn't fight! But I hadn't formed a very high opinion of them.

Lance Bombardier William Harding
6th Battery, 2nd Regiment, Royal Artillery

We visited a French battery on an exchange visit, and we saw the French sentries with their arms crossed against their rifles, leaning up against the wall. Their rifles looked rusty. When the battery gave its demonstration to us, it didn't seem to work together as a unit. The feeling I got was that I wouldn't like to have to rely on them in any trouble. They were very pleased to have us here; there was much hand-shaking, and back-slapping, lots of *'les Boches non bons!'* But that's all very well when there's no fighting, isn't it?

Captain Peter Barclay
2nd Battalion, Royal Norfolk Regiment

We had no great confidence in the Belgian army, I'm afraid to admit. This lack of confidence was well-founded, because when the Germans did invade, the Belgian resistance was next to nil.

Sergeant John Williams
6th Battalion, Durham Light Infantry

The Phoney War was a dream time. We must have been mad to send all those men across. I don't know what we expected. We were in an innocent state. We were doing what we were told, and we had our officers, and we knew all our lads, and we thought all was right with the world. When I look back now, I shudder. I could almost burst into tears.

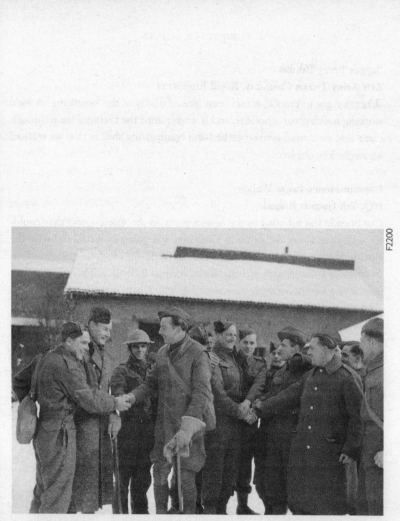

Captain Peter Barclay is congratulated by men of the Royal Norfolk Regiment following the award of the Military Cross for conspicuous gallantry during a night patrol, January 1940

Sapper Percy Beaton
218 Army Troops Company, Royal Engineers

When we got to France, it had been like a holiday at the beginning. A hard working holiday, but a holiday, and it wasn't until the German breakthrough came and we started getting shelled and bombed and shot at that we realised we might lose our lives.

Captain Henry Faure Walker
HQ, 7th Guards Brigade

Our brigade was listening to the news reports on the wireless, and they couldn't understand how the Norway campaign was going so badly, and why the British troops were being seen off as they were. There was great questioning as to whether a similar sort of thing was to happen in France. The brigadier was a great one for encouraging mess meetings which gave an opportunity for any soldier – however junior – to ask any question, put forward any view, or air any grievance, without any fear of being disciplined. It was a very good safety valve, and it gave us a good indication as to what the chaps were thinking, and what state of morale they were in. We became very conscious that the men were upset and considerably worried that the war was going so badly. There was a wave of questioning that went through our brigade, and had an effect throughout our division. However, on the morning of 10 May, this anxiety was forgotten...

Private Victor Burton
1st Battalion, East Lancashire Regiment

We were making our usual preparations to go to the café when we noticed one of the lads in the corner going down his shirt seams – we said, 'What the hell are you doing?' – and he said, 'I'm catching lice.' We said, 'You dirty so and so,' but he said, 'Don't call me that! Look in your own shirts!' and it turned out that all the palliasses the French had given us were full of lice. We couldn't do anything about it then, and we just went out and had our usual couple of drinks. I went to bed that night knowing we were going to be lousy if we didn't get sorted out – but then the blitzkrieg started. At four o'clock in the morning, bombs were going off.

Captain Anthony Rhodes
253 Field Company, Royal Engineers

Four times we had thought the Germans were invading during the Phoney War, but on each occasion it collapsed and we were back in our billets. When the same thing happened on 10 May, people said, 'Another of these bloody things. We've got to leave our comfortable billets and go and sit on the frontier.' We thought it was the same story as usual – then we realised it wasn't.

Captain Peter Barclay
2nd Battalion, Royal Norfolk Regiment

We'd prepared for the German attack through Belgium – but we had little forewarning. The first news we had was early one morning. We heard an immense amount of shelling and bombing in the distance, and very soon afterwards, the commanding officer received a message to the effect that the attack had begun. He told us to stand by for immediate embussing, because we knew that as soon as that had happened, we'd be going forward to take these pre-planned positions. Within a matter of hours, we were moving forward by transport. It took about eight or ten hours, and we were delayed by the retreating Belgian army, by refugees, and by vehicles that had tipped up on the side of the road, but eventually, we reached the line of the River Dyle.

The March to War

F4508

A British soldier in a dugout near Louvain

F3267

A Bren carrier travels over boggy ground

We could see the pilot as he opened up on us with his machine gun. That was our first initiation into real combat. One minute we were saying, 'Why the hell's that plane got black crosses on it?' and the next moment we hit the deck.

As fierce fighting broke out on the Dyle, the intensive German bomb-ing of Rotterdam led to the surrender of the Dutch on 15 May. A panzer corps under the command of General Heinz Guderian succeeded in breaking through the Ardennes near Sedan, crossing the River Meuse, while, further north, the Allies were soon in retreat from the Dyle. Germany's strategy – one that had initially been considered too risky by senior members of the Wehrmacht – was working to plan. Before the majority of the 14 divisions which made up the British Expeditionary Force had seen action, German forces were sweeping beyond them on their way to the coast.

Captain Anthony Rhodes
253 Field Company, Royal Engineers
The night of the 9th – a lovely May summer evening – I'd gone down for a message to a field company in the 50th Division. I handed over the material and had dinner, and about nine or ten o'clock I set off back, driving on my own in my pickup car. Darkness fell towards ten, and it was a distance of some 30 or 40 miles. Suddenly the whole sky was lit up – when an explosion takes place at night you can see it for dozens, perhaps hundreds of miles. Then I heard anti-aircraft fire – and I hadn't taken my tin hat, so I was rather worried and apprehensive. That went on all the way back. Back with the unit I went to bed and almost forgot about it – it was only the next morning that I realised

41

that it had started. We'd had no information before then that there was going to be an attack on the 10th.

2nd Lieutenant Peter Vaux
4th Battalion, Royal Tank Regiment

I was billeted in a little house, and on the morning of 10 May, I heard a shout below – at about six o'clock in the morning – and I jumped out of bed, and I looked out of the window and it was the technical adjutant who was standing out there, and he called up to me, 'The Germans have gone into Belgium and you're off to Brussels at once! You're to report to the orderly room, now!' So I did. Very quickly. Me, my batman, and Sergeant Strickland were off to Brussels. It took me two or three days to drive there in my little 8-cwt truck. I reported and a man said, 'Ah, you're from the 4th Tanks? You're with the 1st Army Tank Brigade, and you're to go into the Forest of Soignes.' He showed me the map squares we were to go into.

Captain Gilbert White
1/6th Battalion, East Surrey Regiment

I was in bed at Wattrelos, and suddenly there was a great air raid. I looked out of the window; searchlights were flicking across the sky, there was a hell of a commotion. I got dressed quickly, went across to battalion HQ immediately, and there was great consternation. Signals were coming in and we couldn't get a clear picture in any way, but most of us realised that the Phoney War was over and that the Germans had begun some sort of military operation.

Sergeant Leonard Howard
210 Field Company, Royal Engineers

We were billeted at an *estaminet* quite close to Douai. At four o'clock in the morning, we were awakened by bombing, and we went out into the road. I can see Eric now, a great tall boy of six foot five – and we had no pyjamas, so we wore our army greatcoats on top of our vest and pants. We went outside the *estaminet* and we could see the German plane, which appeared to come from over Douai. It flew so low that we could see the pilot as he touched his forehead as he came towards us, then opened up on us with his machine gun. That was our first initiation into real combat. One minute we were saying, 'Why the hell's that plane got black crosses on it?' and the next moment we hit the deck.

Captain Gilbert White
1/6th Battalion, East Surrey Regiment

We moved into Belgium and the Belgians were extremely friendly, cheering us like heroes coming to their rescue. They had remembered what being invaded by the Boche was like – they had been invaded by them in August 1914 at the outbreak of the Kaiser's war. However, due to the rumours that the war was going to come to the cities, people thought they'd be much safer in the country, so the roads were jammed. It was extremely difficult to get through, but wherever we went through a village, our welcome was rapturous.

Aircraftman 2nd Class Arthur Taylor
13 (Army Co-operation) Squadron, RAF, attached to 61st Medium Regiment, Royal Artillery

We journeyed right through the heart of Belgium, travelling through Leuze and Waterloo. Refreshments of all kinds were handed to us all along the route, and we couldn't have had a more cheering reception if we'd already won the war. We finally got to our rendezvous at quarter to seven at night, and our vehicles were covered in flowers.

Captain James Hill
2nd Battalion, Royal Fusiliers

We were mobbed in some of the Belgian towns – and it was all very nice except that I found that they were pinching what they could off the car.

Private Ernest Leggett
2nd Battalion, Royal Norfolk Regiment

As we were moving forward, there were thousands of refugees around. I remember going along this long straight road with fields on either side. The road was filled with children, old people, horses and carts, prams, wheelbarrows, donkeys, anything that would carry a load. We had to take to the fields on either side. The bombers came along and bombed this column of refugees, and the Messerschmitts came behind and machine-gunned them. We were all right because we were in the flanks in the fields – but at that time, they didn't worry about us. They were trying to kill these poor refugees. We saw people and horses and carts blown sky high. It was terrible. I remember seeing people mutilated, blown to pieces. We saw people going up in the air in pieces. We

F4386

Belgian civilians cheer as the BEF advances to the River Dyle

could do something about the animals. We saw a horse that had its guts blown open, and we could shoot it. But there was nothing we could do about the human beings. We couldn't stop and give first aid. This happened for two or three days, and we realised *what the enemy was* that we were going to fight. We realised the mentality they had. I couldn't understand it! These poor people were getting away from them. They weren't fighting them. They had no weapons. It was just murder. That sight is still with me. I still dream about it.

Lieutenant D'Arcy McCloughin
9 Field Company, Royal Engineers

After we had moved into Belgium, we were attacked constantly by low-flying aircraft. We had had quite insufficient practice. The idea of shooting from a Bren, using tracer and taking on low-flying aircraft, had never occurred to anyone and none of us had been trained in it. We were – foolish though it may seem – trying to take on low-flying aircraft with our rifles and even, occasionally, the odd officer tried to fire his pistol at something. This only indicates how ill-prepared we all were for the open type of warfare that we were about to face.

Private Ernest Leggett
2nd Battalion, Royal Norfolk Regiment

We got to Forêt de Marchiennes at midday and the field kitchens came out, and so did the hard tack. Those were the hard biscuits that you couldn't eat because they took the roof of your mouth away. They had to be soaked in water before you could do anything with them. They were added to bully beef and there was a big mash made with cans of beans, and it was a horrible mess dolloped into your mess tin; it was terrible but it filled you. We stayed in this big forest until darkness. Then came the most moving time of my whole life. When darkness had fallen, I remember Captain Barclay, the sergeant major and some of the other sergeants coming out with a paraffin lamp. And Captain Barclay said, 'Righto lads, gather round. I've got something to tell you. We're now at war. As you were marching, you saw the bombers coming over. They tried to bomb us before we got out of Orchies, but we're here…' He gave us a fatherly talk, and the last words he said were, 'Now more than ever before will your training stand you in good stead. Keep your heads down and spirits high, and from now on, when you aim your rifle to shoot, you shoot to kill.' They were ominous words. He then said, 'Best of luck, lads!' and after that we formed up and marched into the darkness.

Aircraftman 2nd Class Arthur Taylor
13 (Army Co-operation) Squadron, RAF, attached to 61st Medium Regiment, Royal Artillery

On the 11th, reveille was at 5.30 and the first news that we had was that Winston Churchill had become Prime Minister. I think people were pretty well thrilled. Nothing seemed to be happening before, and with Churchill we thought we'd be on the right side. We weren't very much impressed by Chamberlain, after what we thought was the sell-out at Munich.

Captain Anthony Rhodes
253 Field Company, Royal Engineers

Just before dusk, we saw the first bit of real war – a dogfight. A Messerschmitt came over and a Hurricane took it on, high in the sky. Everybody started cheering – although what happened in the fight, I don't know. Both aircraft disappeared. We went up that night through Aalst, which was on fire. That was the first time I'd seen what a bombing attack could do. There was a wretched Belgian woman outside her house, which was reduced to a pile of rubble. We stopped and tried to comfort her – but all of Aalst was on fire.

Captain Peter Barclay
2nd Battalion, Royal Norfolk Regiment

My job, commanding A Company, was to take up position on the enemy side of the River Dyle, with the rest of the battalion in position on the west of the river. I was holding about 600 yards, and it commanded the main road. And my orders, basically, were to 'Give 'em a bloody nose, old boy, and then pull out.' I remember all this very vividly, because there was a small château in the area of my company position, and there was a garden party going on, with a maypole and children whirling round, and Madame was exercising her role as hostess superbly. She was horrified when I told her that we were going to dig trenches in and around her garden. 'As long as you don't upset the rose bushes, and interfere with the rhododendrons, I suppose I can't stop you,' she said. 'Well, I should certainly send all these kids home,' I said, 'because there's going to be all hell let loose here in the next day or two.' 'Not to worry,' she said, 'my husband will let me know if there is any need for alarm.' I asked where he was. 'Brussels,' she said. I told her there was no chance of speaking to him as all the lines were down – but the party went on anyway, and we dug our trenches in among it all.

Captain Henry Faure Walker
HQ, 7th Guards Brigade

As a matter of courtesy, I paid a call to the nearby Belgian battalion commander, and announced myself. I asked him if it would not be a good idea if we coordinated our plans. I received a slightly hostile reply from the commander who said, 'I have received orders from the King to defend the sacred soil of Belgium, and I remain here to the death!' 'Very good, colonel,' I said, 'I quite understand. I would like to point out that *we are also here* to defend your sacred soil. We will do all in our power to achieve this mutual object. If you look into that house over there, you will find the headquarters of 1st Battalion Coldstream Guards, and I am sure that Colonel Cazenove will be pleased to liaise with you and discuss your plans...' A few hours later, I happened to be passing the Belgian position, and there was not a Belgian to be seen. They had buggered off. That was the last we saw of any members of the Belgian army.

2nd Lieutenant Peter Martin
2nd Battalion, Cheshire Regiment

I recall going that afternoon to the village barber and having a haircut. It seemed a sensible thing to do before the start of a battle.

2nd Lieutenant Richard Annand
2nd Battalion, Durham Light Infantry

I had been told that the Germans wouldn't be arriving for another week. I happened to have some very delicious asparagus with me. Unfortunately the Germans came the next day, and we never enjoyed the asparagus. Our company was on the left bank of the Dyle. The men in the forward section asked me, 'Can you tell us where we are, sir?' I said the nearest village was called La Tombe and their faces fell a bit. 'It's our tomb, is it, sir?' The following day, all those men were dead.

Captain (Acting) Humphrey 'Bala' Bredin
2nd Battalion, Royal Ulster Rifles

On the day the Germans arrived, I was sitting with my batman about 100 yards on the enemy side of the bridge, looking down a long straight piece of road, and I was in a chair reading a newspaper. The crowd of refugees had thinned out, and the colonel of the 15th/19th Hussars came past, and said that I could expect the enemy to arrive pretty soon. I thanked him very much, he wished me good luck, and I carried on reading my newspaper. A little while later, my batman said, 'Can you see? I think there's somebody coming!' I got my binoculars and I saw a German motorbike and sidecar coming up the road. I told my batman and another soldier to wait for a moment or two until these Germans were in reasonable range and then to open fire, before joining me back in front of the bridge. This they did, and then all three of us went back to our platoon position, and told the Royal Engineer NCO to blow the bridge.

Captain Peter Barclay
2nd Battalion, Royal Norfolk Regiment

The Germans' advance guard consisted of motorbikes and sidecars with machine guns mounted on the sidecars. These were obviously the 'forward eyes' of the moving formation, and we caught them completely by surprise, and knocked out about four or five of them. We let them get jolly close before we opened fire, because we wanted to get as many as we could. I think the leading one was only about 150 yards away on the road to the flank, and by that time, there were other motorbikes within range.

2nd Lieutenant Peter Martin
2nd Battalion, Cheshire Regiment

All hell was let loose on the river bank. We'd never been in action before and we suddenly became aware of a very unpleasant smell in the air. We had to crawl across a bit of ground swept by bullets, and we were wondering if we were being gassed. I suddenly remembered we were wearing brassards on our arms which were gas detectors – they were supposed to change colour if you were being gassed. But I had no idea what colour they were supposed to change to. With the aid of a torch, we looked at each other's brassards and instead of brown they were yellow, so we whipped on our gas masks and went on crawling. Then I felt a nasty stinging sensation to my hands, so I thought this was probably mustard gas. We eventually arrived at the platoon position on the Dyle – where no one was wearing gas masks, and they wondered why the hell we were. It turned out that all we had smelled was cordite from bursting shells – which we had never experienced before – and when we looked again at our brassards, we realised they were yellow from the clay which we had been crawling through.

Captain Henry Faure Walker
HQ, 7th Guards Brigade

I had my baptism of shellfire. None of us – and this was a great fault in our training – had been prepared for receiving shellfire. Nobody had warned us what it was like, and what was dangerous, and what could be ignored. So every time we heard a shell whistling towards us, we thought it was coming straight for us, and we lay down on the ground, or jumped into the nearest ditch. It was a very undignified procedure – because many of these shells were completely harmless. We found that so long as a shell was more than 25 yards away from you, you were very unlucky if it did you any harm. But this lack of training was remedied very soon after that.

Lieutenant D'Arcy McCloughin
9 Field Company, Royal Engineers

I was sitting on a camp chair that I carried about with me, and shaving from an electric razor attached to a battery, with a small mirror which had been pinned to a tree. A shell arrived unexpectedly, and the next five minutes I spent underneath a lorry – as I think everyone else did. We became a bit more orderly after that. I left the mirror, the chair and the razor and returned to a safety razor. That was my baptism of fire.

Captain (Acting) Humphrey 'Bala' Bredin
2nd Battalion, Royal Ulster Rifles

For the next three days there was violent fighting and the Germans did everything they could to break the line in our area. My battalion was the left-hand battalion of our brigade, and there was a battalion of the Grenadier Guards on my right. The enemy had been very well trained – but they were trained *so well* that they were predictable. In front of us, to our right, there was a four-storey building, but to our left, the ground was completely open. There was a hillside, sloping upwards away from us, covered in what looked like allotments. At the top of the slope was a row of houses. The enemy sent people to find out where we were. A certain amount of desultory fighting started and gradually they decided what they were going to do, and they made a big attempt to occupy this building to our right.

What played into our hands, was that the Germans proceeded to occupy the allotments. Almost every man in the battalion was a first-class shot, and we'd recently been issued with Bren guns, and our marksmanship really told. The enemy had the usual shaped German helmets, but they were polished, and they showed up very nicely for us to shoot at. They did the usual business of running in ones and twos with a gap between each, but they hadn't reckoned with our marksmanship. The other stupid thing they did, they hid behind these little wooden allotment shelters, not appearing to realise that bullets can go through wooden shelters. So we caused a very large number of casualties, and this started to bring them to a halt.

We were getting casualties. They had a weapon – it turned out to be a very heavy machine gun – but we couldn't work out what it was. It made this noise – 'G'doonk, G'doonk, G'doonk', so we ended up calling it the G'doonka gun. The real danger was when they started getting into the large building in front of us to our right. They started putting snipers on top of it, who could look down into our positions. Very sad to say, my batman was killed by a bullet straight through his head which came from this building.

We had two chaps in a post in front of the railway, and they were getting into a lot of trouble. One of them was badly wounded, and one of my corporals did a marvellous thing. During a lull, he went to help the other chap to pull the fellow in, so we were able to evacuate that position. The chap was brought back and he survived. But the corporal didn't survive. He was killed the next day by a tremendous rush of the enemy – which nearly succeeded in overwhelming us. The corporal manned his Bren gun, firing magazine after magazine, and he stopped that particular attempt almost single-handedly. He was recommended for a Victoria Cross.

It became clear that the Germans were preparing for an assault on our position. I thought there was only one thing for it: to get our artillery firing what we called an 'uncle target'. It was something Montgomery had more or less invented. It was a system whereby all the guns of a division could all be brought to bear on one spot for two or three minutes. The telephone was still working, and I telephoned to say, 'Please bring down an uncle target on to a spot approximately 100 yards in front of our position.' This meant that the 72 guns of the division would be brought on to the house. I realised that one or two shells would probably fall on us, but we reckoned that it was better to be killed by our own shells than to be overrun by the enemy. The shells came down. Only about two fell behind us – and none of them fell on our position. The noise was quite staggering for three minutes, and the building disappeared. After it finished, there was an incredible silence from the enemy for some time, and the only noise one seemed to hear was slates slithering off roofs in the neighbourhood. But it seemed to put paid to whatever the Germans had been planning for that day.

The next day was relatively quiet. There was a certain amount of sniping, and an attempt by the enemy to get behind us, in what they thought was a gap between my platoon and the right-hand Grenadier Guards platoon. But the Guards managed to shove them back. Then we received orders to withdraw. We realised that the Germans had broken through away to our right, and we had to withdraw so as not to get cut off. The withdrawal showed how well and carefully we'd been trained. We took off after dark, doing the usual thing of leaving one or two men behind to pretend to the Germans that we were still there by firing the odd shot for an hour or so. These were men with individuality who could cope by themselves. Then their job was to sneak out and follow our tracks and join up with us. I remember marching through the gun lines, a mile or two back. They were firing to cover our withdrawal, so that the enemy would keep quiet at least until the guns had stopped firing. The whole place was lit up by the gun flashes as though it was day. Then the guns themselves would have to thin out, leaving one or two firing, and withdraw just as we'd been doing.

Captain James Hill
2nd Battalion, Royal Fusiliers
When the Belgians went on the left and the French withdrew on the right, we then had to start withdrawing. But at that stage of the game there was no question of a retreat to Dunkirk or anything like that at all. It was our job to get the refugees off the road to let our own troops move, so we used to have a ruling that we would set up camps for the refugees – internment pens, really – and at three o'clock the foot people would get off the road – they were

A soldier finds a vantage point in a hole in a farmyard wall

F3020

whacked anyhow – and at five o'clock the bicycles and the horse-drawn transport, and at eight o'clock the cars. The Germans spotted this and they'd go and machine-gun and drop bombs on all these refugee pens, which was simply ghastly, terrible. The carnage and horribleness of it all – but that's all part of the cruelty and unpleasantness of war.

Captain Peter Barclay
2nd Battalion, Royal Norfolk Regiment

On 14 May, we received the order to pull back over the river. We received the order on a line telephone. Communications were very poor compared with the situation later in the war. If the line telephone had failed, we would have relied entirely on flares from Very pistols, which was very unsatisfactory. When darkness fell we pulled out and we covered the bridge-blowing party after we'd crossed over. The demolition of the bridge was carried out by a party of Royal Engineers who were with us to do that. But throughout the action, my men were marvellous. It was a well-trained battalion, made up of reservists who had only recently left the battalion. So they all had the spirit of the regiment at heart.

A Fighting Retreat

Soldiers of the BEF under attack from German aircraft during the retreat from the River Dyle

The importance of this counter-attack was paramount in all our minds
– it had to be successful. This was Lord Gort's last ploy.

The Allies' advance into Belgium had allowed Hitler's panzer divisions to bypass the great majority of Allied troops as the Germans raced through the Ardennes. The success of the panzers was due neither to superiority in numbers (the Germans had fewer tanks than the Allies) nor to superior technology. Rather, it was due to a brave and risky strategy, to the concentration of tanks within units rather than spread out, to the importance placed on speed and momentum of attack, and to the support provided by the Luftwaffe's Junkers 87 (Stuka) dive-bombers. The Allies were forced to respond to the German breakthrough with successive withdrawals in an effort to prevent themselves being fatally outflanked. I and II Corps of the British Expeditionary Force withdrew to the River Escaut on 19 May, and Lord Gort, the commander-in-chief of the BEF, subsequently increased his defence line to seven divisions, with two in reserve.

On 20 May, Gort received a direction from the British Cabinet to move his troops south to Amiens. To do so would have risked the annihilation of the BEF; he ignored the direction. Instead, he resolved to resist German attacks on the Escaut, and to mount a counter-attack at Arras, to be carried out by two battalions supported by 72 tanks. The counter-attack made no breakthrough, but its initial success demonstrated how vulnerable the Germans might have proved had Allied strategy been different.

As the days passed, the BEF grew vulnerable to encirclement; from Army Group B – its original foe – in the east and north as the Belgians fell back, and from Army Group A swinging around its rear in the south and west.

Several days earlier, Gort had promised the French that they would mount a fresh counter-attack to the south – but now he changed his mind. Such a counter-attack would risk the destruction of the BEF. Instead, on 25 May, he gave orders to prepare a defensive perimeter around Dunkirk. The BEF would attempt to break for the largest harbour on the Channel coast. This decision to evacuate would ultimately save the British Expeditionary Force.

Apart from Gort's wise and courageous move, the BEF's other stroke of fortune was the decision (taken on 24 May by General von Runstedt, commander of Army Group B, and confirmed by Adolf Hitler) to halt the panzers when they were only 18 miles from Dunkirk. There were a number of possible reasons for this decision: the panzers' supply lines had become over-extended; the infantry needed time to catch up; the panzer divisions could now be conserved for future operations and Hermann Goering's Luftwaffe would be able to step in and play a decisive role in the forthcoming victory. It has been suggested that Hitler allowed the BEF to escape, out of respect for the British and from a belief that Britain was about to enter into negotiations. This seems unlikely, given that Hitler personally reversed the order three days later. Nevertheless, those three days allowed the BEF to strengthen Dunkirk's perimeter defence, and to move huge numbers of men closer to the coast. And they allowed British troops to believe that escape might just be possible.

Captain Stephen Hollway
Field Park Company, Royal Engineers

Any pullback and any retreat is bad for morale – but the order to pull back from the River Dyle wasn't all that bad, because nobody foresaw an evacuation to Dunkirk. We thought the reason for our pulling back was that the Belgians had completely crumbled, so there was an enormous gap to our left flank, and we could be surrounded there. The Germans had gone in very heavily on the French to our right, and were being very successful – so there was a big gap forming.

Captain Gilbert White
1/6th Battalion, East Surrey Regiment

The Belgian army were withdrawing through our positions and they were, to put it mildly, an absolute rabble. They were completely disorganised, demoralised – and they were streaming back in their thousands. They weren't marching – they were slouching – utter dejection. Many of them hadn't got their rifle – they'd obviously thrown it away. They hadn't got their tin hats – they'd probably thrown those away too. We did contact two officers, and asked, 'What the hell are you doing? Where are you going?' 'Oh, we're going back to reorganise.' That was a load of absolute nonsense. They were just fleeing.

Sergeant John Williams
6th Battalion, Durham Light Infantry

At one stage we were mixed up with a whole lot of Belgian troops. I was talking to them, and one of them said, 'Be careful about talking to those soldiers over there. They're Walloons!' A bit later, another one warned me about talking to the Flemish ones. They hated each other more than they did the Germans!

Captain Anthony Rhodes
253 Field Company, Royal Engineers

On the 14th we got the order to withdraw – but we had no idea what had happened. We were simply told we were to withdraw back to the River Escaut – which meant going back through Brussels and taking up another water line. I've never forgotten the contrast between the reception on the morning of the 11th, and when we went back the other way on the 14th – people standing around looking at us in utter dejection. They were silent – they knew that the Germans were coming, and they knew what they were in for.

Captain James Moulton
General Staff Officer, Grade 3, Operations Section

Lord Gort had established his forward command post at Wahagnies, and I was there for a few days. I was on night duty at the time that the news of the Sedan breakthrough came through. I remember pointing it out to Gort when he came into the office in the morning. Gort became increasingly admirable in the course of the battle – nothing seemed to disturb him. At this stage the French were bubbling with confidence. Gort looked at the map and didn't seem too concerned. It was a bit worrying, but you had confidence in this great French army – and they kept on telling us that they were such good soldiers. Goddammit, they ought to be able to do something about it.

Captain (Acting) Humphrey 'Bala' Bredin
2nd Battalion, Royal Ulster Rifles

One does not easily forget the march we did from Louvain through Brussels. We were pretty tired, and the people of Brussels were sorry for themselves, and very sorry for us, and they were trying to get our men to drink glasses of beer all the way along the route. I had to tell some of these people, 'For goodness' sake, please stop giving my soldiers beer! They won't be able to march, and they won't be able to fight!'

Captain Anthony Rhodes
253 Field Company, Royal Engineers

As we went back, our general staff officer hadn't put on his tin hat. Instead he'd got on his red hat with a red band. As he went through the suburbs of Brussels, a sniper put a bullet through his head – finished him. Our colonel said, 'There you are, you see. Officers – put on your tin hats! Don't look as if you're an officer, because you'll be the first person to be shot!'

Private Albert Dance
Rifle Brigade

When we were in the general area of Brussels, this captain came round and said, 'You may not know it – but you're on the very slopes of the Battle of Waterloo.' We were told to dig trenches all along. That night, I was propped up in the trench, listening to this tremendous noise. I was trying to make out what it was. First it sounded like men marching, then I could hear the clop of hooves and then engine noises. When dawn came up, I looked across to our left and saw what looked like the entire French army retreating past us.

Private Harry Dennis
1st Battalion, East Surrey Regiment

Some of us wandered into Brussels and went into a café and spoke to the people. We asked the landlord of the bar what he thought about the Germans coming, and he said, '*Allemands venirent – c'est la guerre.*' That attitude was pretty prevalent at that time – acceptance. The Guards Brigade, coming back from the Albert Canal, passed through Brussels and it was the first sight we had of almost-vanquished troops. They looked really ragged and they'd had a real mauling. Up to that time we hadn't been in action at all.

Lieutenant D'Arcy McCloughin
9 Field Company, Royal Engineers
When we got the order to withdraw from the Louvain area I suppose it didn't come as a surprise – it was presented not so much as a withdrawal but just as a move – although obviously we were going away from the enemy.

Captain Peter Barclay
2nd Battalion, Royal Norfolk Regiment
We moved back into reserve, a considerable way behind the river, and we dug in straight away. Within three hours, we had a complete dug-in, camouflaged, reserve company position, with the French to our right. We were, at that time, the right-hand battalion of the BEF. I was sent for by my colonel who was in rather a state, and he said, 'The Germans have crossed over the river on the right!' It was very strange – because the adjutant didn't seem to know anything about this. But the colonel said that he'd had a message from a Brigade dispatch rider to this effect, and he said, 'I want you to recapture that village over there!' 'That's a French reserve position,' I said, 'and if they're over in that village, they must be within visual range of any enemy...' But the colonel said, 'You've got to go and recapture it!' The adjutant was as amazed by this as I was – but if your commanding officer tells you to go and recapture a village, then you go and recapture a village...

So we prepared a fire plan, with artillery coming down on this village hot and strong, and mortars, and machine guns from good positions to the flanks, and we started our attack. There was no retaliatory fire coming at all, which seemed very surprising – but I thought that the fire plan must have been extremely effective. I was just getting ready for the final assault, when a British carrier emerged from the village. I thought the Germans had captured a British carrier, and had started using it, so I got our man with the Boys anti-tank rifle, and I said, 'Train on that carrier, but keep your safety catch on, and don't fire until I tell you!' And as the carrier came close, I could see the chap in front had a British tin hat on, and he proceeded to stand up and wave a

A sapper presses the plunger and blows a bridge at Louvain

A British soldier leads an old woman to safety from the ruins of her wrecked home in Louvain

walking stick about. 'No German would ever do that…' I thought. In fact, this chap turned out to be the commanding officer of the Royal Scots, Colonel Money. He yelled at me, 'What the devil do you think you're up to?' I said, 'We are just recapturing this village.' 'Well, what do you want to do that for?' he said. 'I was in the middle of the best meal I've had since war broke out – with the brigadier in charge of the French brigade in the sector – and suddenly your shells start pouring through the roof and bring a delectable meal to a summary halt! You'd do far better to stay away from me until you get things sorted with your battalion!'

I went back to my battalion the following morning, and it turned out that my commanding officer – who had been in a very high state of nervousness – had imagined the whole thing. The Germans had not crossed over the river, but he had been convinced that they had captured the village, and that it was the reserve company's job to retake it. I felt particularly sad about this commanding officer; he was a very delightful man. I had served under him during peacetime a great deal, and he was the best peacetime trainer I've ever come across. He was good because he had a very sensitive mind, and he understood how soldiers reacted. But his sensitiveness couldn't stand up to the rigours of war and he cracked. During the First World War, he had been evacuated from supposed shell shock, and it was a most awful pity that the lesson wasn't learnt. He could have been used purely on the training side during the Second World War. As it was, he was given various staff jobs, but he was never the same man again. I mean, he knew that he'd let the side down, and it really worked on his conscience, and he died not long after the war.

Private Harry Dennis
1st Battalion, East Surrey Regiment
On the afternoon Jerry reached Brussels, they started attacking across the river. All the canal bridges were still intact, but on the other side of the canals, in Brussels itself, all the roads were mined so they couldn't get across. One German vehicle that tried to come across got blown sky high. Then in the evening the main bridges were blown, opposite the royal palace. We could see the German troops from where we were, in the warehouse on the opposite side of the river. Our chaps attacked them with small arms and mortar fire. Half an hour later we got our orders to get in our vehicles and away. We pulled

out. This surprised us. We wondered why it was so – but we were told to get on the road. We got to Oudenaarde early the next morning.

Private George Lambert
9th Battalion, Durham Light Infantry

My 'christening' was when one of the dispatch riders was killed by a mortar shell on the roadside. He was badly mauled, and I was one of the ones that had to bury him. Not a very pleasant task when you're not used to it, but we did our job and buried the lad there and then, and the sergeant took his tags, and the officer came and said, 'There's a glass of rum for you, but don't expect it every time.' That was when I realised that things were going to happen. I was actually sick.

Private David Elliott
141st Field Ambulance, Royal Army Medical Corps

I can remember treating one particular man. He was very large. His shoulders were so broad that they were over the side of the stretcher. He had been machine-gunned across the abdomen, and he had a terrible injured arm. When we undid the bandages, we found that his arm was almost severed at the shoulder. The bone was sticking out. He was unconscious. Myself and another corporal were alone. We didn't have any doctors with us. We sent for one of the MOs and a very young doctor came – not one of our regulars – and I didn't know him at all. He examined the wounds and said the arm was useless, but he didn't have his sterilised tools, and he refused to take the arm off. So I opened the panier, and with a pair of scissors, I cut through the skin and flesh. It was the only thing to do. There was no bone at all, and I left him with a jagged shoulder, which we put a big field dressing on. What has stayed with me is the weight of that arm. I carried it out into the night, and threw it into a ditch, and it was the weight of it… I'm certain that poor man died. He was only barely alive when the ambulance came to take him further back.

Captain Stephen Hollway
Field Park Company, Royal Engineers

We got to a place west of Brussels, but by that time, we'd realised that things had gone seriously awry. We'd heard the rumours that the Germans had broken through in the south and the rumours had been reinforced by seeing

French troop trains moving across our front. They were being moved to reinforce the northern armies and reinforce the gap. We were all horrified at the equipment and the morale of the French troops – they were dirty, their equipment was mostly First World War. Many of the reserves were still clad in their red and blue 1914 uniforms. It seemed quite clear, as the retreat went on, that the French army was disintegrating.

Stephane Hessel
Served with French Army
It is quite true that morale was poor in the French army. It grew worse by the weeks. My unit was a very valiant one, but it was very much the exception. We mostly had the feeling that this war didn't lead anywhere, and that things were happening too slowly. Everywhere, there seemed to be a lack of real stamina. What had happened in Poland was awful, and we did not trust the Soviet Union because of the Nazi–Soviet pact, and morale was bad. It became worse and worse as we withdrew, because we witnessed superior officers getting away quickly and leaving their men behind. There was a complete disruption of the fabric of the French army. There was no sense that orders were coming through to organise a retreat in a proper manner. We retreated as we could; people were lost on the roads. The surprise effect of the German attack was such that whatever morale could have remained, disappeared very quickly.

2nd Lieutenant Peter Vaux
4th Battalion, Royal Tank Regiment
We passed a French sergeant with his crew, and I told him about the presence of Germans in the Saint Amand area. I said, 'They're two miles away and coming. Are you sure you won't come?' 'No, no, no,' he said, 'I will stay and see these people off.' Of course he couldn't see them off, but I've always felt that was a marvellous piece of strength of mind from that sergeant with his conscript crew. So, you see, all the French army wasn't dud.

Captain Peter Barclay
2nd Battalion, Royal Norfolk Regiment
We were pulling back gradually from river line to river line. Withdrawal was the order of the day. We were never once molested in our withdrawal, which I was thankful about, because we were nearly always a rearguard company, and

you had a horrible fear of getting one up the pants as you were coming out. As we were withdrawing, one's picture as a company commander was a very limited one, and it seems sad that one didn't know more of the bigger picture. But, quite honestly, we were so involved in our own concerns that we didn't thirst for the bigger picture. The food and water situation was still good. We had a marvellous quartermaster, and a most efficient transports officer, and we never seemed to go long without some sort of meal. Maybe there wasn't hot food every night, but the soldiers never had empty bellies. And their morale was remarkable. One felt terribly proud of the way they reacted. They were positive they were in good hands, and they never failed to see the joke in whatever ghastly job they had to do. It was simply amazing.

Private Ernest Leggett
2nd Battalion, Royal Norfolk Regiment

We were falling back all the time, but I didn't realise that the whole BEF was falling back. I thought we would be going forward again at a later date. As we came back, I remember the devastation of the towns and villages. They'd just been brought to the ground. There was water, smoke and fires in the streets, and the terrible smell of death from the houses. There was desolation everywhere. The trees had been uprooted, or the tops had been shelled away. It was like walking through hell. This had all been happening *behind* us, and we were walking back through it.

Captain (Acting) Humphrey 'Bala' Bredin
2nd Battalion, Royal Ulster Rifles

The sequence of the campaign became much the same each time. You withdrew from your position. You moved to a new position where your commanding officer told you where you were to go. You dug in as quickly as you could. And before you had dug in properly, the enemy had arrived, and you had to fight. You were usually along a river or a feature that was defensible. At about this time, one of the company commanders was wounded, and I was put in command of a company. I knew extremely little about how to command a company, but you learn very quickly when you have to step into a wounded man's shoes. Even my two or three days fighting in Louvain had given me some experience of what *not to do* – even if I didn't know enough about what *to do*. We gave the Germans an extremely good run for their money. Each time they attacked, our rifle and light machine-gun shooting was so good that they were very surprised. There would be a halt for about 24 hours, until they received reinforcements or extra artillery, and the same thing would happen again.

Private Ernest Leggett
2nd Battalion, Royal Norfolk Regiment

One night, we marched 25 miles in the darkness. People have said that you can't march while you're asleep, but I can tell you here and now, you *can* march while you're asleep – because I've done it. You wake up when you bump into the man ahead of you, or the man behind bumps into you.

Captain Henry Faure Walker
HQ, 7th Guards Brigade

We made it a rule that when we were moving along a road in vehicles – our main method of movement – our lorries travelled with an interval of between 50 and 100 yards between each one. This meant that only one lorry could be bombed at a time, and it was hoped that this would deter the German pilots from any attempt at mass bombing. Of course, it had the great disadvantage of occupying an enormous road space by a comparatively small number of vehicles. So our leading vehicles might arrive at their destination before our last vehicles had left their starting point.

Captain (Acting) Humphrey 'Bala' Bredin
2nd Battalion, Royal Ulster Rifles

One day, we had to do a daylight withdrawal. We were withdrawing through fields of corn, crouched down so we couldn't be seen. When I lay down for a minute's rest, I looked up and noticed the corn stalks being cut off by enemy bullets. It's always stuck in my mind.

Private Edgar Rabbets
5th Battalion, Northamptonshire Regiment

I don't think we were really surprised when we were ordered to withdraw from Brussels, because we had no tanks or artillery – and infantry aren't going to stay very long when people are coming along with tanks and attacking them. Also, the Belgians didn't want Brussels damaged in any way, so they declared it an open town. The only civilian I spoke to in Brussels was a chappie who came across with some bottles of Whitbread's beer from a local café, and he presented them to me with his compliments. Clearly he wasn't too distressed about things.

Lance Corporal Kenneth Carver
5th Motor Ambulance Convoy, Royal Army Service Corps

We weren't getting supplies through, so we ransacked shops for food – and if the shops were empty, we tried houses or farms. In most towns and villages we found that people had just got out of bed and left because of the onrush of the German army. Very often you would walk into a shop and find it completely stacked with groceries, and you could take what you wanted.

Private Ernest Leggett
2nd Battalion, Royal Norfolk Regiment

Before our field kitchens were set up, we were on the move again. The only thing we could eat was the produce from the fields, or anything we could find in the houses as we were passing through. In the cellars, the French used to cure meat, like legs of ham, and we could help ourselves with that. I can only once remember having a meal supplied to me by my company, and that was when someone said, 'Here you are! Catch!' and it was a tin of beans and I had them cold. The only water I had to drink was out of the ditches which we lit a fire and boiled. It was terrible but we had to have something. We were vagrants. And that's not in the regimental history...

Lance Corporal Kenneth Carver
5th Motor Ambulance Convoy, Royal Army Service Corps

We didn't use the word 'looting' as such, but it was a factor. If you wanted bedding, pillows, sheets, blankets, food, you picked it up and used it. One farm we went to was empty, so we stayed there for several days. We killed one or two cows, pigs, sheep and chickens and then we heard a noise one day. Under the farm we found the owner with his wife and two daughters. They came up and cooked for us for a few more days.

Private Edgar Rabbets
5th Battalion, Northamptonshire Regiment

Once ordered to withdraw, we marched all night. There was a big slip-up here with the transport. It was supposed to meet us just outside the town, but

Private Sidney Nuttall (on the left) later in the war, serving with airborne forces

then we were told that they'd been delayed, and we should meet them an hour further on. We were told this pretty well all night – and we never saw any sign of transport at all. We were still marching long after daylight broke the next morning. We'd been marching from eleven o'clock at night, and we were still marching at eleven o'clock the next morning, with very few breaks because people find it difficult to get started again. It's a lot easier to let them keep marching.

Captain Anthony Taylor
15th/19th The King's Royal Hussars

We had withdrawn to a place a few miles west of Brussels, where we had some fairly hard fighting. We now wanted to retire over the river – but when we got to the bridge we wanted to retire over, we found that the Germans had come round our left, and were sitting on it. I was the adjutant, and I had to find the next bridge to the south, so I went off in my light tank to try and find it. However, shortly after I'd turned to the south, I suddenly saw three or four German armoured cars on the road in front of me. I was behind the guns, and I fired at these armoured cars with everything I could. They put down smoke, and we chased them. The tracks of our tank were very worn by then, and we were going pretty fast down this road, and when we came to a sharp turn, the tank went off the road into soft boggy ground.

We tried to set fire to the tank, which we were not successful in doing, and we went on foot towards the river. By this time, the Germans were coming from all directions, and there was firing from every direction. I had the two men of my tank crew with me, and we lay in some scrub, and I told them to keep quiet. I hoped we could stay there until dark. I dozed off – I was very weary, having been fighting for several days. The next thing I knew, there were three German soldiers pointing rifles at my head. I didn't know what to do. I didn't like to put my hands up, and I vaguely fumbled for my revolver. They might easily have dispatched me there and then – but they didn't. They merely walked up and took our arms off us, and we were taken to a house in a nearby village. We were on the whole well treated by the Germans. When we got there, one of our men – Trooper Haig – was there, and he had a terrible wound in the stomach, and the Germans took a lot of trouble to make him comfortable. They brought him pillows to rest on and water for him to drink.

Sapper Percy Beaton
218 Army Troops Company, Royal Engineers

The British troops were despondent. There were no two ways about it. The Jocks, for example, they're good fighting soldiers, and they were furious that they hadn't got the arms to hold the Germans back. They said, 'We could have held them back! They're a load of young, inexperienced soldiers, and we could have mowed them down, and they would have run.' I think we were all despondent at the time because we expected better things of our army.

Private Robert Brown
2nd Battalion, Royal Norfolk Regiment

The Germans were more ruthless than we were. Whatever they wanted to do, they did it, no matter who was in the way. We were still fighting a kid-glove war. For example, we wouldn't lay a telephone wire through a churchyard; we would go round it. But the Germans used the church as a defensive position, or for observation.

Private Sidney Nuttall
Royal Army Ordnance Corps attached to 1st Battalion, Border Regiment

We were driving back, and as yet I hadn't fired a shot. When I say I hadn't fired a shot, *I really mean that*. I'd never fired a shot in training, because I hadn't been trained. We were considered more or less non-combatants. I took a message to C Company, and while I was there we came under attack, and I was told to stay with them. I was given to a lance corporal who set me up on the bank of a canal. A chap said, 'Can you use a rifle?' I said, 'Well, I can shoot a gun, but I've never fired a rifle.' He said, 'Do you know how to load it?' I said, 'Yes,' because we'd mucked about with the things. He showed me a house, and he showed me the edge of a wood on the other side of the canal. He said, 'If you see any German soldiers in that area, fire at them. But only if you see them in that area.'

It was a lovely day, beautiful sunny weather, and that made it much nicer than if it had been raining or snowing. Eventually I did see somebody come out from behind the house. Now, I'd never seen a German soldier, but after a good look at him, I thought, he must be one of them, so I aimed the rifle at him and pulled the trigger. It went bang, and the chap kept on walking. He never even ducked. He just walked into the wood. The lance corporal came

71

down to me, he said, 'Did you just fire?' I said, 'Yup.' He said, 'What did you fire at?' I said, 'A bloke coming across.' 'Did you hit him?' I said, 'No.' He said, 'Give me a look at your rifle.' So he took my rifle, he said, 'Oh God! Your sights are set to 600. The shot must have gone miles over his head!' He put my sights down to 100 yards, and said, 'Anything you can see, you can hit him at 100 yards.' And eventually, I did hit somebody.

Private William Ridley
9th Battalion, Durham Light Infantry
We marched back from Brussels to Lille. Everything was like in a dream, and we were getting Stuka-ed and machine-gunned. We came across some civilians who were loading a truck up with dead bodies. That was the first time I'd seen dead bodies, and what struck me, when the cart was pulled away, everything on the cart just moved like jelly.

Sapper Percy Beaton
218 Army Troops Company, Royal Engineers
When we were on the retreat, I think the French got the impression that we were leaving them in the lurch. The roads were packed with French people, and we were on lorries, sort of forcing our way through the crowds, pushing people off the road. Sometimes when we went past, they used to shake their fists at us, much as to say, 'We've got to walk and you're all riding!' It was sad for them.

Lance Corporal Kenneth Carver
5th Motor Ambulance Convoy, Royal Army Service Corps
We would go through a very thick crowd, and you'd see a clenched fist being shaken at you, saying, *'Pourquoi? Pourquoi?'* And you had to accept it. They wanted to know why we were running away and leaving, but we could not answer for the simple reason that we didn't know.

Private William Ridley
9th Battalion, Durham Light Infantry
The refugees were pathetic – we were more annoyed than anything with them, because we just couldn't get through them – and where there was a crowd, the Stukas used to dive-bomb.

Flying Officer Roland Beamont
87 *Squadron, RAF*

The German attacks on the civilians on the roads were absolutely deliberate. It was part of a tactical policy to jam the roads and prevent the Allied armed forces using those routes to reinforce their front. If you jam the roads with refugees and overturned vehicles and slaughtered horses, the reserves are going to take longer to reach the front.

Flying Officer Harold Bird-Wilson
17 *Squadron, RAF*

On our first sortie on 18 May, we were told that the Germans were strafing refugees on the road south of Lille. We flew into the area and saw thousands upon thousands of refugees walking along the roads with horse carts and bicycles – women and children. To know that the Germans were strafing people retreating like this was a double shock.

Flying Officer Peter Matthews
1 *Squadron, RAF*

I was shaken to the core when I first saw German fighter pilots machine-gunning the crowds of civilians on the roads. It wasn't just bombers that were strafing – it was Messerschmitt 109s and 110s. That didn't seem to me to be a fighter pilot's job in life.

Lance Corporal Lawrence Greggain
5th *Battalion, Border Regiment*

Out of the sky came a formation of Stuka dive-bombers, and we all raced for cover. Along with a French civilian, I dived into a ditch at the side of the road. I went in almost head first, little realising that it was an open sewer. The civilian, probably knowing this, went in feet first. As I stood up, I saw what I took to be a football rolling across to the other side. My immediate reaction was, 'Who the hell is playing football at a time like this?' I then looked to my right. The French civilian's body was falling towards me – headless.

Private Ernest Leggett
2nd *Battalion, Royal Norfolk Regiment*

Stukas had – we didn't know this at the time – special sirens attached which made this hellish scream, and the bombs they let loose had sirens in their tails. It was the most hellish, terrific noise you could ever encounter. I threw myself down on the bank, spreadeagled, and I shook just like a jelly. The noise was so penetrating and so ominous: it was devilish. Our sergeant major came round and said, 'That effect is exactly what the enemy wants! The noise is there to get you like this! The noise won't hurt you! Now pull yourselves together!' And we thought what blasted fools we were to be taken in like that… but honestly, it was the most devilish noise.

Werner Roell
German Junkers 87 (Stuka) pilot

The Stuka was the sharpshooter amongst the bombers. Whereas the horizontal bombers dropped an enormous amount of bombs on an area, the Stuka had a small target and with a small number of bombs, it could erase a target of importance. A bridge was a typical target. Of course, Stukas were slow. They had to be sturdy because they came out of the dive sharply. And the pilot had to be accustomed to that. It was easy to black out when you redressed the plane because the blood went out of your head. You could hear in the earphones when you were down to 1,000 metres and then you started redressing the plane and you levelled off about 700 metres above the ground. The Stukas had sirens in front of the wings, one on each side. When the speed was increasing during the dive, the sirens started making a terrific noise. And we had air brakes which would not let us go over 650 kph. There were also cardboard whistles on the tail rudders of the bombs so that when the bombs were released, the bomb itself started whistling. That gave quite a psychological effect but all these things worked only at the beginning of the war. After that, people developed resistance to it.

Captain Gilbert White
1/6th Battalion, East Surrey Regiment

As we moved back by motor transport to concentrate near Oudenaarde on the River Escaut, we saw what we thought to be a group of nuns dressed in black and yellow sashes, and they turned out to be Germans. They suddenly opened fire, much to the amazement of our A Company commander. He returned the fire and they scarpered off. We also came across four British soldiers who'd been taken prisoner. They'd been stripped of their uniforms and eventually found

F4499

A Belgian mother and her three children amid the ruins of the bombed town of Enghein

their way back to our lines. Presumably the Germans were using their uniforms to impersonate British soldiers. The Germans' methods of subversion were excellent – they caused panic and spread rumours. This was all to create confusion, to block the roads and to make it more difficult for the BEF to move – and they were very successful in doing this.

Sergeant Leonard Howard
210 Field Company, Royal Engineers
We had prepared bridges on the Escaut for demolition – but the actual charges weren't put in place until about 16 May. We built bridges with chambers in their abutments to take prepared charges. It seemed an awful thing to build a bridge, and make provision for destroying it at the same time. On one occasion what appeared to be two nuns pushing a pram came over one of the bridges over the Escaut Canal that we'd prepared for demolition, along with a lot of refugees. These nuns got to the other side and then they pulled a sub-machine gun out of the pram, with which they machine-gunned the bridge, including the civilians. Naturally when we saw this, we shot them – and they proved to be men.

Captain Stephen Hollway
Field Park Company, Royal Engineers
We were trying to clear the evacuation route between Renaix and Tournai when the Germans appeared – and that was a surprise – but you'd learnt not to be really surprised at anything, to be honest. They turned up in the most unexpected places. Our problem at that stage was getting our troops back in good order so that they could take up a new line and fight.

Sapper Percy Beaton
218 Army Troops Company, Royal Engineers
On the retreat, we had this spell of blowing up bridges. On one particular bridge, we were told to blow it at one o'clock after a French cavalry unit had crossed it. It came one o'clock and we gave them 'til quarter-past one and we blew this bridge up, and it blew four shops up as well. The people protested like mad. And the cavalry unit showed up after we blew it. They were just standing there speechless, stranded on the German side, and then the old Frenchman started rattling on at us. We couldn't understand a word he was saying, but we had given them a quarter of an hour, and they happened to be late.

Captain Stephen Hollway
Field Park Company, Royal Engineers

Renaix was a key town, one of the centres which led to the Kerkhove Bridge, which was the only bridge which wasn't blown. I got messages to say that the Germans were approaching from the west, and I remember thinking that I had only myself and two policemen with revolvers – and there wasn't too much we could do to stop them. Then an officer from the Gordons came up from east of the town. I told him the position, and he promised to put his anti-tank guns in. Just as the situation was getting crucial, to my delight and amazement, up came, at full gallop, a troop of 25-pounders with their horses. There was a long village square with trees in the middle, and in the far right-hand corner there was a road where the Germans were coming. I looked at our 25-pounders – and I thought to myself, 'I'm never going to see this again – horse-drawn artillery going into battle over open sights.' They dashed up the end of the road, slewed round the corner, undid the traces, back came the horses, and the guns opened fire straight down the road. I would think it was probably the last time that horse-drawn artillery went into battle like that. It was a marvellous sight. You might have felt whacked and tired and dead – but you thought, 'By God, if people can do that, life's worth living!' And it certainly was for me after that.

Captain (Acting) Stewart Carter
2nd Battalion, Nottinghamshire and Derbyshire Regiment

During the march to Kerkhove we heard that the bridge on the river was going to be blown, so the adjutant was sent ahead on a civilian motor bicycle to prevent this being done before we got there. We arrived 20 minutes before it was due to go up, but the adjutant succeeded in persuading the demolition party to delay blowing it up until we had got through. It was with great difficulty that he did this, as there were reports of fifth columnists and German officers dressed in British uniform and speaking perfect English. We advanced on both sides of the road, and we could see the adjutant talking to the East Surrey officer.

Now, the East Surreys had been told that any armed body coming up was likely to be German – which was quite reasonable – and at a distance of 200 yards, you might well think we were the enemy, so the forward companies opened fire on us and we all took cover in the ditch. Major Temple got up to go forward and talk to them, but I pulled him back into the ditch just in time as their Bren gun opened up. Eventually the adjutant prevailed and we marched across the bridge.

As the last soldier got on to the road, they blew the bridge up – which very sadly was covered with a lot of civilians – cars, vehicles and horses, who were blown into the river. They did everything they could to stop these civilians getting on the bridge, but they just charged in after us. They were panic-stricken – and it was a very terrible thing. But the Germans were very close behind us.

Sapper Percy Beaton
218 Army Troops Company, Royal Engineers
When we were blowing up the bridges, the French housewives used to be doing their washing in the river, and beating it on the stones. They used to carry on unconcerned. We told them that we were actually going to blow the bridge, and they used to just put their washing back in the baskets and saunter away casually. They took it in their stride.

Private Sidney Nuttall
Royal Army Ordnance Corps attached to 1st Battalion, Border Regiment
Someone once said that war is 80 per cent boredom and 20 per cent terror – but they never mentioned humour. Without humour, people would have a hell of a job dealing with the boredom and the terror. As a case in point, we moved in to take over from some regiment, and we were walking down the road in the middle of the night. The people we were relieving were coming up the road. It was pitch black, no sound, just the feet going. Suddenly a Lancashire voice comes from the other side, 'I shouldn't go up there mate, they're killing one another.'

Private Ernest Leggett
2nd Battalion, Royal Norfolk Regiment
We arrived at the River Escaut late at night on 20 May, and we gathered around as a company in one place and on the next morning we took our positions. It wasn't a big river, about 20 yards wide, and on the other side was a wood so thin I could see through it. Our company was told that we would have to disperse from right to left. The headquarters – comprised of Captain Barclay and CSM Gristock, and others – stayed on the right-hand flank. The rest of us went down to the left.

Captain Peter Barclay
2nd Battalion, Royal Norfolk Regiment

Our positions on the Escaut were on a wide front. After a few hours some Germans appeared on the far bank, totally oblivious of our presence in the immediate vicinity. I told my soldiers on no account were any of them to fire until they heard my hunting horn. A German officer appeared with his senior warrant-officers and got his map out, and then they withdrew into the wood and we heard a lot of chopping going on and we saw the tops of trees flattening out. They were cutting down young trees; there were bits of concrete lying across the canal and they were so placed across the canal that with suitable lengths of timber, pedestrians could get across.

Eventually they emerged from this plantation with a number of long hurdles made from saplings and they proceeded to lay these across the rubble and concrete blocks in the canal. We kept quiet and they still had no idea we were there. I reckoned we'd wait until there were as many as we could contend with on our side of the canal before opening fire. SS troops with black helmets started to come across and we waited for a posse of them to accumulate on our side. They were still convinced that there was no problem about adversaries in the area – they were standing about in little groups waiting for guide parties to get across. I reckoned we'd just enough to contend with so I blew my hunting horn and my men opened fire with consummate accuracy, disposing of all the enemy personnel on our side of the canal and also on the bank on the far side. This brought hostile proceedings to an abrupt halt.

Private Ernest Leggett
2nd Battalion, Royal Norfolk Regiment

My section took over a building that had been an old cement factory. The roof was missing but we were able to get up on to a veranda on the second floor. We could see into the woods, and we could see the Germans forming up about 150 yards away. Then we saw them coming at us through the wood. They had light tanks, and they were firing everything at us. We were firing back. We let them have all we'd got. I was on the Bren gun at that time, and we killed a lot of them. They came up almost as far as the river and we really gave them hell – and they retreated. But we found the Germans attacked us again. And they were repulsive – their tanks were coming over their own dead

A German soldier lies dead in a trench, May 1940

men. We couldn't understand why they did that. They were using the smaller type of tanks, but even though the river was small, they couldn't cross it. We managed to keep them on their side. They attacked us three times, and three times we sent them back. In our cement factory, we were coming under a lot of fire. Artillery and machine guns – but the mortars were the things that were really causing the damage. It was terrible being under mortar fire. You can hear the things 'pump off' and the next thing is the explosion.

Captain Peter Barclay
2nd Battalion, Royal Norfolk Regiment

We came in for an inordinate amount of shelling, and not long after that I was wounded in the guts, the back and the arm. We'd had several casualties before this so all the stretchers were out. My batman, with great presence of mind, ripped a door off its hinges and in spite of my orders to the contrary, tied me on to it. In fact, had he not done this, I probably wouldn't be here to tell the tale. At the time I thought, 'Now you've done this you're going to have to carry me round on this door – and you've not only got my weight to contend with, but the door as well.' It took four people to carry me, but they took me round to deal with what had become a very threatening situation from our right flank, where there should have been one of our units, but instead of a friendly unit being there, suddenly we were fired on by Germans from our side of the canal. I put my sergeant major, Gristock, in charge of a small force of about ten men, including a wireless operator and a company clerk and various other personnel from Company HQ. He was not only to hold my right flank, but deal with a German post that had been established not far off to my right.

Private Ernest Leggett
2nd Battalion, Royal Norfolk Regiment

I was looking along the line at our company headquarters, when I remember hearing machine-gun fire, and I looked along the river and I saw a figure I recognised – Sergeant Major Gristock – and he was crawling across this open ground on his elbows with his rifle in front of him. There were at least three other men behind him. They were moving towards a German machine-gun nest in front of them that they were trying to take out. I saw him putting up his rifle and I heard him fire at least three shots, and there was covering fire from the men behind him. I then saw another German machine-gun crew hurrying along, and setting up a position on the German side – but behind Gristock, so they had a flank view of him. He couldn't see them. I remember him reaching back, and throwing grenades. I saw his arm coming over. Then I heard the machine gun on the flank firing – but something happened that I had to turn away, and I didn't see any more. I later found out that Gristock got a broadside raking into his legs, and he won the Victoria Cross for this action. But at the time, it didn't register with me the extent of what he did. We were all killing Germans.

Captain Peter Barclay
2nd Battalion, Royal Norfolk Regiment

With that heroic display of his and the good work done by the rest of Sergeant Major Gristock's tiny party, the two enemy groups that had crossed the canal were disposed of. Then the reserve company of my own battalion came up and made good that right flank. I think I passed out then and the next thing I remember I was in a first-aid post with Gristock, who was in a very bad state – but not so bad that he didn't appreciate some jellified brandy pills that we were given. That cheered him up no end. They were delicious and very welcome. From there on I was evacuated and so was Gristock.

Private Ernest Leggett
2nd Battalion, Royal Norfolk Regiment

There was a lull in the fighting. Everything became quiet. Out of my section, in the end, there was only myself, two other privates, and a lance corporal. Out of 25 of us. We had suffered heavy casualties – and there were no wounded. The others were all dead. We sat down, and smoked and talked. And every time we saw a German moving in the distance, we shot at him. The lance corporal said to me, 'Nip across! See if the bastards have gone from our left flank!' I left my rifle near a wall, and I walked across the floor of this building, and the next thing I knew I'd hit the ceiling, and then I heard a loud bang. I came down and hit the floor. I realised that I'd been hit. It was one of those blasted three-inch mortars and I'd been hit. My left leg was absolutely numb, my back was numb from the waist down, I couldn't move my legs, and all I saw was blood all over the floor. Two others ran across to me, one said, 'Bloody hell, Ernie! You've had it!' I later found out that a piece of shrapnel about three and a half inches long and an inch and a half wide had gone in through my left buttock and out through my groin and caused a big cavity. It had gone straight through me. My pals got their field dressings and they bunged one into the wound at the back, pushed it up, one into the wound at the front and they tied the other two on the outside. Fortunately, I was numb and I had no pain – but I thought I'd had it. I thought of my home and my family, and what they were going to do when they heard the news of my death.

They dragged me out, and carried me downstairs to the railway line. I was still numb, and they'd taken my trousers off, and all I had on was a rough old pair of pants. I couldn't walk. All I could do was crawl. And I knew that if I had six inches of cover, I was safe from rifle fire and machine-gun fire. All I had to worry about was from above, but the rails afforded me six inches of cover. I crawled and crawled, and they were bombing from above, and I was being covered with earth. As I was crawling, I was pulling myself along, and I became conscious that my fingernails were being worn down and my hands were bleeding. I was like a wounded animal, determined to get away. It took me ages to get to the company headquarters, and as I was almost at my last gasp, there was one hell of a big explosion, and I was covered with earth, and I said, 'Please, God! Help me!' I don't know how long I was out, but it was a long while, and next, I remember my hands and arms being tugged, and someone was saying, 'Bloody hell! It's Ernie!' I looked up into the faces of two bandsmen who had taken the job of stretcher-bearers. They pulled me out – and I remember them putting me on a stretcher, carrying me away, putting me in the back of a truck. I was still numb, and we were driving over bumpy ground. I was unloaded, and a medical officer bent over me, and I saw a nun bending over me with one of those big flowery hats the French nuns wear, and the MO was talking in French to her, and he got a syringe out of his bag. 'Just a prick, old boy,' he said, and I can't remember anything else.

Captain Peter Barclay
2nd Battalion, Royal Norfolk Regiment

I was evacuated from a first-aid post to a larger medical rendezvous. I had a darling little black mongrel dog who wouldn't leave me, and she was lying on me, preventing anybody getting near me. They cut off my trousers – which I thought was a most awful waste of a reasonable pair of battledress trousers – and my little dog was so concerned about this that they had to put a bag over her and take her away. I never saw her again – it was too awful.

Four of us were put into a tradesman's van and we'd gone some little distance when the driver brought the vehicle to a very abrupt halt and turned the van round unceremoniously. The van had an open back and I found myself looking at a German tank sitting about 20 yards away in the middle of the road. We had a Red Cross painted on the side of the van and the chap forbore to fire at us, and so we went on our way until we reached a station where the stretcher cases were loaded on to a hospital train.

Private Ernest Leggett
2nd Battalion, Royal Norfolk Regiment
In my lucid moments, I remember being placed on a hospital train. Every time I woke up, I got another needle to put me out, and this carried on for quite a while. It was a very hazy period – but the morphine had taken the pain away. I was taken off the train and put on an ambulance. I remember waking up on the beaches at Dunkirk – on a stretcher in the dunes. I had nothing on me except a filthy old blanket and dirty bandages. I was given jabs every so often. I remember shells and bombs. I was very hazy, but when danger became very close, I can remember people falling on top of me – to shield me from further harm. That's comradeship.

I woke up in bed in a ward with other people around me, and a nurse said, 'It's all right. You're OK now! You're in hospital in England.' The surgeons had plugged the worst wound all the way from the back to the front, and said that I would be OK. They told me it was a miracle – because this shrapnel was red hot, and as it went through me, it turned and its jagged edge scraped the femoral artery in my groin. Had it punctured it, I would have been dead in three minutes. They said it was a one-in-a-million chance of me being alive. I've also got an eight-inch scar on my leg, my left thigh was wounded all the way up, I had a fracture of the spine, and I have a shrapnel scar on my forehead. I must have been one hell of a mess. The next thing I remember, someone touched me, and there was my dear mother by my bedside. She said, 'How bad is it?' I said, 'I don't know, mother.'

I had been in hospital for three or four days, when the sister came and said, 'There's someone in the next ward who has ordered that he should see you.' I asked who it was and she said, 'Wait and see...' so they lifted me out, and wheeled me in, and I was greeted with, 'Hello boy! How are you?' It was Sergeant Major Gristock! He told me that his legs had been amputated from the hip: he'd been so shot up by the broadside machine gun. I noticed that on his bedrail was a line of 10 or 12 bottles of ale. It went through my mind that if they were allowing a man in his condition to drink, he must be in a very poor way. And he said, 'Do something for me, boy!' I said, 'What's that?' He said, 'Fill this up for me.' And I poured beer into a pot with a spout, and held it to his mouth, and he just supped it, and said, 'Beautiful! Pour another one in!' and I did that every day.

I told Gristock that I'd seen what had happened to him, and he said, 'The bastards! But I wiped them out!' We talked about the company, the men, about how fortunate we were to get away. 'You know, boy, we were wiped out? All but seven of us! The company is non-existent.' I said that I'd heard. We talked about the old days, and we did this every day, and I'd help him to drink, and then the horrible morning came when they didn't come and get me, and I said to the nurse, 'Take me through to see my sergeant major,' and she said, 'No. Sorry.' He had died.

Private Harry Dennis
1st Battalion, East Surrey Regiment
We were on the Escaut for two or three days. While we were there, we crept out of the lines, and got on to the road where there were a few buildings. One of them was an *estaminet*, and one of the lads wanted to have a look. There was a wooden cellar cover in the pavement, so we broke it open and went inside. Lo and behold, there were barrels of beer – full. And also, up in the corner, there were some wooden crates. We undid one of these and they contained bottles of champagne – untouched. We said, 'We can't leave this here! Good lord, if we don't have it, the Germans will!' So we lifted it all out, took it back on the road and waited until dark. I brought the staff car up, and we loaded up one barrel and three crates of champagne, and took them back to headquarters. The wounded, waiting to go out the next morning, tapped the barrel and had some beer, and all of us had a drink of champagne.

It wasn't a matter of looting – it was only for food and drink. I never saw any looting, though there were plenty of opportunities in some of the villages where houses were empty, and which blokes could have broken into. We also found a farm where the farmer had legs of salted pork and dried bacon down in the cellar, and we took some of those and distributed them. Many a soldier has eaten chicken, boiled whole, out of a can that had just had four gallons of petrol poured out of it. We can tell you what petrol-flavoured chicken tastes like.

Sapper Percy Beaton
218 Army Troops Company, Royal Engineers

There was no actual panic but people were sometimes a bit uncertain because you'd hear a rumour – some French-speaking person would say to you, 'The Germans are five miles down the road and they're advancing fast,' and we wouldn't be prepared to move. So we'd be thinking to ourselves, 'Are they five miles down the road or *aren't* they? And if they do come, what do we do?' Because nobody had told us what to do. The fifth column used to cause a lot of despondency because you didn't know if it was true or not. You could turn around and say, 'Oh, it's a load of lies. It's only the fifth column!' But there was always the fear that it might be the truth for once.

Stephane Hessel
Served with French Army

In France, there was a minority – not very large but influential – that was on the side of the Germans. The fifth column. People who disliked the Republic, who disliked democratic institutions in France, did all they could to have France weakened in front of the assault of Fascism. Many people felt that the way the fascists treated the economy, morale, nationalism, was the right thing to do. And there were quite a number of Frenchmen, particularly in the higher bourgeoisie, who felt it was better to have a fascist regime than communism or *forme populaire*. There were no great numbers of these people but they furnished the background of collaboration in later years.

Captain James Hill
2nd Battalion, Royal Fusiliers

The Belgians and French were very conscious of the fifth column in their own countries – and you never really knew who to believe. The Belgians would tell you that a group of people were fifth columnists, and you'd not know whether they were or weren't. Once a lot of notices suddenly appeared all along the telegraph posts – they were all the same and it was said that they had been put up by the fifth column to mark the route for the German armour as it came through. But I couldn't believe that that was so.

Private Edgar Rabbets
5th Battalion, Northamptonshire Regiment

We *did* come across some fifth-column activity. There were some Belgians – or they may have been Germans who had been planted there – and they were doing some farming. They were ploughing a field, working down two sides so that the lines formed an arrow pointing to our headquarters. No farmer ploughs his land that way. This was for the benefit of aircraft, which duly arrived and plastered the headquarters out of existence. We lost our first colonel through that. After that, if I noticed anybody ploughing wrongly, he got shot. I shot two men who were doing that. Drawing an arrow on the land. They knew what they were doing, and I knew what they were doing – so there was no need for discussion.

Lance Corporal Lawrence Greggain
5th Battalion, Border Regiment

I still feel fully justified in what I did in the circumstances I am about to describe. I was in the battalion orderly room, which was a pillbox, and two of my lads appeared with a large civilian between them. He was a most revolting-looking individual. He stood over six feet tall, must have weighed over 20 stone, and was wearing a dark blue suit. His face was large, fat and podgy, with close-set little piggy eyes, and a small slit of a mouth. 'Who the hell is this, and where did you find him?' I asked. 'He was in a cottage overlooking our reserve trenches, sitting in a window with a Martini .22 rifle, and a box of ammunition beside him. We have been getting lads in the reserve trenches shot in the head with a small-calibre rifle, and the window faced that way. There were some empty shells on the table, and the barrel of the rifle was still warm. It had obviously been fired.' 'Why didn't you bring the rifle and ammo along as evidence?' 'Never thought of it, Corporal!'

We questioned the man, who stood and leered at us. We could not get him to say anything. We had already had trouble with Belgian fifth columnists, and it was possible that he was one of them. Remembering some of the atrocities they had committed, I was thinking, 'I'll soon wipe that grin off your face, you bastard!' The adjutant had followed all the conversations, and tried again. Nothing. Turning to me, he just said, 'Get rid of him!'

We marched off down a country lane. I turned to the two escorts and said, 'Well, which one of you two buggers wants to shoot this bastard? You?' 'No, not me, Corporal.' 'Well, you?' 'No, not me, Corp.' 'You do realise he must have shot some of your friends? Always the bloody same. Leave all the really dirty work to the NCOs.' It was hard to say whether this Belgian understood what was being said. He was poker faced the entire time. But at this point, some German bombers flew over, and he jerked his thumb in their direction, and uttered the only word we got out of him. He said, 'Bosche!' and gave a kind of insane giggle. It was the last laugh of his life.

'Pay attention! You will march ahead with the prisoner. I shall give the order "Prisoner and escort, halt!" He understands nothing, or so it would seem. He will not halt, and I shall shoot him. Understand?' 'Yes, Corporal.' And so it was. A single shot through the heart, and another through the side of the head for the *coup de grâce*. I sent my lads off on their respective duties, and reported back to the adjutant. 'Prisoner tried to escape, sir, I had to shoot him.' 'Did you bury the body?' 'No, sir, it rolled into the ditch at the side of the road.' 'Well, make sure your men bury it properly.' 'Yes, sir.' But there was no time for such niceties. Almost at once, we were moving out, retreating still further. I really disliked what I did, but felt justice had to be done.

Lance Corporal Kenneth Carver
5th Motor Ambulance Convoy, Royal Army Service Corps

If anybody saw a light at night, one was told to think of a fifth column. There were all kinds of rumours. On one occasion I travelled with a convoy over the canal outside Dunkirk, and when I got to the canal that evening I was stopped by some military police who said, 'You can't go any further! The bridge is blown!' I had been over that bridge previously. When I turned the convoy round I met some more military police and told them what had happened. They said, 'Stop here,' and they were gone for a while. When they returned they said they believed that the two MPs were German parachutists – fifth columnists. The next day, we travelled on over the bridge.

Private Edgar Rabbets
5th Battalion, Northamptonshire Regiment

There *were* German infiltrators – in British uniforms – who were well briefed and knew the regiments in the area. They'd come along and say they belonged to a regiment on the right or left flank of where you were. For some reason they were usually majors. I suppose the idea was that a major had sufficient authority to transmit orders. They would tell us to take up new positions, five

Belgian refugees – with their meagre possessions – flee from the German advance

or ten miles away from where we happened to be at the time. They claimed that they were going to move a short while after we did. This was an obvious ploy to create a gap. When they were challenged to produce their papers, they couldn't. I took one back to the unit he claimed he belonged to, and as the colonel didn't know him, that was the end of that one. I shot him.

Lance Sergeant Robert Green
2nd Battalion, Bedfordshire and Hertfordshire Regiment
In the early part of the war there were stories about German paratroopers coming down dressed up as nuns and all sorts of codswallop like that – rumours and myths. Well, one night, it got darker and we were getting ready to withdraw, when one of the lads came up and said, 'You know, there's a woman round the back of this house showing a very keen interest in what's going on.' I said, 'What about it?' He said, 'Well we've had all that heavy shelling – and this woman's got a remarkably masculine cast of features. We've been suspicious of her all afternoon.' So I said, 'We'll have to go and find out – and there's only one way we can do that.' We were just on our way round to find out if this character was in fact male or female when the order came – 'Get fell in!' So we never did find out whether she was male or female, for which, I might allow, I was rather thankful, because it would have fallen to my lot to check.

Captain James Hill
2nd Battalion, Royal Fusiliers
A number of infiltrators came down by parachute – I saw them quite often – but you couldn't do very much about them. Some of the Belgians used to get very fed up, and one or two of them scythed off the heads of some of these chaps. I thought that was fair justice. But the fifth column people were a nuisance: people would bring me in suspected fifth columnists. The only reason they brought them to me was that I was probably the only mark of authority in that part of the world. This happened all the time. If I thought that a chap was a really bad sort, I'd tell the Belgians to hold him in prison. I couldn't shoot him – there was no point.

Private Edgar Rabbets
5th Battalion, Northamptonshire Regiment
Another thing the Germans did to demoralise us was to drop leaflets. I saw one of these leaflets at Dunkirk, telling us we were surrounded and we should

give up, but nobody took a lot of notice. We knew we were surrounded, but I don't think anybody had any idea of giving up, at least not without a fight.

Private William Ridley
9th Battalion, Durham Light Infantry
We went down into Petit Vimy, and as I was standing on the ridge, I looked towards Arras, and saw a huge black cloud of planes – hundreds of them. I thought, 'Oh no, there we go again. We're going to get a right bashing.' Then I looked to the other side on the left, and there was another black cloud, and I thought, 'Oh good, here's the RAF! This'll sort them out!' But unfortunately the two masses of planes joined together and came down and bombed us.

2nd Lieutenant Ian English
8th Battalion, Durham Light Infantry
At Vimy, we were told to get as much sleep as possible as we were going to be mounting a counter-attack. I think we were fairly resigned; it was fairly obvious that we were going to have to do some fighting sooner or later.

2nd Lieutenant Peter Vaux
4th Battalion, Royal Tank Regiment
We came back and rejoined the regiment at Petit Vimy. I told the colonel that I'd made contact with the Germans. I told him where they were. And he smiled. 'I'm afraid,' he said, 'that's out of date, now. We are going to make contact!' He told me how the Germans had broken through, and were running somewhere through Arras, and he said that we would counter-attack. We would be getting orders in the morning. I asked, 'Is this the real thing, colonel?' And he said, 'Yes, Peter, it's the real thing this time.'

Captain James Hill
2nd Battalion, Royal Fusiliers
The importance of this counter-attack was paramount in all our minds – it had to be successful. This was Lord Gort's last ploy.

Flying Officer Roland Beamont
87 Squadron, RAF
We started getting orders to take alternative targets of opportunity – which

meant columns of troops and vehicles which could be positively identified as hostile. That meant making ground attacks with machine guns, which weren't a particularly effective weapon against vehicles. These attacks were on troops coming up those long straight roads in the area of Arras.

2nd Lieutenant Peter Vaux
4th Battalion, Royal Tank Regiment

We reached a railway line at Dainville. Our tanks all lined up on a ridge just short of it. We went up the crest and over the top straight into the side of what we later discovered was Rommel's 7th Panzer Division. It was a most extraordinary situation because they didn't know that we were coming. There were masses of half-tracks and lorries and motorcycles and anti-tank guns on tow. And everything worked as it should. The gunners all fired and the German lorries burst into flames. A German motorcycle was just in front of me, and the driver was trying to start the engine, and he was kicking away with his kick-start and he couldn't get it going. My gunner was laughing so much that he couldn't shoot the gun. Eventually the German threw the motorcycle into a ditch and ran away. We hadn't fired on him at all.

Lieutenant Colonel Peter Jeffreys
6th Battalion, Durham Light Infantry

My great impression of the counter-attack was the action by the 4th Royal Tanks, they were all regulars, but they were thrown into the battle in a very haphazard manner. They had travelled on their tracks for a very long way before this engagement, but they were so full of cheer and go, and my word they did a terrific job against the back of that German force.

2nd Lieutenant Peter Vaux
4th Battalion, Royal Tank Regiment

I came to a crossroads where there was lorry with a great big 'G' painted on the door. I remember thinking – in the silly way one does – 'G is for German' and at that moment the driver, who sure enough was wearing a field grey uniform, jumped out of the driver's seat. I said to my gunner, 'Shoot!' and he shot the lorry which burst into flames. Then he swung the turret round and fired at the German soldier who ran down the street, zigzagging with the tracer bullets flying on either side of him. He disappeared into a garden – and we hadn't hit him. And unbelievably, a woman came out of a house, emptied a bucket into a dustbin, and went back in again. She must have watched the whole thing from her kitchen window, and waited her turn to empty her bucket. Anyway, the effect on my driver was interesting. He only had about nine days to live – but he would have nightmares about that German soldier over the next few days. He would wake up and shiver, and say, 'How dreadful it must have been for him with those bullets coming past him!'

2nd Lieutenant Ian English
8th Battalion, Durham Light Infantry

Our orders during the counter-attack were that our two battalions should reach the Arras–Doullens road – but we encountered German tanks and infantry a long way before we got near there. When we reached the Arras–St Pol road, we saw a column of German vehicles lying in the ditch, all shot up, and quite a number of dead about, with some wounded and some prisoners. This German column had been engaged by armoured cars earlier that morning, and also by the 7th Tank Battalion, which was moving ahead of us. Our rifle companies had marched quite a long way, and it was very hot – everyone was just slogging along – and the sight of this German column having been attacked did a tremendous lot for our morale, everyone had their tails up.

2nd Lieutenant Peter Vaux
4th Battalion, Royal Tank Regiment

I remember some wretched German small weapon – I suppose some 2cm thing – fired at us. The blooming projectile went in one side of my turret and out the other. Just in front of my gunner and myself. It left two holes. The gunner and I looked at one other, and without a word, he bent down and picked up his small pack and took out of it a pair of rather smelly socks. He gave one to me and I stuffed one in my hole, and he stuffed one into his. It seemed somehow a bit better that way.

2nd Lieutenant Ian English
8th Battalion, Durham Light Infantry

We came under very heavy fire from German positions on the Arras–Doullens road itself – especially mortar fire. And then we were attacked by Stukas.

Several of the troops were caught in the open, just as they were getting into position. This was the first time we'd been directly attacked and the whole thing was very frightening, as they come down in a nearly vertical dive with a tremendous scream – and they appear to be aiming their bombs right at you. Then they strafed us with machine guns – and this went virtually unopposed apart from one man firing his Bren gun at them. Then the truck behind him got hit, and he went into the ditch. This attack went on for about 20 minutes, and there was tremendous smoke and dust and confusion, and everyone was absolutely pinned to the earth. Then they went off. I think we had three trucks damaged and about ten men wounded – the material damage was virtually nothing, but the effect on morale was absolutely amazing. Everyone was really shattered. It really took an awful lot of effort by the officers and NCOs to get anyone moving again. They really had to be kicked to get in position. They seemed to be numbed – absolutely shattered.

2nd Lieutenant Peter Vaux
4th Battalion, Royal Tank Regiment

I motored through a lot of our tanks, of which I suppose there must have been 20 or so of all three squadrons. But they weren't moving, they weren't shooting, and the guns were at all angles. Then I saw that some of them had men hanging out of the turrets or out of the driver's seat, or lying beside the tanks. All these tanks were dead. I told my driver to reverse, and I stood up on my seat in the turret, so I was exposed from the waist upwards. I was shouting to the driver to do this and that, and shouting at the gunner to do the other. But what I little knew was that behind me a German soldier was lying on the ground with his rifle resting on a kitbag, drawing a bead on my back. I didn't know this – but Captain Cracroft did. It wasn't until we got back to England that his gunner told me that Captain Cracroft drew his revolver and shot this man in the throat before he could pull the trigger. After that, we pulled out of what was really a valley of death, and we picked up quite a number of tank crews as we went. There must have been half-a-dozen men clinging to the outside of one's tank.

2nd Lieutenant Ian English
8th Battalion, Durham Light Infantry

A Company had taken quite a number of casualties, so the commanding officer pulled them back to Warlus, and we took up a position for all-round defence of the village. This took a bit of organising, because the men were just sitting about after this air raid. The German pressure became more intense as the day went on, and there was quite a lot of shelling and accurate mortar fire. We were suffering a few casualties – the CO was wounded in the leg, but that didn't seem to make a great deal of difference to him. He just went round a bit more slowly than he had before, as he organised things. Darkness was beginning to come down, and the village of Warlus was burning from the shellfire and there was a lot of smoke and confusion. We learnt that the company commander of A Company had been wounded and taken prisoner, along with several of his men.

2nd Lieutenant Peter Vaux
4th Battalion, Royal Tank Regiment

A number of our tanks rendezvoused at a crossroads in Achicourt. It was getting dark, and we heard a tank coming towards us. Trundling along – clatter, clatter, clatter. I was in the turret of my tank, and Captain Cracroft was leaning against the running board, smoking. My gunner had been turned out of the tank and replaced by Major Fernie – who was to take over the regiment. Captain Cracroft walked across the crossroads towards this tank. He waved his mapboard up and down in front of the driver's periscope, and the tank halted. The hatch cover opened – and out popped German helmets. It was a German tank! Cracroft ran back as fast as he could to his tank, and everybody opened fire. The Germans' shots must have gone over our heads, and our shots must have gone over theirs. Captain Cracroft – I think it was him – called out, 'We must pull out of here at once!'

There was absolute chaos as we pulled back because there was a very narrow railway bridge at Achicourt with a bend in it – and we went over that. There was unbelievable confusion. There were our tanks, there were Bren carriers that belonged to the Durham Light Infantry, there were German motorcyclists. It was dark and it was noisy. And we had no ammunition left. We'd used it all up. After a while, we reached the Arras–Doullens Road, but instead of crossing it, we turned left, and when I looked out we were quite alone on a road I didn't recognise. We were heading south-west towards Doullens, and a lot of traffic started coming the other way – and it was all German traffic. The Germans didn't react to us. It was quite dark – and we didn't have insignia in those days. As long as we kept moving, there was no reason why anybody should know who we were.

A driver of the Royal Tank Regiment looks out through his hatch

Unfortunately, we got to a crossroads where a column of German half-tracks were backing out. They were right across the road while an angry German officer directed traffic. I didn't really know what to do. But my driver, Corporal Burroughs, had the answer. He drove quite deliberately and slowly into the back of a lorry. There was an expensive crunch, and loud shouts from the German soldiers in the lorry. The German officer swore at us, told the lorry to pull forward, and told us to get the hell out of it. And we drove on. He never knew us for anything but a German tank.

2nd Lieutenant Ian English
8th Battalion, Durham Light Infantry

We were under constant attack, and the brigadier ordered that the battalion should withdraw as it was running up against opposition which was very much greater than it could cope with – but it was some hours after that that we actually withdrew. We went back the way we'd come, to Vimy which we reached at around five in the morning. At Vimy we moved further along the ridge to Givenchy, where we took up defensive positions. The next day was fairly quiet, then at about three the following morning we were ordered to withdraw to Carvin. It was extremely slow going – the roads were absolutely packed with vehicles and refugees. We then got word from our signals officer that a French Algerian division were manning the La Bassée canal, and were very hard pressed. I was sent into Carvin to report to the French at their divisional headquarters – there must have been a dozen or more French officers, all poring over maps on the table and everyone talking at once. I stood there with the liaison officer for a moment, then somebody saw us, and there was tremendous excitement. 'Ah, bravo! Les Anglais!'

2nd Lieutenant Peter Vaux
4th Battalion, Royal Tank Regiment

By now, the driver was saying, 'It's a matter of minutes before she runs dry of petrol.' We found a village and we pulled in spluttering and baled out the tank. We destroyed it as best we could, and we disappeared into an empty house where we spent the night and the next day. We soon discovered that the village was called Fransu – and it appeared to be deserted. In the house, we found a tin of condensed milk and a child's school atlas, and we saw that we were about ten kilometres from the Somme. We guessed that the Germans were heading for the coast, that the Somme might well be guarding their left flank, and that if we could only find the Somme and cross it, we would probably find French or British troops on the other side.

So that night, we took our food in a basket we found in the house, our overcoats, our compass and our strange little map. We set off, walking across country, to the nearest point on the Somme – a village called L'Étoile. We reached it just as it was getting dawn. We hid in the forward edge of a wood looking down on the river. We suddenly heard a rustling in the trees, and out sprang a German officer brandishing a pistol. He shouted to us to stand up, and put our hands up. We did, and he came across and took the major's pistol and Burroughs' revolver. He came to me and tore my binoculars from my neck – but he forgot about my pistol. He said, 'Go on! Move on!' So on we went, Burroughs leading, me next, the major, and then the German. He told us to move faster. Burroughs did, I carried on the same, and the major stopped. The German turned on the major, and took a shot at him. I swung round with my pistol – and I shot at the German. He turned his attention to me – and we shot at each other. I fired five shots, and the fifth hit him well and truly in the chest, but he kept on running at me, shouting and shooting, until he collapsed against me, and I put the sixth shot into him. Down he went.

We turned and ran as hard as we could. We hid in a ruined abbey a mile from the river. While we were there, getting hungrier and hungrier, and weaker and weaker, an elderly Belgian gentleman – Monsieur Gilis – appeared. He said, 'All the refugees know that you're here. And there are notices up all round here, saying "Wanted for Murder. Three British". The refugees know that you're wanted for murder, and the notices say that anybody who helps you will be shot! You must go!' He explained that the only place to get over the river was where the railway line crosses it, as it was built on the only bit of hard ground, and he offered to take one of us in civilian clothes to do a reconnaissance that afternoon.

So he went off and came back with some country clothes, and gave them to me. He and I went together, and everything went well until we got to the river bank. There was a German sergeant major there, in charge of a position. He asked to see my identity card – and Monsieur Gilis turned on this German like a tiger. He said, 'You are a most unpleasant race! Here is this lad, an honest half-witted country lad. Only speaks Flemish. He's come all the way down from Belgium, pursued by you and your horrible Stukas! How would he have an identity card?' And the German said, 'Get out of it!' So we noted where the path led down to the bank, and went back to the abbey, where Monsieur Gilis wished us luck.

Now the situation was that Burroughs was not a good swimmer, so it was agreed that I would help him across the river, and the major would swim with our clothes done up in a bundle. We waited by the river bank until we had worked out the pattern of how the sentries went up and down the bank. We realised, after a while, that once the sentry had passed, there wouldn't be another for about ten minutes. As soon as one had passed, we slipped into the water, and started off. We had completely overlooked the fact that we were almost tottering with fatigue and lack of food. The result was that Burroughs couldn't swim at all. I lacked the strength to get him across to the other side – and he slipped from my hands. The major got across. I became unconscious but I got across. When he was across, the major concluded that Burroughs and I were drowned, and he put on his uniform, hid the others, and set off due south with our compass. I spent a long time looking for Burroughs, but I didn't find him. And then I set off up the hill, naked except for my pants.

After about a mile, walking uphill on gravel, my feet getting very cut, I came to a roadblock – where I was challenged in French by a sentry. I called out that I was a British officer. He stuck his rifle into my stomach, and said, 'You don't look like one!' After a while, I persuaded him, and I was taken to battalion headquarters, and there was the major, dressed in his uniform. From there, we were handed over to a British escort who took us down to Rouen, where we were interrogated. I was fitted out with new battledress, and after a couple of days, we were sent down to Cherbourg and shipped home. Corporal Burroughs had been swept down the river to a place called Pont-Remy, where he was pulled out, and buried by the French in a little cemetery there. Every year, they still put a little wreath on his grave.

2nd Lieutenant Allan Elton Younger
61 Chemical Warfare Company, Royal Engineers
We were given a sector in the south-east of Arras to defend between two main roads. The 1st Battalion, Welsh Guards were in charge of the defence of probably the whole of Arras and certainly of this sector. And they had two posts, one on the main road going due east, and the other on the main road going south-east. I was asked to fill in between these two posts, covering a sector, I

suppose, of about a quarter of a mile. There were several roads coming into my sector from the expected direction of attack – south-east – so the first thing I did was to get some anti-tank mines to put in the road; we had no way of stopping a German tank if one had come other than our Boys anti-tank rifle – which we didn't really expect to be able to stop too much.

So I went to GHQ, and found out where to draw up mines, and then placed them in these various roads. But there was a disaster on the first night. I'd put double sentries out to make sure that no French vehicles – or British for that matter – went over these mines. Some time in the middle of the night, I was woken by the most appalling bang. And it turned out that a huge French civilian lorry had come along and refused to stop when the first sentry, Sapper Kirkbride, tried to stop him. He absolutely refused to take any notice of him. The second sentry, Sapper Calvert, moved out in front of him to try to get him to stop – but he didn't stop. And he went over one of the mines. Sapper Calvert was standing in front of him and he was killed. Sapper Kirkbride was luckily screened by the vehicle. The vehicle was destroyed, the whole of the front of it was blown up, but the driver, who was very high off the ground, appeared to be all right, and just disappeared.

The lorry just stayed there. We couldn't move it, and we had to lay new sentries. And there wasn't much time until we stood to at dawn. And then the day's work began, and I went to a garage that I'd spotted, and I requisitioned all the cars that were there. I placed them, blocking the road, behind the anti-tank mines, so that this couldn't happen again. I had some arguments with some of the French car owners, of course, but I felt that this was a necessary action to be taken in order to defend Arras. I gave them some receipts that such-and-such a car is requisitioned by the British Army for the defence of Arras, and left it at that.

All the time, refugees were pouring down the roads. I don't think they knew which direction to go in. Some were going north, some south, some east, some west. But I noticed after about the second or third day that the refugees on the main road had stopped. I went to see what had stopped them, and I asked some of them what the matter was. There was a group of oldish men there, and one of them said, very excitedly, 'There are some detonators on the road!' That was his word – 'detonators'. And he pointed to where he meant. I went up to look at these, and they appeared to be pencils. Ordinary blue, sharpened pencils. I leant down to pick one up, and the man grabbed my wrist, and said, 'No! No!

No! This is a known trick by the Germans! They're detonators, and they're very dangerous!' So I took another look at them, and they certainly didn't look like detonators to me. They looked like pencils. Eventually, I picked one up, and this little group of Frenchmen all fell back, and I threw it over a wall – and nothing happened. They *were* pencils. I then picked the rest up, and we all shook hands, and then the flow of refugees went on.

After that we strengthened our defences. We dug trenches for the sentries, and we got sandbags to put in the windows from which we could shoot at attacking Germans. In the meantime, the Germans were bombing Arras, and we heard horrifying stories from the Welsh Guards on the main roads about how they had been strafed by German fighter-bombers. The thing was, we never saw the RAF or French Air Force.

Lieutenant D'Arcy McCloughin
9 Field Company, Royal Engineers

From time to time either shelling or bombing caught up with the animal population and we saw some nasty cases of horses careering about in agony because part of their backside had been torn off. In one case I found a pig that had been badly wounded and I felt I ought to try and put it out of its misery. Pigs do make an awful noise when they're stuck. My only means of doing it, as I'm not a very good rifle shot, was to try and charge it after holding a pistol to its head, but that's easier said than done. I had to fire quite a lot of shots before I managed to kill it. I think we all felt that if we saw wounded animals, we ought to put them out of their misery or they'd only die a lingering death.

Private David Elliott
141st Field Ambulance, Royal Army Medical Corps

We were suddenly bombed, and there were dead cows laying about, and one or two mooing at us in pain. We had no casualties among ourselves, and we managed to persuade the doctors to let us have some stitching material, and we tried to stitch these cows up. It was something to do…

Captain Gilbert White
1/6th Battalion, East Surrey Regiment

We had to withdraw from the Escaut as part of the overall plan of the 2nd Corps, and we started withdrawing on 22 May, and deployed along the River

Lys. We were in a very uncomfortable position – too far stretched – but we did manage to take two prisoners. They were absolutely cock-a-hoop – on the crest of a wave. It was just their bad luck that they happened to be captured, but they knew that they were going to push us back into the sea. Their tails were right up, and they were arrogant. 'This won't last for long – we shall soon be reunited!' They were as cocky as hell.

Major William Reeves
3rd Battalion, Royal Tank Regiment

We withdrew into Ypres, and spent the next day there, doing nothing but waiting for orders. There was a conference in a little café just under the Menin Gate, during which time the gate was being shot up and shelled. It was strange to see the First World War memorial being shelled again, splinters being knocked off it before our eyes.

Brigadier William Fox-Pitt
2nd Battalion, Welsh Guards

One day, the Chief of the Imperial General Staff, Field Marshal Dill, rang me up and talked to me personally, and said, 'I've got rather a hot one for you. You've got to go out and hold on to Boulogne as long as you can. There's very little information as to what's happening.' So I organised the brigade again, and the two battalions were sent to Boulogne. We went over in destroyers, and I took up a line outside Boulogne with the Irish Guards on the right and the Welsh Guards on the left. We were supposed to have a French division in front of us, but it never materialised. We held Boulogne for 24 hours until we were very heavily attacked by tanks, and then we withdrew, very well covered by the destroyers. I got the whole of the Irish Guards off, and I got the Welsh Guards, bar two companies, off. The destroyers kept coming back and forth, taking us off. Wonderful. Two companies were put in the bag.

Armament Quartermaster Sergeant Frank Hurrell
3rd Army Field Workshop, Royal Army Ordnance Corps

We were in a hamlet near Hazebrouck, and two men went out on a recce and said the way looked more or less safe up the road, so the colonel decided we'd leave all our vehicles in the village, and we'd break out, going in Indian file on each side of the road. We did this – but we had no idea where we were going.

A captured German pilot is assisted by men of the Border Regiment

The officers had had their briefing, but it was never passed down to anybody else and we were all just like a lot of sheep, following the leader. We'd gone about a quarter of a mile, when suddenly there was gunfire sprayed right the way through the ranks. It came from four German armoured cars positioned on a hill. As soon as the firing started I hit the ground and threw myself to my right to get off the road. What I'd thrown myself into was not a ditch, but part of a quarry, and in so doing I damaged my knee. I didn't realise I'd injured myself until five minutes or more later, because of the impact and excitement. I picked myself up and found my leg was injured and my trousers were badly torn. I looked around, trying to find out what was happening and how many men were still OK. Eventually five us got together in the quarry, and decided to go to our right – as the enemy was on our left. Although the night was dark, there was a moon with clouds flitting across, and every now and then there was bright moonlight so you had to be very careful that you weren't suddenly exposed. I was dragging my injured leg and using my rifle butt to help me along, and there were several others limping as well. We met another six or seven of our own fellows who had been in the rear of the column. We had a little council of war and decided to split up into three parties and go in different directions.

Major William Reeves
3rd Battalion, Royal Tank Regiment
We engaged a German panzer division at Guines, where we were overpowered and outgunned. The German fire was very accurate and we had seven tanks knocked out – or 'brewed up' as we called it. You could see them burning on the crest of the hill. We had orders to withdraw and form up again at another position between Guines and Calais. Later on we withdrew again to a position to the west of Calais just before it got dark. From there we could see the German tanks moving to the south of Calais and coming nearer and nearer. The orders were then to withdraw right into Calais and reform, then await further orders.

Calais at that time was very eerie and sinister. The civilians had all disappeared, and there was quite a heavy atmosphere. Calais had had several bombing raids and a lot of houses had been knocked down and the streets were full of rubble. The shops had all been looted and there were Frenchmen wandering about half-tight as they'd had so much wine to drink.

We thought a bombing attack was coming at any minute, so we just settled down and tried to reorganise before it got dark. Then when it was just getting dark, further orders came through that we were to proceed to Dunkirk, and that mine was to be the leading squadron – a cruiser tank and three light tanks – as the advance guard on the route through Gravelines to Dunkirk. I was to report back by wireless if there was any resistance on the way.

I started off with my three tanks ahead of me, in the moonlight. We were five miles along the road when suddenly a road block was reported in front. Lorries had been towed across the road and the point tank said he thought he couldn't get any further. I went up and had a look – there were two lorries which had been pulled across the road, blocking it. We tied a tow rope on to one of the lorries and reversed to pull it out of the way, but there were no indications as to whether the road block was defended or not. We managed to get through, but in another mile we came to another similar block with lorries and old carts put across the road – and again we broke through it and carried on. By that time there was no going back and unfortunately the wireless had broken down, so there was no communication to battalion headquarters in Calais.

Soon after that we came across my point tank again, and he reported soldiers on either side of the road, lying down bivouacking and having a meal. He thought they were French troops and he asked what to do. I said he should carry on, and I'd come up and see who they were. When I got there I saw that they were German troops on each side of the road. A panzer group was spending the night there, having put up road blocks.

Peter Williams leant over his tank and started to speak to them. I caught up with him and said, 'For God's sake, move on fast as you bloody well can!' I decided it would be fatal to start a battle there or open fire – we'd have been finished on the spot. We drove on with the troops on either side of us, with vehicles and tanks, all brewing up for the night and bivouacking. They didn't take any notice. We waved to them and they waved back: they must have thought we were German tanks.

We went through at least a mile of this, but then they began to get suspicious. One German dispatch rider came up behind my tank and shone a torch on the number plate, then speeded off, having evidently understood what had happened. We kept driving and eventually came to a bridge over the canal at a place called Marck. You could see on the canal that there were strips of mines joined by metal across the top and obviously if you ran a tank over these, they would explode and probably blow up the tank and the bridge as well. We expected that the bridge would be defended, and were expecting at any minute to be attacked from the rear by the German formation we'd just driven through. Sergeant Cornwall said, 'I'll get out of the tank, put my tow rope on these mines and reverse – take them off the bridge.' This was very gallant and brave of him and he got awarded the Military Medal afterwards. He got his rope on to the mines and very gradually drew them off the bridge and away to one side of the road in his light tank. This allowed us to pass over the bridge, but no sooner had we got to the other side than we ran into coils of anti-tank wire – which was even worse.

This wire got round the sprockets and tracks of the leading two tanks and stopped them dead, so we had to carry out a further operation to cut the wire. That took at least half an hour. We reached Gravelines without further adventures at about five in the morning. We reached the River Aa, which eventually proved to be the western perimeter of the Dunkirk withdrawal. We crossed the bridge and got our four tanks to the other side – and I got in touch with the French commander. He asked me if we would help him with the defence of Gravelines the next day, as there was bound to be a battle there – and I agreed. The first thing we did was to carry out a recce of the river, looking at the bridges, which were very badly defended. With great difficulty we persuaded the French to pull up the main drawbridge over to Gravelines.

We took up positions along the river, covering the bridges. My own cruiser tank covered the main bridge and the other tanks, a bit further down, covered the other bridges, as a German attack was expected at any minute. Sure enough, the French commander was right, because the bombardment started on Gravelines at about eight o'clock. German formations began to move up and plastered the town with mortars and shells. So we waited and my tank took up a position on the quayside where they unloaded vast quantities of timber from the barges. Luckily there were large blocks of timber all along the river on the quayside, going up towards the bridge. It must have been about nine o'clock when we saw some refugees approaching on the other side. They couldn't cross it but they were all putting their hands up. Suddenly a German armoured vehicle drove up to the bridge on the other side, only 300 yards away.

The Germans shouted to put the bridge down for them to cross – and that was our chance, because with our 2-pounder gun we got on to this vehicle and got a direct hit, blowing the thing up. The Germans all baled out and got into a block house on the other side of the road. We put another shot into that and knocked it down – I think several were killed and the rest dispersed. Very soon another tank drew up behind it and we managed to get a direct hit on that, and after that another, so we got direct hits on two tanks and an armoured vehicle and completely blocked the road. Meanwhile, they were shooting back and also mortaring the town and the canal bank. It began to get a bit hot, so I withdrew my tank back into the town. They didn't seem to go to the other bridges – they were only concentrating on this main one, so I got two of my other tanks up and went back into the town and down a road converging on the bridge which gave us a different view. We got in some very good shooting and managed to dispose of about five tanks and two armoured vehicles. That seemed to stop them getting across, but the battle raged on until about midday.

Then the Green Howards arrived, and they thought we were German tanks. One of their infantrymen fired a Boys anti-tank rifle at my tank and put a bullet through the bottom, which wounded the gunner inside. He had to be taken out, and they provided a sergeant gunner, who volunteered to come into my tank and operate the gun in any further exchanges. He did very well. I showed him in about ten minutes how to operate and load the gun, then we went back and carried on shooting up the vehicles on the road.

Towards the evening the fighting died down. It seemed clear now that the order had come through at midday for the Germans to halt on that line. But we reckoned that we stopped them crossing that river between eight o'clock and midday.

Private Edgar Rabbets
5th Battalion, Northamptonshire Regiment
We got to the River Yser on 24 May, to the west of the bend of the river. I used to go out for a few hours at a time, carrying a .303 rifle and a few rounds of ammunition so that I could stop any German snipers. They preferred to work in twos, and my job was to try to find them and see them off. In contrast, British snipers tended to work alone, and I was the only one in our unit. It was up to you to look after yourself. On a typical foray you would roam around on your own in an evacuated village. You were looking for some movement somewhere.

Lance Corporal Lawrence Greggain
5th Battalion, Border Regiment
I was in charge of the battalion sniping section. With the help of glasses, my

eyesight could cope; I had a lot of shooting experience. My first job was to eliminate an enemy sniper who, ahead of their own lines, had got himself a good 'hide' on the top floor of a big old three-storey house at the end of a wood. This meant dashing from tree to tree, in order to get a good position to shoot him. It was quite frightening dashing from tree to tree. The tree trunks were not very big in circumference and did not provide adequate cover. He had obviously been sniper-trained, and knowing he was to be hunted out, must have changed his position. As there was little we could do, a light anti-tank gun was brought up, and a round put through each upstairs window.

Private Edgar Rabbets
5th Battalion, Northamptonshire Regiment

On one occasion a German sniper had got himself up inside a roof and knocked a few slates away. He'd got a good field of fire. He was in the centre of one side of a square, and his mate was in the corner. They covered the whole square that way, with one protecting the other. The first one, in the centre of the square, had shot at one of our officers who had exposed himself, so I found out where the flash had come from, and went up into a house opposite and shot him from a bedroom window. Then his mate had a go at me but he was too weak and I shot him. He didn't wait until he saw me, that was his problem. He saw the flash of my rifle and must have assumed, wrongly, that I was a lot nearer the window than I was. We didn't bother about retrieving bodies – the first one was hanging out of the roof as he dropped forward.

Lance Corporal Lawrence Greggain
5th Battalion, Border Regiment

There are very few foolish snipers – only dead ones. A trench dug on top of a gigantic anti-tank trap towering over 20 feet above the neighbouring fields gave me an excellent view of the surrounding countryside. In the middle distance was a small village. A German panzer tank squad could be seen approaching the village, but so far, the day had been quiet, with literally nothing to shoot at. Lying in a shallow trench with nothing to eat or drink is far from pleasant and I was both uncomfortable and rather bored. I was getting almost somnolent, when suddenly a shot rang out, and a heavy body fell into the trench beside me. Very shaken, as I had not heard anyone approach me, I was astonished to recognise the person as a young second lieutenant from D

Company. The poor devil had been shot in the stomach and was bleeding profusely. He was still conscious, and giving a wan smile, said, 'Sorry to drop in on you like this, corporal.' Those were his last words. He was in the most terrible agony, and died in my arms in less than half an hour.

In sniping, you usually dispose of your victim with a shot through the head, and normally this means instant death. But seeing this nice young man die so horribly, embittered me so much that I determined to shoot at their stomachs from then on. By this time, I could see that the panzer tanks had drawn up in the village square. They were 500 or 600 yards away. They drove in and lined themselves up, and then the staff car came in with its major general, who did the 'Heil Hitler' bit. I thought, 'Well, this won't do any harm...' so I took a potshot. He clutched his chest and collapsed into his car. So a patrol was sent out to eliminate snipers. Luckily for me, the large expanse of ground meant that they had to advance at the double without cover. In extended order, they approached my position at a fast run.

'Do not open fire too soon,' I told myself. I carefully followed their progress over the open ground. Their officer, a young lieutenant, was on their right flank. I sighted on the officer, and the next time he got up to run, I shot him in the stomach. This produced a withering return of fire, but they were unaware of my exact position, and it all went very wide. The sergeant was a big man – an easy target. He was my next victim. My third shot got one of the privates. This left a corporal and six rankers. Two further shots took out the corporal and another private. It was rather like shooting at the moving targets on a fairground rifle gallery. Without anyone in command, the last five turned and fled. Running away, they presented ideal targets – and I made sure that no one made it back. That's the sort of day you don't forget.

Private David Elliott
141st Field Ambulance, Royal Army Medical Corps
Information started coming on the grapevine that the NAAFI in Lens had been abandoned, and stuff was there for the taking. We were fairly disciplined, and we continued driving, but we suddenly saw a small army truck come round the corner fairly fast with some Scotsmen in it, and they were all drinking brandy out of bottles. They threw us bottles out of these large crates. I suppose the depot had been raided – but it was probably fair enough as it had been abandoned.

Sister Catherine Mary Butland
5 General Hospital and 159 Field Ambulance, Royal Army Medical Corps
I was working as a nurse in the operating theatre. It was impossible to keep track of the number of patients we operated on. Every man requiring surgical attention was brought straight to the theatre, with no pause for clearing up. As one man was removed from the operating table, another was put in. Instruments were washed and flung into a bowl of pure Lysol. We kept on one pair of rubber gloves until they split, just scrubbing them in Lysol, and washing them off under the tap. At one point, the noise we had thought was the blowing of the methylated spirit sterilisers was actually the school being attacked from the air.

Late one night we were told to evacuate, and we went out one end of the village as the Germans entered at the other end. The next morning we were fetched by our quartermaster with an ambulance, and we rejoined our own casualty clearing station in Woumen, which was just over the border in Belgium. At this clearing station we had two operating theatres and there was a constant stream of casualties coming in straight from the fighting area with, in many cases, bits of uniform stuck in their wounds. All that had to be cleaned out. You tried to find the entry point of the wound, and the exit point, and you scooped out any fragments of shell within that area. If a man had a fairly minor wound, you could deal with him while he was unconscious – but if he was severely wounded, you would need him to regain consciousness before you could start. Our problem after the men were treated was that we had nowhere to evacuate them to, so you had stretchers all over the place, including in the toilets. Everywhere you went you had to step over stretchers. Feeding them was a problem too, but if a man was badly wounded he didn't need much except a cup of tea – and they could always manage that themselves.

Private David Elliott
141st Field Ambulance, Royal Army Medical Corps
In a barn, where everyone was sitting very quietly, I saw a French colonial soldier in leather breeches sitting on the floor. His knees had been injured; he had shrapnel holes through them. We cut away his breeches, and put some dressing on his knees. He said, '*Cabernet, cabernet...*' and he kept on saying this. Finally, he pointed to his bottom with his finger and I realised that the man wanted a bedpan. So out we went to the truck, and unpacked a bedpan, and we lifted him on to it, and it was great relief to him. The smile on his

face… He sat there straining away, and when he signalled that he'd finished, we lifted him off again, and there was a tiny little marble, like a rabbit dropping, in the pan. He was so grateful, and he kept saying, '*Merci, merci.*' That's the sort of thing that happens when somebody is in shock.

Private William Ridley
9th Battalion, Durham Light Infantry
We marched off Vimy Ridge on the only road not occupied by the Germans, and into Provin, and right along the path on the windowsills were bottles of wine and liqueurs – and there was one of our lads who was a real boozer, and he picked this bottle of what looked like custard, and I picked up a bottle that looked like water, and I stuck it in my pocket. We come to a big factory and they said we could rest there, and it was full of great big bales of cloth. I said I'd see what it was in the bottle. It must have been pure alcohol, because I took one sip of it and that was it. I didn't want to know – it was pure alcohol. The other lad, who loved his beer, he'd picked this bottle up that he thought was advocaat, and it was olive oil – which didn't please him a bit. But I just fell asleep immediately I hit the deck, and when I woke up somebody had got my bottle, and by the smell, they'd smashed it on the floor.

Private Edgar Rabbets
5th Battalion, Northamptonshire Regiment
I went out and found a German military policeman standing at a crossroads. He was standing there directing a unit into a new position. I shot him, taking, as my target, a point between the eye and the ear – it was the best place to kill them – especially with a German helmet. It just lines it up for you. Rather than go for the heart, it's a nice white target, and you know that once you've hit him in the head, he's dead. I could feel sure of hitting anything at up to 400 yards. I pushed his body out of sight and ran back and told my unit where this new German unit was coming from. He had given himself away by continually looking up the road where he was expecting the unit to come from.

Lance Sergeant Robert Green
2nd Battalion, Bedfordshire and Hertfordshire Regiment
We halted at the roadside and sat down on the edge of a ditch with our feet in the bottom of it. In front of us was a field of ripening corn. One of our

F4529

Men of the 4th Battalion, Border Regiment take up a defensive position

trucks passed by with someone riding on it and the next thing I heard was a burst of automatic fire and blue smoke over the top of the corn. I thought, 'It can't be – we're miles from the Germans!' As I sorted this out in my mind, blood started to splash all over my boots and run down into the bottom of the ditch. What had actually happened was that there was a bloke marching along with a Bren on his shoulder, with a magazine on it with a change lever at automatic. On the truck was a fair-haired kid – a pretty young soldier – and he called out, 'Give us your gun. I'll carry it for you.' This lad handed up the Bren by the barrel. The kid on the truck picked it up by the pistol grip with his finger round the trigger. When the bloke leg go, the weight of the barrel dragged it down and it dragged the trigger against the kid's forefinger. He hadn't sufficient sense to let the gun drop, and it fired at two blokes sitting at the side of the road. One chap was hit in the backside, chopping off about half of his backside, and the other was caught across the upper part of the thigh, straight through to the bone. I yelled for stretcher-bearers and they came up, put a field-service bandage on his leg, but he was dead in seconds.

Private Edgar Rabbets
5th Battalion, Northamptonshire Regiment
I saw four German light tanks approaching. I'd found a Boys anti-tank rifle, and I tried using it – but it had no effect whatsoever. I was firing at a range of no more than 200 or 300 yards, but I might as well have been using a peashooter. I hit the tank – it probably gave him a headache, but that was about all. It simply didn't penetrate. I could understand why this thing had been abandoned. I abandoned it too.

Captain James Hill
2nd Battalion, Royal Fusiliers
I remember Lord Gort arriving at the headquarters – you couldn't but be impressed with him. He stood about six foot seven, an enormous great man of rather severe mien. This tremendous conference was going on and the air was heavy. I think on great occasions when decisions which affect countries are made, you get an atmosphere – and I remember the atmosphere being heavy and dark. That was where the decision was made to evacuate the BEF.

Captain Anthony Rhodes
253 Field Company, Royal Engineers
In the evening, the colonel summoned us all into a cellar in Armentières and said – and this was a great surprise for us – 'We are withdrawing from France. This is going to be a very difficult retreat, an amphibious operation,' then he laughed. 'We have the precedent of Sir John Moore at Corunna and we must try to do the same.' Then we realised that we had been beaten – or at least expelled from France.

Captain James Hill
2nd Battalion, Royal Fusiliers
There was a happy memory for me at this time. I was sitting on the thunder-box outside in the wood and I heard this whistle and I thought, 'By George, I know what that is! I've always wanted to see one of those!' It was a golden oriole.

The Trap Tightens

A battery concealed in a wood

Early on the 29th, we heard the word 'Dunkirk' mentioned for the first time.
Everywhere you looked, you could see fires burning, black smoke,
and aircraft bombing and machine-gunning.

In London, the British Cabinet was considering the wisdom of entering into peace negotiations with the enemy. On 25 May, the Foreign Secretary, Lord Halifax – known as the 'Holy Fox' for his piety and love of hunting – had attended a meeting with the Italian ambassador who suggested that Mussolini could broker negotiations between the two countries. Halifax believed that Britain ought to consider making concessions that did not compromise her independence. Winston Churchill disagreed. 'Nations that went down fighting,' he said, 'rose again – but those that surrendered tamely were finished.' For Churchill, any concession insisted upon by Hitler would amount to a compromise of independence. The Cabinet agreed. Nevertheless, it was clear that talk of Britain's independence risked growing hypothetical, unless the British Army could somehow be rescued from its predicament.

As ministers were discussing Britain's political future, the trap was tightening around her army. On 26 May, Calais fell to the Germans. On that day, Lord Gort and General Blanchard, commander of the French First Army, agreed to create a defended perimeter around Dunkirk. Unknown to the French, Gort viewed Dunkirk as the BEF's springboard to escape from France. British troops were to defend the canal line from Bergues to Furnes to Nieuport and then to the sea, while the evacuation took place. In the week before the evacuation began, almost 28,000 non-essential members of the BEF – or 'useless mouths' as they were described by one general – had been brought back to Britain. The

Admiralty hoped that Operation Dynamo, organised by Vice Admiral Bertram Ramsay, would enable another 45,000 troops to cross the Channel to safety.

In the meantime, the men of the BEF drew back towards Dunkirk in a state of tiredness, hunger and, often, disorder.

Captain Gilbert White
1/6th Battalion, East Surrey Regiment

By 26 May we had learned that the BEF was virtually surrounded, with our backs to the sea. It became apparent that we would be pulling back and evacuated, although no firm orders had come down to the battalion to this effect. The whole picture looked very gloomy. We were already thinking, 'Thank goodness there's the Channel to go to, where the navy will be meeting us, and we will no doubt get back home.'

Sergeant William Knight
No 1 General Base Depot, Royal Engineers

We got a picture of how the battle was going by listening to the BBC on the wireless – and the impression they gave was that the British were advancing backwards and the Germans were retreating forwards. But we were not really taken in by this because it was so obvious what was happening. We were being pushed tighter and tighter all the time and no amount of explanations could alter that.

Lance Corporal Edward Doe
2nd Battalion, King's Royal Rifle Corps

We assembled in Calais on 23 May. The town was already alight. Flames were soaring in the air. It was terrific. We all had the same reaction – 'What the ruddy hell are we doing here?' We were told by the commanding officer that we were to hold up two German armoured divisions and stop them getting through into Dunkirk. We were deployed inside the town. We crossed over the canals, and we could clearly see the brigadier's headquarters – the Citadel – on our right. But everywhere was burning. The whole town was alight. It was a question of where to take refuge. Most chaps took refuge in the places that had already been bombed. Every house in Calais had a cellar.

On 24 May, we were advancing in open formation up a main road, when, all of a sudden, and where it came from I didn't know, a machine gun opened up. I was fortunate, along with a few others, that I was in the middle of the formation, because the left and the right simply disappeared! They just went down. By God, I was scared. Where you ran to was your own business. Us in the centre got away with it. I shall remember that to my dying day.

2nd Lieutenant Philip Pardoe
2nd Battalion, King's Royal Rifle Corps

On the morning of Saturday 25 May, the thought of surrendering to the Germans at Calais simply hadn't dawned on myself, or, I think, on any of my platoon. We treated it as a really good joke. The prospects – so far as we looked forward – were that either we should be reinforced and we would break through the German lines, or if the worst came to the worst, we should be evacuated. The idea of surrender simply never dawned on us.

I was in a hole in the ground, about four feet deep. I heard a shell coming, and I remember thinking, 'My God, this is it!' and sure enough, it must have landed a question of feet away. I was completely covered in by sand, absolutely winded, thinking my last hour had come. But gradually, I started moving each limb in turn, and found that I was not hit at all. And once I got my wind back, I was quite all right. But I can remember one soldier who really began to crack under the shelling. I remember him shouting, 'We can't hold out under this much longer!' and I remember the sergeant dealing with him very peremptorily. Apart from that, it was just a question of gritting one's teeth, keeping one's head down, and sticking it out. It was a very unpleasant couple of hours. Subsequent to the bombardment, the German advance began. It was just where I'd feared – on the high ground. An urgent message came through from the company commander, telling me that the French were not holding up this advance. We took up position on a cliff, and we got a wonderful shoot. We could see the Germans running across into some scrub, and we must have inflicted fairly considerable casualties on the Germans there

Lance Corporal Edward Doe
2nd Battalion, King's Royal Rifle Corps

On the 25 May, the German infantry put in their attack, and gradually drove the pockets further and further inland toward the dock. They were closing in on all sides, mopping pockets up. The infantry was bunched up behind the tanks. Following behind in bunches, using the shelter of the tank. And once these tanks started blasting, there was very little you could do. You couldn't stop a tank with a rifle bullet. I found myself with a group of others being driven back towards the canal. I actually fired the Boys anti-tank rifle for the first time. It was a terrifying weapon. To even fire it, you had to hang on to it like grim death, because it would dislocate your shoulder if you didn't. I fired at a tank coming over the main bridge about 50 yards away, and I couldn't miss. It hit the tank – and knocked the paintwork off. That's all it done. It just bounced off, making a noise like a ping-pong ball. After that, an officer said, 'Leave that blasted thing there, Doe, and get the hell out of it!' We left the gun there and we scarpered.

2nd Lieutenant Philip Pardoe
2nd Battalion, King's Royal Rifle Corps

My great fear was that when darkness came, the Germans would realise how ridiculously small our force was – about a dozen men – and would overrun it. But they didn't make any use of the darkness. That Saturday night, there was no activity on our front at all, and we were able to snatch a few hours' sleep.

Sunday morning started with a dive-bomb attack on the Citadel. It was a most dramatic thing to watch. I remember a drone in the distance, getting louder, and out of the sky, in perfect V formation, came these planes towards us. One by one, these Stukas peeled off, and dived vertically towards their target. It was an absolutely breathtaking sight. As soon as the Stuka attack was over, the German advance started along the high ground, running along by the cliffs. The first I knew, I was aware of enfilade fire and I realised that we were outflanked. The company commander gave the order for the company to withdraw as best it could. We fell back 300 or 400 yards. Our orders were to defend to the last man. As simple as that.

There was an hour's lull, and suddenly one saw figures with the unmistakable silhouette of a German helmet running along the high cliff. And we realised the Germans had got in behind us once again. It was at this point that the commanding officer got into my shell hole and said that we should break up into small groups and try to make our way out of Calais. To join up, if possible with our forces to the north. Further resistance was at an end. I collected three riflemen together, and we set off in a northerly direction through the town, to see how far we could get before we bumped into the Germans.

Bugler Edward Watson
1st Battalion, Queen Victoria's Rifles
I saw a fellow from the King's Royal Rifles who had a bloody great hole in his back. Probably from a lump of shrapnel. This fellow was crying and lying on the floor. There was a sergeant major standing over him, shouting at him to get up. I was standing there aghast. I'd never seen anything like this before, and much to my amazement, the fellow did get up, and was able to walk. I thought that this sergeant major was a rotten sod – but he really made the fellow move.

We were somewhere near the clock tower at Calais. We were given instructions to cross the square, go over the bridge, along a road, and into some houses. I vividly remember running across the square. It was like a cowboy film. It was a cobbled square, and as I was running along, I could see the bullets down by my feet, and the puffs of dust coming up as the bullets ricocheted. I looked down once, and then didn't look down any more. I just ran on.

2nd Lieutenant Philip Pardoe
2nd Battalion, King's Royal Rifle Corps
We got, I suppose, half a mile, when we came to a big square, and as I looked cautiously round the corner, I saw a group of Germans in the middle of the square with armoured vehicles. They spotted me, and there was an immediate rush into their vehicles. We beat a hasty retreat down the street, and we dived into the cellar of a house. And then, for some reason, instead of lying down in the cellar we made our way up to the first floor of the house. And there we lay on the floor of the bedroom. Don't ask me why. We just did. We heard the German vehicles coming down the road, pouring machine-gun fire into the next door house, moving on to ours, stopping outside, and pouring their fire into the cellar, and then on to the ground floor. This was a dreadful moment as we waited for fire to be poured on our floor… but they moved on.

Bugler Edward Watson
1st Battalion, Queen Victoria's Rifles
The fellas found some wine in the basement of a house and they really started drinking it. I'd never tasted wine before. I didn't like it very much, this red

stuff. It tasted very bitter. We were drinking it out of bowls – there were no glasses – and the officer said that if he found anyone drunk, he would shoot them. 'You can drink as much as you like,' he said, 'but if you're drunk, then I'm going to kill you.'

The officer – his name was Banbury – pulled his cigarette case out, and he had a photograph of his wife in it. He said, 'I want you to take this cigarette case, Watson. This is my wife, and the address is on the back. When you get home, I want you to give it to her.' I said, 'Why are you giving it to me?' He said, 'This is in case I don't get home.' I said, 'What about me?' He said, 'I know you'll get home. I might not.' It made me feel good – as if he knew something I didn't know.

I needed to go to the toilet. I was really bursting and it was outside in the open. There was mortar fire all round, but after a while, I really couldn't stand it any more and I had to go. I ran out to the loo and opened the door and found a dead Frenchman sitting on it. I promptly slammed the door, ran back inside and did it in one of the corners of the room.

After a while, someone called out, 'Gas!' and a funny smell started coming through into the basement. We thought the Germans had dropped gas and everybody whipped out their gas masks except one soldier who didn't have one. This soldier went over to an old Frenchman and took the man's gas mask off him, saying that he'd rather the Frenchman die than him. So our officer pulled his revolver out and made the soldier give the gas mask back to the Frenchman. Turned out it wasn't gas – but it was one hell of a panic.

Lance Corporal Edward Doe
2nd Battalion, King's Royal Rifle Corps
What amazed us was that when you looked at the German soldier, he had his jackboots on, a belt round his uniform, a canister at the side, but he wasn't lumbered down. He wasn't tied down with packs and equipment like we were. Furthermore, he was armed with an automatic. He could just point it and let go! We had to fire a shot and eject the cartridge and reload again. We were not only outnumbered in Calais, but out-armed in every way.

Bugler Edward Watson
1st Battalion, Queen Victoria's Rifles
Some Germans came round the corner with an anti-tank gun. We were a

hundred yards away from them, at an angle. They were loading their guns and firing away, and we were in a beautiful position. I said to the officer, 'What do we do?' He said, 'This is your job, Watson!' Some of the other fellows were probably not as accurate a shot as I was. He said, 'You must kill! There mustn't be any missing, because if you miss, they'll know where the shots are coming from!' The position of the windowsill was so that I could rest the rifle down and get a very good aim. It was a bit frightening at first, but after a while, it felt quite fun, just to kill them. I vividly remember the look on the faces of the people you hadn't killed, who couldn't work out where the firing was coming from. After four or five of them were dead, they pulled the anti-tank gun away and went back round the corner.

The Germans started coming up the street and our officer gave the order that it was every man for himself. I asked him what he meant. He said, 'You can do what you like. The thing is to get away. No one's in charge.' I said, 'Really?' 'Yes,' he said but then looked at me and said, 'I want *you* to come with me!' 'No!' I said 'I want to go on my own!' He said, 'You come with me!' So we went out the back of the house and the German snipers were going at us, but we got over the wall. We went into another house and there was a German sniper sitting at the window, with his back to us. My officer shot him straight away. I'd never seen it before at such close quarters. There were no questions – no 'What are you doing?' – just 'BANG'.

2nd Lieutenant Philip Pardoe
2nd Battalion, King's Royal Rifle Corps

We lay on the floor in that house for about half an hour, and we thought we were all right. We hoped to stay there until darkness, and then carry on up north. But then we became aware of German shouts, and we suddenly heard in the next house a section of Germans searching it. This was, I think, the worst decision I'd ever had to make in my life: what to do. We knew perfectly well we could kill the leader when he came into our house. But then what? What good was it going to do? We knew how many Germans there were around us. The inspiring and yet daunting thing was that I knew that whatever I decided, those three riflemen would accept absolutely. This was a decision which no training at Sandhurst had prepared one for. I told them to put away their weapons and leave it to me. And when the Germans came into the house and shouted, I went downstairs with my hands up. The others followed. This was, to me, the most dreadfully shaming moment in my life, and I wondered whether I was the only person in the whole regiment who'd made the decision this way. Yet, it seemed to me that once one had been told that all organised resistance was over and that we'd to try to escape, then to sacrifice the lives of these three chaps for the sake of shooting one or two Germans was going to achieve nothing.

Lance Corporal Edward Doe
2nd Battalion, King's Royal Rifle Corps

We were in the shed for about ten minutes. And all of a sudden, everything went quiet, and we heard a voice somewhere at the back of the shed saying – in perfect English – 'Come out! You haven't got a chance! If you're not out within five minutes, we'll blow you to pieces!' So all of us just walked out. We just left our rifles where they were, and we went out with our hands in the air.

Bugler Edward Watson
1st Battalion, Queen Victoria's Rifles

We were finally taken prisoner. There was yelling outside the house, and they threw some hand grenades in. They were shouting, 'Tommy, for you the war is over!' They must have been taught to say this.

2nd Lieutenant Philip Pardoe
2nd Battalion, King's Royal Rifle Corps

At the end of the battle at Calais, we felt that this was defeat with a capital 'D' and to no purpose. Some prisoners joined us about a month later, and told us about Churchill's speech in the House of Commons, about how he attributed the salvation of the BEF to the delay imposed on the German forces through the defence of Calais. It wasn't until then that we realised what we'd achieved.

Private Samuel Love
12th Field Ambulance, Royal Ambulance Medical Corps

I had spent 21 days guarding the surplus store in the grandstand at the race-course at Marcoing. There must have been millions of pounds' worth of stuff there – blankets, steel helmets, drugs – the idea being that they would call for it as they wanted it. But it didn't happen like that, because we got cut off from the 4th Division. On 26 May, some artillery people arrived while I was cooking for everyone, so I made them some char. A bombardier said, 'You see those 25-pounders over there? We've got to start firing them at eight o'clock and keep firing until eight o'clock tomorrow night, and then we spike them and get out.' I nearly shit myself. Frightened me nearly to death. The lance sergeant was in Lille with a lady, so I said to one of the chaps, 'Go over to Lille and get that little bastard back here! He's got a job to do!' When he was back, I said to him, 'You go over to that major and ask him how we're going to get out!' – because we'd got no transport. He came back and said the major couldn't do anything for us, so I went over to see him. We had a real set-to, and eventually he said, 'The last convoy comes through here at eleven o'clock tonight. Get on it if you can.' That was how we realised that things had gone badly wrong.

Lance Sergeant Robert Green
2nd Battalion, Bedfordshire and Hertfordshire Regiment

At Wytschaete our carrier officer – a bloke called Young – got hold of two very tired-looking individuals and said, 'Here, these two are deserters. Put them under arrest.' So I grabbed them, and said, 'Give us your ammunition. If Jerry gets through I'll give it you back, but as far as you're concerned, you're under arrest and you stay here.' I went back to Porky Young and said, 'Sir, do I have to hang on to these two? There's stragglers from every regiment in the British Army round here. Why pick on those two?' He smiled and said something non-commital and faded away into the distance. So I went round to these blokes, gave them their ammunition back and said, 'Get lost. It's ridiculous me holding you.' They weren't really on the run, they were just lost, I think.

Private Harry Dennis
1st Battalion, East Surrey Regiment

I was given a message to take back to the commanding officer of the Berkshire Regiment, and deliver it in person. When I eventually found the Berkshires, I came across a lieutenant who looked as if he'd been put through a mincer. I told him I was looking for the commanding officer of the regiment – and he said that was him. The message was to take up a battalion frontage, and he gave me a verbal message to take back to my colonel, that he would do the best he could, but his battalion was down to 87 men.

Corporal Charles 'Bert' Nash
2nd Bulk Petrol Transport Company, Royal Army Service Corps

Having brought five tankerloads of petrol to the Calais Marck Aerodrome, I was rudely awoken, at four o'clock in the morning, by the sound of shells. A quick investigation revealed that on the horizon, silhouetted against the dawn skyline, was a row of black objects. These turned out to be enemy tanks, and they were firing at the aerodrome. I roused the men – and I must admit I didn't quite know what to do. I certainly wasn't expecting this sort of thing. The situation was resolved for me when the colonel of an engineer unit turned up. He said, 'Who's in charge of these water tankers?' I said, 'I am in charge of these five vehicles, sir – but they are not water tankers. They are petrol tankers and they contain 100-octane aviation fuel.' To my amazement he said, 'Goody, goody, just what I can use.' He then said, 'Corporal, I want you to tell your men to open the cocks on your tankers, and flood the petrol out on to the ground. We're setting fire to this bloody place. There are Jerry over there, and they're not going to get hold of anything while I'm around.' I said, 'Excuse me, sir, do I get you right? You want me to cascade petrol all over the floor, and you're going to set fire to the vehicles and cargo?' He said, 'That's right, Corporal.' I said, 'Can you give me a signature for this?' He said, 'Who the bloody hell do you think you're talking to? I'm a colonel, and you'll do as you're bloody well told. I'm also instructing you to take your men, and whatever you can salvage of their personal belongings, and go to the town of Dunkirk. The British Army is pulling out of France!'

2nd Lieutenant Peter Martin
2nd Battalion, Cheshire Regiment

We went from river to canal to river all the way back until we were told we were heading for Dunkirk and evacuation. As my battalion hadn't been troubled desperately by the Germans at all, it was incomprehensible.

Signaller Alfred Baldwin
65th Field Regiment, Royal Artillery

On the retreat we slept wherever we dropped off. On the night of the 27th it had poured with rain, and an artillery shell hit our truck and blew it up, so we lost all our gear. During that night we slept on the ground, round the guns, in the pouring rain. Next morning at dawn, our second-in-charge came round

The BEF in retreat; a soldier living in the field

and was shouting his head off about everybody being asleep, and he gave instructions for all the gun sergeants to give us some PT to wake us up. That illustrates the attitude of the officers to us…

Private Albert Dance
Rifle Brigade

We were going back and back until we got to a town called Hazebrouck. The town was empty of French people and then suddenly the RSM turned to us and said, 'You, you, you. There's an ammunition train pulling into the railway sidings and it's got to be destroyed. Take all the hand grenades you want.' We got down there and sure enough, there were German troops unloading the wagons. We got as near as we could and threw a hell of a lot of grenades and then scarpered. It caused a lot of pandemonium, if nothing else. As we ran, we lost each other but I remembered the route back. When I got back to Hazebrouck, there was no sign of my battalion or the headquarters. I realised that they'd gone on again.

I tried to figure out which way was north and as I was walking down the road, I heard a motorcycle. I took cover in a doorway and I saw this German motorcycle and sidecar come round. Then one or two others joined them and they stood pointing up the road. I had a rifle but I could see an anti-tank weapon in front of me. There was one round in the breech and as these Germans stood talking, I aimed at the sidecar and fired. There was a tremendous recoil, and all I could see was that everything disappeared. It must have hit the bike and splattered all over the place. I ran like mad, and the others came round and started firing at me, so I ran into a house. The door was open and there was bread going mouldy on the table. I rushed through to the back, and on the table in there was a naked body of a very old man who'd been dead for days. I rushed through the back and climbed over fences and walls until I got to the outskirts of Hazebrouck.

Lance Corporal Lawrence Greggain
5th Battalion, Border Regiment

The irregular meals and shortage of food played havoc with the bowels – quite appalling. Normally, I'm very regular and my bowels are very good, but I don't think I had a proper meal, and I can't honestly can't remember having a bowel movement all the way back to Dunkirk.

Private Albert Dance
Rifle Brigade

I was completely alone and I went on for a day, hiding whenever I saw Germans on the road until I came across a party of eight British soldiers – all odds and ends who'd lost their units. There was a corporal with us and he said that we couldn't go any further and we should give up. 'I'm not giving up! I'm getting back! My sweetheart's back in England!' I could see a forest ahead and I thought if we could get into there and head north we'd be all right. The light was going but I said, 'If we go now, we can make the forest.' We made it to the forest and then we came across a muddy trail. On a nearby tree was a daub of red paint. This paint ran right the way through the forest. It was a guide mark for the British troops who had been through. It took us a day to get through the forest but when we came out, we could see British troops on the road. We'd gone right through the Germans.

Lance Corporal Kenneth Carver
5th Motor Ambulance Convoy, Royal Army Service Corps

The refugees continued to present a very sorry picture indeed. It was heart-rending to see the people with all their worldly belongings on their carts, shoulders, wheelbarrows, perambulators… You had to push these people aside while trying hard not to cause casualties, but invariably you pushed a cart or wheelbarrow into the hedge, and your instructions were to keep going and not to help people at all. It was heart-rending. These people were travelling for miles and miles with no food or water, and no accommodation. When I finally got home, I said to my parents, 'If the Germans arrive here, stay in the house. You have a roof, you have water, you have somewhere to sleep. Once you're on the road, you haven't got anything at all.'

Trooper Ernest Cheeseman
5th Battalion, Royal Tank Regiment

We came across a man and wife on the road. The man was pushing his bicycle with an unbelievable assortment of parcels on it, and his wife was heavily pregnant. Because of standing orders, we were told on no account have anything to do with refugees – but we couldn't leave this woman. We stopped, put her on our lorry, and told her husband we would leave her at a convent we'd spotted early in the day. We drove off, but we were still in open country when a muffled shout came from the back of the lorry, and my sergeant shouted to stop. I pulled up, and the sergeant shouted, 'Get yourselves a smoke, lads!' What the hell was he doing? What was going on? I was there with the rest of the lads at the side of the road, smoking and trembling. My nerves were sticking a foot out of my body. I was thinking, 'What's behind that line of trees? Is it Jerry? Do you think he's training his guns on us? Bloody hell!'

Then it happened. It was like the cry of a vixen fox – but it came from the back of our lorry. It was a newborn baby girl. One of our lads who was very keen on horticulture and knew the Latin names, called her Viola Tricolor – wild pansy. It was a sort of oasis among everything, it certainly took my mind off the things I'd seen and done.

Private William Ridley
9th Battalion, Durham Light Infantry

During an air raid, we went down in the cellar of a house for half an hour, and when we came, a sergeant told us to look for any casualties. We found one officer who wasn't dead, but as we lifted him on to a truck, his back fell away. I went over to another lad who was down on one knee with his rifle in his hand. 'Are you all right, son?' I asked, and he was motionless. I touched him, and he fell over. One body was lying face-up with his tin hat and pack on, and his rifle in the crook of his arm. You'd think he was lying to attention. There was another one I couldn't move, so we went to get a shutter off one of the houses, and brought it over. We tried to lift him on, but when we lifted the top part of him, the bottom half stayed where it was. It was only the buttons on his battledress and his pants that were keeping his body together. I lifted what I thought was the end of the shutter – but it was the bone in his leg. That's the only time I felt as though I was going to be sick. We took him and did with him what we did with all the others: we dug a hole in someone's garden and tipped them all in.

Captain Gilbert White
1/6th Battalion, East Surrey Regiment

My overriding impression at this time was one of great tiredness. The battalion would fight all day and then, perhaps for two days on end, patrol at night and then withdraw by motor transport at night. It was an exceedingly exhausting business.

Captain James Moulton
General Staff Officer, Grade 3, Operations Section

At one point I had to take some orders to a brigadier – and he'd put his head-quarters in the worst possible place in the village, near the crossroads, as they were always Stuka-ed. He was in such a state of sleeplessness he couldn't understand what I was telling him. He said, 'I'm sorry – I'm going to hand over to my senior gunner now. You'll have to pass the order to him.' It just shows what lack of sleep can do to you. I meant no disrespect to him – he had been on the go the whole time and could no longer make sense of what was being said to him.

Private William Ridley
9th Battalion, Durham Light Infantry

As we marched along, we heard the sound of music coming from one of the gardens. It was a piano going like the clappers. We investigated, and there were three or four soldiers sitting round a piano with the shells flying all over the place.

Lieutenant Colonel Peter Jeffreys
6th Battalion, Durham Light Infantry

The movement back was fraught with difficulty. On my way from Armentières to the Bergues Canal, I was in an unarmed vehicle, and I found myself suddenly shot at by some guns which whistled over the car. I told the driver to go a bit faster – which he did, only to find some German tanks coming towards us. We jumped out of the car, threw ourselves into the ditch, and hoped for the best. Three tanks came on, as well as some others to our right which put about five shells into the car, and then moved on. This left me, my driver and the orderly room sergeant on our feet and miles from the Bergues Canal.

These tanks had just broken through at random, and when we walked further up the road, we found a battalion of the Sussex Regiment which had been very, very severely handled by these tanks. They had just driven up the road, firing their machine guns, and had inflicted the most dreadful casualties. There were men with terrible wounds lying about the sides of the road, crying out for water. And there was nothing we could do. The situation was fairly depressing but by extraordinary luck I came on a vehicle with a sapper

Panic on the streets as Armentières burns

captain, and I told him I'd had my car shot up, and that I must get to the Bergues Canal. To his eternal credit, he agreed to lend me his pickup.

We piled in and his driver drove us to the canal where we met up with the battalion. On the way, we managed to get into a little village, where I found a medical officer, and I was able to direct him down the road to where he could attend and evacuate as many of these chaps as possible. It was a dreadful sight and a shattering experience.

2nd Lieutenant Ian English
8th Battalion, Durham Light Infantry

The first time we knew we were nearly surrounded was at a place called Steenvorde. We took up positions in a field facing east – and we were suddenly fired upon from the west. The next day, 29 May, the brigade withdrew to Woesten, where we were one of the forward battalions. Once again the carrier platoon was sent forward to be eyes in front as a light screen. Eventually the enemy came up as expected, and I withdrew the carrier platoon back to the battalion and from there we were ordered back to the Dunkirk perimeter. Just as we were doing this, the Germans attacked, and there was tremendous shelling and mortaring and an infantry attack which worked round and more or less surrounded our C Company. The majority of them – those who weren't wounded – were taken prisoner, so we lost the great majority of a company in one action.

At Les Moeres we were told to destroy our vehicles, which seemed the most terrible order. One could see the reason for it later on – Dunkirk was so crowded with troops of every sort, and the number of vehicles had to be kept down to a minimum. The carriers were spared, so we had them with us until we got to the beaches.

2nd Lieutenant Allan Elton Younger
61 Chemical Warfare Company, Royal Engineers

On 28 May, we got the astonishing order to leave our vehicles and march to a place called Mont des Cats, near Poperinghe. It took most of a day to march there, carrying just our packs. We'd left everything else. At Mont des Cats I was allocated a sector to defend. After a while some German tanks appeared – and we thought that was it. They came out of a wood about 500 yards in front of our position, and fired a few rounds. Very early next morning, I was woken up by my runner and told to report to company headquarters. I was told to hand over our positions to some infantry who were coming in, and we were to march back to Dunkirk. Before we left, I realised we were missing two of our men, so I told my sergeant to take the section back to Dunkirk by whatever route he felt was best, and I went to look for these two men. I ran across another 2nd Lieutenant, Hugh Davis, who was also searching for some men who couldn't be accounted for. He'd also sent his section off, but as we failed to find these men, we decided we'd have to abandon them.

Private Victor Burton
1st Battalion, East Lancashire Regiment
When we got rid of the trucks I had plenty of bandoliers round me for ammunition, and my rifle, gas mask and helmet. I'd also got lots of tins of cigarettes which I'd put down my blouse, and I had no underwear on, so they were cutting into my chest. In them days I was a heavy smoker – and my nerve was shattered, so I wouldn't get rid of the cigarettes even though they were cutting my chest open. Eventually we got to a place, where we were told we would be doing the rearguard. HQ took over the farmhouse and we were in positions round it, laid flat out. I was with my mate Phil – we travelled together. The 88-mm were coming in, and I heard a tinkle on my helmet, and a bit of shrapnel dropped on my hand. I turned to Phil by my side, and said, 'Hey, I've been hit, Phil!' And when I looked, the back of his head was blown in.

Private Frank Curry
1st Battalion, East Lancashire Regiment
There was some movement in the woods, and my little dog Blackie jumped out at me, yapping, as though to say, 'There's someone out there!' [*Curry had befriended Blackie earlier in the campaign and had been looking after him on the retreat.*] The next minute, a shot rings out from one of my comrades – who shot Blackie dead. When I turned round in disgust, he said, 'The bloody stupid thing! The enemy's here, and he's giving the game away!' It broke my heart because I'd become very familiar with Blackie. But sadly – or what can I say – this same chap who killed Blackie was killed by a sniper before we got to Bergues. And the sadness when I lost Blackie was – more or less – on my mind when this chap got shot.

Lance Sergeant Robert Green
2nd Battalion, Bedfordshire and Hertfordshire Regiment

On the night of 28 May we had been given to believe that we could afford to have a bit of a rest because the East Surreys were out in front of us, holding the line. Well, it turned out that the East Surreys hadn't been in front of us at all. Nobody was in front of us. We had just been dead lucky that nothing had happened during the night. Just before dawn we assembled the company – and our orders were, 'Get your packs. Get anything you want out of them – and chuck them away.' There were all sorts of rumours flying around. Why were we smashing up vehicles and chucking away packs? My first impression was one of absolute shame. I remember saying to a mate, 'You know, Stan, it's going to take us 50 years to live the shame of this thing down!' But before I had time to get too emotional, we had to move on again. Although we didn't know it at the time, this was because the Belgians had surrendered up on the northern flank, left a gap. The Germans were coming in behind the British Army's left flank. Something had to be shoved into that gap to hold it – and that was our brigade.

Captain Harold Ervine Andrews
1st Battalion, East Lancashire Regiment

We were in defensive positions when a couple of very smartly dressed Belgian officers came and told us that they had now left the war and ceased hostilities. They were a neutral country, and we had to be out of our area or they'd come back and intern us. Luckily the company commander on my right was a splendid chap – he had also been warned to get out – so when the Belgian officers came back, they found they were facing a couple of Bren guns and quite a number of men with fixed bayonets, whereupon they made a courteous retreat.

Private William Ridley
9th Battalion, Durham Light Infantry

As we were about to take up our new position, the company sergeant major said that we hadn't to worry, as there were no Germans in the vicinity. So we marched across a ploughed field – and a machine gun opened fire and scattered the earth around us. Which increased our pace considerably. When we got to the position, we were made to dig a hole for our sergeant major, and he occupied that hole for the next three days. The only time we saw him was when the

135

grub came out – and that only happened once or twice. Anyway, the sergeant major said to one man, 'I want you to go back and report to the company sergeant major that we've been fired on.' And this man refused! He told him again, and he refused again. But instead of making that man go, the sergeant major went to another soldier who also refused, saying that the other man had been asked first, and he should go. I was so ashamed watching all this, that I volunteered to go. All I had to do was retrace the steps over which we'd come. I nipped down and I was fired on twice altogether, but I got back safely.

Signaller Alfred Baldwin
65th Field Regiment, Royal Artillery

Early on the 29th, we heard the word 'Dunkirk' mentioned for the first time. Everywhere you looked, you could see fires burning, black smoke, and aircraft bombing and machine-gunning. There was a tremendous amount of artillery fire coming down on us, but we had no equipment and no shells, so we couldn't give any defensive fire at all. After one raid, we heard screaming coming from a gun tower, and when we opened the door, there was one of the gunners. He'd got a smashed foot and been put in the gun tower by his mates, but when the air raid came they'd just left him there. I was down to just one chap with me, so the two of us took poor old Paddy out of the truck, and we humped him on our backs for quite a distance up the road. In a field we saw a couple of French army horses – so we took them, got him on the back of one, and plodded on northwards. Eventually we got tired, so Ernie had the second horse, which was a lovely great big white creature. Later during the day when my legs were aching, I jumped on the back of this old horse with Paddy.

We approached Poperinghe, and entered it by a side road. As we joined the main road, we saw a French artillery unit, which suddenly gave the signal to gallop and off they went – and our horses, being French army horses, recognised the sign and they started galloping with them. We had no bridles or saddles, so there we were, hanging on the back of these horses going at full gallop through Poperinghe. We held on and eventually the French artillery galloped off and then the Stukas came over again. We saw some big concrete drainpipes by the side of the road, and we dived off the horses and dragged Paddy with his smashed foot into a drainpipe. It was no protection at all, but we lay there until the raid was over. When we came out, my poor horse had had his leg blown off by a bomb, so I shot him where he lay, and we started off again.

We came to an *estaminet* and outside was a mass of bicycles. Inside, getting very drunk, was a mob of French soldiers. I didn't connect the two at the time, and I helped myself to a bike. All of a sudden the French soldiers – who were a cycle unit – came chasing up the road, shouting and shaking their fists at us. Obviously they wanted their bike back, but without a word of French, I just pointed to Paddy's foot which was bandaged up but well soaked in blood, and they accepted that and let us keep the bike.

Leon Wilson
French gunner – served with 229 Heavy Artillery Regiment
We reached a small village ten miles from Dunkirk. There were six of us, and when we sat down to rest for a couple of minutes, I saw a shop with bicycles. I said to the chaps, 'Unfortunately, I know it's horrible to do a thing like this, but let's break into the shop, and take a bicycle each, and that will help us to get to Dunkirk much quicker.' When we got into the shop, we found some bread that must have been a month old, and we thought it was wonderful! We soaked it in water, and we split it up, and it was the first piece of bread we'd had.

2nd Lieutenant Allan Elton Younger
61 Chemical Warfare Company, Royal Engineers
We hadn't gone more than a mile towards Dunkirk when we saw some troops standing in the road in front of us. I suddenly realised that they were Germans from their helmets, and they were equally unsuspecting, but when they saw it was a British car they started to rush for their weapons. Luckily there was a road off to the right, and we whipped the car round and drove off as fast as we could towards Poperinghe. When we got there, it was being bombed, and there was dreadful carnage. We couldn't get our car through the town, so there was nothing to do but abandon it.

Private Samuel Love
12th Field Ambulance, Royal Ambulance Medical Corps
The Luftwaffe were dropping all their shit on Poperinghe. God, what a bloody mess. I don't think there were two bricks left standing on top of each other. I stopped a brigadier and asked him how to get out of Poperinghe – and he said, 'You tell me!' Then this young lance sergeant said, 'I'm stopping for a rest.' So I said, 'You can have all the bloody rest you like, sonny, but I'm keeping on!'

A British lorry in flames having been hit by a German bomb

I don't know how this lance sergeant got his bloody stripes. He wasn't worth them. When I explained the situation to him, he got the fear of Jesus in him, and we set off for Dunkirk. I walked miles with a big valise on my back, because in a doctor's house in Poperinghe I'd seen all this medical stuff going begging. It must have been £200 worth. But we couldn't go straight. You had to go where everyone else was going. We went where the redcaps directed us.

Captain (Acting) Humphrey 'Bala' Bredin
2nd Battalion, Royal Ulster Rifles

The British Army often has a dislike of the Royal Military Police. The army feels that they are too strict in peacetime. Well, I can only tell you that I have the most tremendous admiration for them in war, because at every crossroads – which the Germans knew were important to us – there was a military policeman in his white gloves and red hat, exactly as if he was directing traffic in London.

Private Samuel Love
12th Field Ambulance, Royal Ambulance Medical Corps

The redcaps were wonderful – right from Marcoing there were redcaps – at every crossroads, telling you which way to go or what not to do. They did a real good job, because if it hadn't been for them there'd have been no end more casualties than there were, with people taking the wrong road.

Captain (Acting) Humphrey 'Bala' Bredin
2nd Battalion, Royal Ulster Rifles

The military policeman had a fair idea of how many shells would come from the Germans in the next minute or two, and whether there would be a gap when no shells would come. So he would motion the traffic to go through when he felt that no shells were likely to fall, and then he'd stop it when he reckoned there was bound to be shells in the next minute or two. At one of these places, we heard that the man on duty had been killed a moment or two earlier, and a new man had stepped out of a slit trench, and taken his place. I've never lost my admiration for the Royal Military Police.

Lance Sergeant Robert Green
2nd Battalion, Bedfordshire and Hertfordshire Regiment

We were coming along the road in our truck, and immediately behind us was the Company CO's HQ truck. The German artillery got a range on us – a long bracket, then a short bracket, getting closer. Everybody pulled up with a screech during the next salvo which landed right in the middle of the road. My company commander was sitting in front of me, and he got a lot of small splinters in the face. It didn't incapacitate him, but it must have been very painful. I had my legs open – and a great thumping piece of shell splinter had passed between my knees. The unluckiest bloke of the lot was on his motorbike. The last shell blew his guts out. He took one look at himself, pulled his revolver out and shot himself.

Sergeant Leonard Howard
210 Field Company, Royal Engineers
We had to cross between two buildings, and the Germans had the road covered for enfilade fire. Only one person could cross the road at a time, and you had to pick your spot and take your chance. I crossed behind a driver, Wheeler, and when he was some eight feet in front of me, he was hit in the stomach by machine-gun fire. I had no option but to hold back my run across the road to allow him to drop in front of me. As I got almost up to him, a further burst of fire took the top of his head off right in front of me. Had it not been for him, I would have had that burst. I always think that poor Wheeler, who'd bought it anyway, saved my life.

Private Frank Curry
1st Battalion, East Lancashire Regiment
I was thinking, 'If the Germans come, I'm dead.' We were all in ones and twos, and I was imagining hundreds of Germans. What was going to happen? Paddy used to say we should all learn a bit of German. I thought I should learn, 'Schnell!' or a bit of 'Wie geht's?' or something.

Reverend Cyril Scarborough
4th Battalion, Royal Sussex Regiment
I was in a barn with a lot of troops when someone came in and said, 'Now keep calm! We've been captured! So come out quietly with your arms above your head!' I was thinking, 'Blimey, I've seen this in the cinema, but I never thought I'd take part in it…' So we all lined up, and we were marched away. A soldier said to me, 'Do you think they're going to shoot us, sir?' and I said, 'Oh

no, the German army's very correct,' but when we were marched off the road and lined up in front of a big ditch, I did feel a little uneasy. So began a three-week straggle into Germany. It was a very tiring time. There wasn't much food about. The civilian population always tried to give us water. They put it out by the side of the road, and I remember some of them putting out raw sticks of rhubarb as well, which were very welcome. On one occasion, some girls tried to bring us water, but their fathers stopped them, afraid that the Germans might take measures against them. We walked a lot of the way, but we were sometimes crowded on to lorries. There was one very unpleasant incident, when we were pushed into a cattle truck so that you just stood without moving. It was a most unpleasant night.

Bugler Edward Watson
1st Battalion, Queen Victoria's Rifles
We couldn't make our way any further. My officer told me to tear all our papers up. We were herded up quickly, and the Germans were very rude. I honestly didn't know if I was going to be shot. They went through my pockets and then they sent us back behind their lines. At first, I was very impressed with the German soldiers – they looked professional compared to us. But after we had been marched to the rear, we saw their reserves, and these reserves looked like something from the Crimean War. It wasn't the same German army we'd just seen. It was all horses and carts, all higgledy-piggledy.

Massacres

Private Alfred Tombs

They started throwing bombs everywhere,
and they fired the automatics into the barn.
There was no end of firing, and after a while, nobody moved.

As the BEF withdrew to Dunkirk, its rearguard fought desperately to keep the way open for its escape. Significant numbers of British troops were taken prisoner during the fighting. On two known occasions, British prisoners of war were massacred by members of the Waffen-SS. On 27 May at Le Paradis, 97 members of 2nd Battalion, Royal Norfolk Regiment were murdered by 1st Battalion SS Totenkopf ('Death's Head') Division's 2nd Infantry Regiment. On the following day, 90 men, mostly of 2nd Battalion, Royal Warwickshire Regiment, were murdered by SS Liebstandarte Adolf Hitler Regiment in a barn at Wormhout. All of these men had surrendered. The commander of the unit responsible for the Le Paradis killings – Hauptsturmführer Fritz Knöchlein – was executed in 1949. The commander responsible for the Wormhout massacre – Hauptsturmführer Wilhelm Mohnke – escaped justice and died in 2001.

Private Frank Curry
1st Battalion, East Lancashire Regiment
The retreat. What do they call it sometimes? An 'orderly withdrawal'? No way! It was panic! Absolute panic! There were all sorts of stories coming in that they were shooting prisoners, not taking them. And I was terrified.

WORMHOUT

Private Bert Evans
2nd Battalion, Royal Warwickshire Regiment

We took up position by the town of Cassel. We had orders that the position was to be held at all costs because an important operation was to take place. Afterwards, we found out that the operation was to be the evacuation of all the people from the beaches of Dunkirk. It was afternoon, and we were entrenched, but we had hardly anything to fight with. Just one mortar and a couple of Bren guns. They started sending over mortars that were dropping just in front, and just behind us. Then their tanks came along, and they spread out, and their infantry was behind the tanks, stretching right the way across. We couldn't go any further, and we had the river behind us. Some people jumped in and swam across the river, but I couldn't swim, so I stayed on the river bank. When they rounded us up, I recognised that they were SS by the markings on their clothes. The lightning flash, the skull and crossbones. They searched and stripped us. We had our identity discs removed, and they took my watch and some papers I had on me. Then they marched us to a barn. They practically doubled us there. There was maybe 80 to 90 people in our party, and we were joined by some more that they'd picked up. When we arrived at this barn, they bundled us into it. I was the last to enter the barn with Captain Lynn-Allen.

Private Alfred Tombs
2nd Battalion, Royal Warwickshire Regiment

In the early morning, we went into position at Wormhout. We only had one gun, and no ammunition; only smoke bombs. We were there for a day, before the Stukas spotted us, and started bombing us. We couldn't use the gun because we had nothing to fire. Captain Lynn-Allen came along and said he'd find out where HQ was. He went off, and came back, and he said, 'Collect as much ammunition as you can, and we'll take up position here.' Then we saw Jerry. Over the mound, we could see the top of a tank, and we could just see a Jerry lifting his helmet up and down. Someone said, 'Shall I put a few rounds through him?' 'No,' said Captain Allen, 'don't do that! He's surrendering!' But the next minute, a tank came over the top, and a blond chap in a black uniform came up. 'It's finished!' he said in English. They stripped us of everything, and then they lined us up against a gable end. They had a machine gun mounted on the road facing us, and I thought they were going to mow us down – but instead, they marched us down the road. As we went, we passed three trucks, and by each truck we saw bodies burning, as though somebody had poured petrol over them. They took us further on, down to a farmhouse. There was this big Jerry officer with peaked cap, jackboots, his trousers puffed out, and a stick under his arm, and as I went into the farmhouse, he kicked me up the backside. We were only in there a couple of minutes before they took us all out again. It was pouring with rain, and they put us in the middle of a field, and left us there with one guard. The next thing I knew, 30 or 40 others came up, and we all got together, and they marched us to a barn and put us inside.

Gunner Brian Fahey
208 Battery, 52nd Anti-Tank Regiment, Royal Artillery
On Sunday 26 May, we left our truck at a farmhouse with the driver, and went and dug our gun position in the corner of a field. We were at Wormhout, and our job was to cover from the edge of some woods until the next gun took over. There was obviously no danger of tanks coming through woods. On the Sunday, it was all very quiet. The next day, it was still quiet, and we went to the farmhouse, and cooked food in turns. We got some sleep; we hadn't had much of that during the previous couple of weeks. We stood down at night, and before dawn, we went back to man the gun again. We were all alert, and then an infantryman came backwards through the hedge that was screening us, and he said, 'They're coming down the road!'

The sergeant in charge of the gun said to me, 'You'd better go and get the truck so we can get the gun out of action!' I made my way round the field, keeping my head down, and when I got to the farmhouse, I said to the driver, 'You've got to come and get the gun out of action!' He said, 'I can't turn the lorry round!' He was all ready to go in the opposite direction. I told him to wait there while I fetched the others. But when I got back to where the gun had been, they'd all gone.

I was on my own now. Everything I owned – my helmet, my respirator – was in the lorry. So I started walking down to the road and I heard a vehicle coming along the road, and I feared it was German so I kept down in the ditch and then I saw that it was one of our army lorries, and it was absolutely full of men. I put my head up from the ditch, and I signalled that they should take me. But they indicated that they weren't going to stop. So I sprang out of the ditch and I got hold of the struts on the side of the lorry to try and get a foothold. As it came into the clearing, this lorry was hit by a fusillade of rifle and machine-gun fire. I was wounded in the left leg, and the lorry caught fire. A lot of the people in the lorry had been shot, and we all dropped down into the ditch, as the lorry burnt itself out. About an hour later, the Germans came along the road with a party of captives from the Royal Warwicks. We were taken as well, and the fit helped the wounded, so I walked with my arms round two members of the Warwicks. They marched us across a field, and they took us to a derelict little barn in the corner of the field. Then, for the first time in the entire campaign, it started raining, and they herded us into this barn. I was so naïve, I actually thought they were putting us in there to shelter us from the rain.

Private George West
2nd Battalion, Royal Warwickshire Regiment

I was in the wood until the signal officer said, 'Come on, West. I can't get through to A Company.' So I went with a reel of cable round my waist towards the meadow. As I went down a slope with Captain Padfield, I heard the rumble of tanks which came round the corner, with soldiers behind – Waffen-SS soldiers. Captain Padfield was shot straight away by a machine gun – but I wasn't hit. Two of the SS came up to me, searched me, and they pushed me over to a road where I met up with another big crowd of prisoners from my regiment. I knew some of them, and we were all led towards this barn, and they crowded us all inside.

Gunner Brian Fahey
208 Battery, 52nd Anti-Tank Regiment, Royal Artillery

There must have been about 100 men in the barn, and then the Germans sur-rounded it, and threw in hand grenades. It was apparent that they were going to murder us all. I suppose the men in front took the full force of the blast, but we all went down like a pack of cards. I heard the noise of the explosion, and it hadn't damaged me – but we were terrified. Then the German officer said, '*Raus*, five men!' And five men were taken out, and there were five Germans in front with rifles, and the officer counted out, '*Ein, zwei, drei, vier, funf,*' and they were shot. I was already wounded, and the feeling I had was that this was so unfair, so futile, and all so hopeless, and I decided that I would be one of the next five. I thought to myself, 'I can't suffer this any longer. I am going to get this over with as quick as I can.' The officer said, 'Out! Another five men!' and I got up and went out. A boy helped me, and we went out and took our positions. I was number five, and they turned us all round, and I was shot in the back. It was like a punch, like a severe blow, and it knocked me over. And I suppose I passed out.

Private Alfred Tombs
2nd Battalion, Royal Warwickshire Regiment
After the second five men were shot, a guard bent down, got one of those stick grenades from his boot, and he slung it into the barn. When I saw him doing that, I dropped on the floor, and two young lads dropped in front of me, and I could hear a machine gun going, and rifle shots, and another grenade, and it all went quiet. One of the lads who was sitting up at the back was screaming, 'Shoot me! Shoot me!' – and they shot him.

Private George West
2nd Battalion, Royal Warwickshire Regiment
They started throwing bombs everywhere, and they fired the automatics into the barn. There was no end of firing, and after a while, nobody moved. I fell underneath two or three blokes, and we heard some trampings of feet going away.

Private Bert Evans
2nd Battalion, Royal Warwickshire Regiment
When the SS man had thrown the stick grenade, it blew the bottom part of my right arm to pieces. At that moment, Captain Lynn-Allen saw the SS guards taking cover from the blast, and he caught hold of my left arm, and dragged me out of the barn. We ran about 200 yards and jumped into a stagnant pond. The captain got over to the far side of the pond, and I was on the other side, and he told me to stay as low as I could, and to keep my arm out of the water. But one of the SS guards must have seen us and followed us, and he fired at the captain at point-blank range, hitting him in the front of the head, killing him. I saw him go under the water. Then he turned and fired at me. The bullets hit a tree, and ricocheted into me. I copped two in the neck. I was

unconscious for a little while – I don't know how long – but I came round, and I went across to where the captain had been standing, and I reached for him under the water, but I couldn't find him.

Private George West
2nd Battalion, Royal Warwickshire Regiment

There was two or three hours in the barn without any noise. I got up, and I could see Private Hall sitting up against the wooden wall, and there was no end of dead men around him. He said, 'Don't go out, Knocker!' but I took no notice, and I went out, and there was a ditch all the way along. I crawled along the ditch, and I saw a soldier of my regiment sitting on the bank, covered in blood with his hand over his chest. I didn't even look to see if he was alive.

Private Alfred Tombs
2nd Battalion, Royal Warwickshire Regiment

When it had all gone quiet in the barn, I got up. I was covered in blood; they must have got the two young lads in front of me. About five of us were alive. Kelly was still alive. His leg was twisted round, and he was going mad in pain. Sergeant Moore was dead. I said, 'What are we going to do?' Someone said, 'Why don't we stay here, and go during the night?' I said that if we went during the night, we'd be shot. I said we should go now. So we went out a little side door, all along a ditch, and we came to a dead end. We decided to run for a farmhouse. As soon as we got to the farmhouse, somebody shouted 'Halt!' and rifles poked through the hedge. A German officer came along, and he spoke perfect English, and he said, 'All right, boys, the war's finished. You'll be in Berlin, and we'll be in London!' And I'll always remember one man; he went down on his hands and knees and cried, 'Don't shoot me!'

Gunner Brian Fahey
208 Battery, 52nd Anti-Tank Regiment, Royal Artillery

When I finally came to, it had all gone quiet in the barn, and I could feel this bubbling in my lung, but I realised that I wasn't dead. The pain in my leg was bad from where I'd been shot earlier in the day, and I started looking for my glasses. I was about 20 yards from the barn, and blood had pumped all over my jacket, and my shirt was soaked, and I could only use my left elbow and right knee. I crawled back into the barn, and there were men in there. Most were dead and some were dying. They told me what had happened: after the Germans had left, some people had gone to get help – but nobody had come.

I lay there with my head on someone's body, and we talked. What we were more interested in than anything else was quenching our thirst. There was no water or food anywhere. This was the evening of Tuesday 28 May, and we lay there all day Wednesday and all day Thursday. I actually had a packet of cigarettes in my pocket, which I passed over, because there was no way I could smoke with my lung. I think at times I lost consciousness, and at others I was delirious, because the time passed very quickly. I think we all actually wanted to die. I prayed that I would be taken because I was so low. One thing I will never forget was one chap who was sitting up, propped against the side of the barn. He'd found a clip of rifle bullets in his pocket, and he was holding one against his head, trying to detonate it with another.

Private Bert Evans
2nd Battalion, Royal Warwickshire Regiment
I was thinking to myself, should I go back to the barn and try to help the others? I had heard automatic firing going on at the barn. But I was bleeding from the neck, and my arm was busted up, and something told me it would have been suicide to go back. I don't think I'd have even reached it. I went in the opposite direction, and I could see a farm about 500 yards away, and I crawled along a gulley towards it. I must have stood up, because I got hit in the right shoulder with a bullet. It didn't bury itself, but just dug into the tip of my shoulder. After that, I kept as low as possible until I reached this farm. When I got there, a little girl screamed when she saw me.

Gunner Brian Fahey
208 Battery, 52nd Anti-Tank Regiment, Royal Artillery
On the Friday morning, there were six of us still alive in the barn, and we heard some activity, and it was some more German soldiers. We thought, 'Well, that's it now…' I didn't realise that there are actually rules for war. But these soldiers were ordinary Wehrmacht, and not the SS regiment – the Liebstandarte – who had captured us. These chaps came and they spoke to us, and we couldn't understand them. One of them spoke a bit of French, and I could speak my schoolboy French, so that's how we conversed. He thought we must have made a futile stand in the barn, and he asked why there were no

guns or helmets. I told him what had happened, and he was appalled. He said, 'You were captured by the SS, and they don't take prisoners.'

Private Bert Evans
2nd Battalion, Royal Warwickshire Regiment

A German officer came out of the farmhouse, saw the state of me, and he ripped a sheet from the line, bound my arm and neck up, put me in a sidecar, and took me to a German dressing station. This medical man had put his overcoat on me, and an officer at the dressing station practically tore the coat off, until he saw the state of me, and then he apologised. A German doctor said, 'I'm afraid you'll have to lose your arm, my son.' He spoke English quite well. The whole of the bone was missing, and the bottom part of the forearm, and they put maggots into it because I had blood poisoning. When they took the dressing off the next morning, the maggots had sucked out all the yellow pus, and the wound was absolutely blood-red clean. I had the arm removed at Boulogne Hospital, under candlelight. The British were shelling Boulogne at the time, and shells were passing over the operating table. I was wide awake the whole time, and I saw them cut through the bone. I think they must have used a freezing process – a local anaesthetic, because it didn't hurt. But after that, the main artery burst, and blood was just pumping out of me like a fountain, and they had to do a reamputation, and I lost my elbow. They took the arm off near the shoulder.

Gunner Brian Fahey
208 Battery, 52nd Anti-Tank Regiment, Royal Artillery

Overall, the thirst had been worse than anything else. For a long, long time, even after the war, I feared not being able to quench my thirst. But I've got over that now. And it hasn't twisted me against the German people. You see, I don't believe that all the Germans are evil or wicked or bad. Any more than I believe that all Britons are great and good and kind. Part of the reason that you get these national conflicts is because people are willing to generalise.

It's very, very harrowing. It's something I've never spoken much about over the years. Obviously my family know about it, but it's something I had to put behind me when I came home. I've not made a career out of being a victim of a massacre. In fact, this massacre changed my attitude to life for the better. One expression I've said many times is, 'They can't shoot you for it!' Most of what I do – what most of us do – pales into insignificance besides that. Nothing else like that is going to happen to me again. It couldn't possibly.

Private Bert Evans
2nd Battalion, Royal Warwickshire Regiment

When I was put in a POW camp, I told the British officer in charge about the massacre. I explained it to him. He said, 'Now, look, tell this story to no one! I know about it, and you know about it, but if the Germans get to know of it, you'll be taken out and you'll be no more. So keep the story to yourself!' So I kept it to myself until April 1943, when I was repatriated. When I first came home, I had a lot of nightmares. I used to wake up in the middle of the night, screaming the place down. I was dreaming about the barn incident, and what I went through. It played on my mind. I could have drawn a complete picture of all the guards, the barn, the position of everything – because it was all so vivid. I had to go to a psychiatrist in the finish, and he told me to take up some occupations to take my mind off it.

Gunner Brian Fahey
208 Battery, 52nd Anti-Tank Regiment, Royal Artillery

I am still enjoying life, but having been a freelance musician, nobody pays me a pension. Wilhelm Mohnke, the perpetrator of the massacre, receives £20,000 a year from the West German government! Ironic, isn't it? I'm glad to say I retain my sense of humour…

LE PARADIS

Private Robert Brown
2nd Battalion, Royal Norfolk Regiment

We were told to take up positions on La Bassée canal outside Béthune. We were told that we were fighting the Germans that had broken through the Ardennes and were coming round behind us. We had to hold them up as long as possible to stop them closing the gap and cutting off the BEF from the coast.

All four companies were involved. We were so depleted in numbers that we had to put everybody in defence, and we held them back until the early morning of 27 May, when we were encountering our first tanks. There were also heavy mortars and artillery fire. Major Ryder – who was commanding officer by this time – ordered all surplus personnel out to the defence of battalion headquarters. So I handed over the switchboard to the wireless operator, and I went out and I was told to go forward to a row of trees, to let Captain Long know if I saw any Germans coming. I was there for some time, and there was no sign of anybody. I withdrew about 100 yards to a farm, where myself and a lance corporal kept watch. Suddenly, we saw a German motorcycle combination with a machine gun mounted on it coming from behind us. Between the two of us, we stopped it coming through, and we had to get back to headquarters to let them know that the Germans were behind us. So we dashed across the road, crawled along the ditch, and gave the information that we had.

I then took up a position in a barn. We knocked holes through the walls which were, by this time, heavily riddled with shrapnel. Mortar bombs were dropping over the barn, behind us. I was with a chap, John Hagan, who said, 'We'll find somewhere a bit more safe,' and we went to the end of the barn, and saw a small brick outhouse. We went in and knocked bricks out for loopholes, and that's where we continued our defence for the remainder of the day. The other side of the farm was stables and cowsheds and barns, and the men there had done the same as us inside, and knocked bricks out for loopholes – so we were more or less an all-round defence.

Towards the end of the afternoon, Major Ryder came round to us, and said there was no way we could get away from where we were, and that ammunition was running very low, and he was taking our opinions as to whether we should surrender or carry on fighting. Some said fight on, others said surrender. I said, 'Let's carry on as we are!' Because the morale was so high. I had no thought of being taken prisoner, or being killed or wounded. We were just firing, and making a joke out of it, really. But eventually, Major Ryder said that there was no point wasting human life, that we'd held them up for three days which was a very good effort, that we couldn't hold them indefinitely, and that we should have to cease firing. But he said that if anybody thought they could get away, then we were entitled to do our own thing. We wouldn't be running away from the battalion – we would be trying to save ourselves.

Myself and two pals decided that we would go out of the door on to the road in the opposite direction to the other men. The smoke from the burning house was going that way, and we thought if we used the smoke as cover, we had more chance of getting away. We jumped into a ditch at the side of the road, and in it was an adjutant lying wounded with the medical officer. When we looked over the top, we could see German patrols were coming up from the village of Le Paradis. So we couldn't get across the road. They saw us and shouted to us to put our hands up – and that was that. We stood there with our hands up until they came up to us.

They had the SS flash, and the 'Death's Head' badge on their helmets. They seemed far superior to the British troops at that time. They had equipment that we'd never seen, and they were all armed with automatic weapons. But they treated us as reasonable as you'd treat an enemy – just the normal knocks and pushes and shouts. When we got to their headquarters, the wounded adjutant and the medical officer were taken into the officers' mess where they were under cover, and we were left outside. That night, there was a terrific thunderstorm, and we were soaked through half of the night.

In the meantime, the men in the outbuildings and stables had gone out into the field – but they were fired on, so they came back. Then they went out again, waving a dirty white towel on a rifle. They surrendered, and they were the ones that were marched away – and massacred.

Private Stanley Priest
Royal Army Service Corps
About 120 of the Royal Norfolks decided to surrender, so the sergeant major put a towel on the end of his Lee Enfield, and he waved it at the door – but at that precise moment, someone fired from one of the windows further down the barn. This rather angered the Germans who thought that the British were up to wicked tricks. Bill O'Callaghan, a signaller attached to the battalion, thought it was purely because the whole thing hadn't been coordinated. He doesn't think there was anything sinister about it.

Eventually, they got out. They were taken to a field beside the barn, they were stripped to the waist and one fellow got a rifle butt in his face and his teeth were knocked out. Then they were marched 400 or 500 yards down a country lane into a meadow. Bill noticed that as they filed into the meadow, there was an officer standing by the gate, and he saw two machine guns had been set up pointing towards a little barn. They were taken to this barn, and made to stand outside it. Bill says he remembers seeing Major Ryder leaning against the wall of the barn, in a bad way. He could see he was dying. And then the machine guns opened up. One boy said, 'I'm not going to die like this!' and he started to run, but the machine guns cut him down in no time. Luckily, Bill – and a man named Bert Pooley – were standing near a little dip in the ground. They dived into the dip, and the bodies of their comrades covered them. That's what saved their lives, although Bill got a bullet through his arm, and Bert's right leg was shattered. They both lay there, not daring to breathe. The Germans finished off anybody who was moving or groaning with revolvers. They came along and shot them. Bill lay next to somebody whose brains had been blown out, and his own face was covered with this fellow's brains.

The massacre took place at half-past six, and Bill lay there 'til it got dark. He thinks he must have fallen asleep, because when he woke up, he heard somebody snoring. It was Bert Pooley. When it was dark, Bill saw that there were still some SS around in the meadow, but he decided he couldn't stop there, so he carried Pooley across fields until they came to a farm. They found shelter in a woodpile, but that didn't seem secure enough. Bert's leg was turning a horrible green colour, so Bill decided they needed a more secure place. They scouted around, and found that the best place was a pigsty with two pigs that had been burnt during the attack two hours before. They crawled in with the pigs.

A day later, Bill was searching for food; he'd found a few eggs, when the owner of the house came back. She saw Bill in one of the doorways. From that moment, things started to move. They got some kind of dressing for Bert's wounds – but the villagers didn't really want the farm owner to keep the two Tommies because of the danger of reprisals from the SS. But she decided she would do what she could for them, and after several days, Bert's leg became so bad that they had to seek medical help. The mayor went to Béthune about six miles away, and he brought back a doctor who said that they must go to the hospital. And so the German authorities were informed, and they finished up in the local hospital. From there, Bert was sent to a hospital at Saint-Omer, and Bill joined the great line of prisoners from the Calais and Boulogne battles on the long march into Germany. And he spent the rest of the war in Poland – but he dared not breathe a word of the massacre because, had he done so, it would have reached the ears of the German authorities and he would have disappeared.

In the meantime, Bert was repatriated after several operations in 1943. All returned POWs had to be debriefed. He told his two debriefers about the massacre, and they told him it was a cock and bull story. The Germans, they said, wouldn't do that! Bert suffered a great deal. Mainly from the pain of the wound. But when Bill O'Callaghan was sent home in 1945, they got together, and they went back to Le Paradis. They dug some bullets out of the wall, and got an affidavit from the French authorities in Le Paradis about the massacre, and the case was reopened. Bill had noticed an officer standing by the gate before the massacre, and he said he'd never forget his face, and when they went round the refugee camps after the war, they came across this chap. It was only about five or six years later, and he was brought to trial and hanged.

Nearing Dunkirk

Hedgehog road blocks in position, ready to obstruct the road from Bergues to Dunkirk

We were so exhausted that if we stood still for a couple of minutes,
we went to sleep on our feet.

As significant numbers of British troops approached Dunkirk, the largest harbour on the Channel coast, they benefitted from a stroke of luck. Senior German generals took the decision not to mop them up with their panzer divisions. Instead, the infantry of Army Group B was entrusted to finish the BEF, while the tanks moved south to prepare to attack the French on the Somme–Aisne line. In the days that followed, the Dunkirk perimeter was defended fiercely by British and French troops. Their role in the escape of so many Allied troops has not always received the recognition it deserves.

Sergeant Leonard Howard
210 Field Company, Royal Engineers

It wasn't until 30 May that we were ordered to make our way to Dunkirk. We abandoned our transport, and the boys and I walked and ran, and we were being shot and mortared. At one stage we had to cross a sunken road, and the enemy had machine guns enfiladed down its length. We were really suffering a terrific amount of casualties, but a good friend of mine – George Parks – stood up and threw a Mills grenade through the loophole of a pillbox which was machine-gunning us. For some reason they didn't shoot him, and he threw his grenade straight through the loophole. I was flat on the deck and so was anyone else with any sense – but he just said, 'How's that for a cricket throw?' He got the Military Medal for that – and so he should. It was one of the bravest things I ever saw.

Captain (Acting) Humphrey 'Bala' Bredin
2nd Battalion, Royal Ulster Rifles

We got to our last real position before getting into the crescent around Dunkirk. It was in the middle of water meadows, with a canal in front. We were feeling very tired, and in the middle of the night, my second in command came round to see that we were all right. I woke up – and it took me about a minute to be able to actually stand up. I staggered around as though I was drunk. And then I was reasonably normal again.

Corporal Charles 'Bert' Nash
2nd Bulk Petrol Transport Company, Royal Army Service Corps

We approached a crossroads outside of Dunkirk with the aim of passing straight over, but coming from our right was a convoy of vehicles. They were earthy war vehicles, half-tracks and armoured cars, not just a little 30-cwt utility like us. I instructed the driver, 'You'd better let these buggers go by – they seem to be more at war than we are. We stopped and six or seven of them lumbered across the road – no form of aggressive action at all – and then the penny dropped. On the side of the vehicles was the German army cross. I can only guess there was no engagement because we were too insignificant.

Lieutenant D'Arcy McCloughin
9 Field Company, Royal Engineers

About two miles outside Dunkirk we were mortared and we picked up a lot of casualties. I was told afterwards that I spent some time shouting and swearing at some sappers who were exposing themselves and not getting under cover, only to discover that they had all been killed.

2nd Lieutenant Allan Elton Younger
61 Chemical Warfare Company, Royal Engineers

As we got closer to Dunkirk, we joined up with all sorts of other people – some French, but mostly British. We crossed a canal and there was a French officer who had laid some defences along the canal bank. He kept shouting at any French troops that were passing to come and assist him, 'Remember Verdun! We must stand here! We mustn't let *les sales Boches* take Dunkirk!' These French troops were very reluctant to go, and when we'd passed over the bridge and gone about a quarter of a mile, I heard a rifle shot. I wondered what it was, and I was told by one of the British behind us that a Frenchman had just shot the French officer.

Private Samuel Love
12th Field Ambulance, Royal Army Medical Corps

We came across an Englishman with a Belgian wife and two daughters, and he wanted us to take the girls with us. But we couldn't. We told him that if we got them to the beaches they wouldn't be allowed on to a boat. But this Englishman just had to carry on. I felt sorry for him.

Sergeant Leonard Howard
210 Field Company, Royal Engineers

We arrived at the outskirts of Dunkirk at five o'clock in the afternoon, having walked and run 40 miles in 16 hours. Occasionally we hadn't been able to move because we were being attacked. Survival was the main object in everyone's mind, but I remember a warrant officer walking down the road, dressed just in his knee breeches and service dress jacket and cap. Tears were streaming down his face, and he said, 'I never thought I would see the British Army like this.' The poor man was absolutely shattered. He was a regular soldier and it reduced him to tears. For myself, at 21 years old, one hadn't experienced death close to you, and it was all a bit frightening.

Corporal George Ledger
8th Battalion, Durham Light Infantry

When we got to the outskirts of Dunkirk, we came upon a whole consignment of dumped arms, lorries and equipment; miles and miles of it. Wherever you looked, the whole place was engulfed with abandoned weapons and machines. A lot of us were sent out to immobilise some of the vehicles. We'd put things into the radiators, or drop a grenade in and smash it.

Lieutenant D'Arcy McCloughin
9 Field Company, Royal Engineers

For some extraordinary reason, I was fixed up by someone with a horse. I was not a particularly good rider, so I wasn't that keen, but perhaps my PU [pickup] was no longer able to make progress. I went a very considerable distance on the horse, for me, without falling off – something like 20 miles – and strangely

Private Frank Curry (on the left)

enough arrived on the sand dunes on the coast where I could see, to my astonishment, the embarkation taking place.

Corporal Thomas Myers
10th Battalion, Durham Light Infantry

It had been a nightmare all the way through. We got outside Dunkirk and it was all blazing. 'We're going to go in there?' 'Yes…'

Sergeant John Williams
6th Battalion, Durham Light Infantry

An awful lot of troops had passed through Bergues, and Colonel Simpson said, 'I think this thing's folded up, Williams. I don't think we can do very much good.' I said to the sergeant major, 'We're supposed to be bloody soldiers! We can't just run off like this!' He said, 'You can talk better than I can,' so I went to the colonel and said, 'Sir, is our job finished?' 'Yes, I'm afraid it is, Williams.' So I said, 'I think there's something effective we can do here!' He pointed to the town marshal's office, and I went in. There was a Royal Artillery officer there, and I told him we had a sergeant major, myself – a sergeant – two corporals and eight men of the Durham Light Infantry, and was there anything we could do? He said, 'Thank God, sergeant. This is fate, you know. My name's Major Lambton, and it's good to meet some infantry who want to do something, and who know what they're bloody well doing!'

Private Frank Curry
1st Battalion, East Lancashire Regiment

We were at Bergues. The mayor had opened the alcohol factory vats, as if to say, 'The Germans are not getting all our good wine!' So the alcohol flowed from the factory into the surrounding fields. I recall vividly, as we were walking, hundreds of British soldiers heading – more like stampeding – towards this ball of fire about five miles away called Dunkirk. One shell must have hit the middle of the field, because the next minute the whole field was on fire. And there were chaps screaming. Literally hundreds of men screaming. Some of them charged out towards us, their clothes on fire. We had kept to the high roads, but if we'd been going through the fields we'd have been burned to death.

Sergeant John Williams
6th Battalion, Durham Light Infantry

I was handed over to an old last-war officer of the Queen's Royal West Kent Regiment, who had an engineer officer with him. We flooded the Bergues canals, and the sea water came in. Then, the officer said, 'We had 111 men last night, and 50 of the buggers have deserted! See what you can do about it!' So I started stopping people on the road, saying, 'Come on you! Get over here!' On one occasion, I stopped practically a full company of the Pioneer Corps with a sergeant major. I said, 'Sergeant major, there's a job to be done here! Fall in!' We were being heavily Stuka-ed, and the sergeant major said, 'We're bloody well getting out of here as soon as it gets dark!' I said to him, 'You should be bloody ashamed of yourself! You're a sergeant major in the British Army, the country's in danger, we're supposed to be soldiers, and you're talking about getting out in the presence of all these men!' The whole lot of them raised their rifles and said to me, 'We'll shoot you if you talk like that!' I had my rifle in my hand, and I was hoping I didn't look the way I felt, and I said, 'The first one who shoots, you won't stop me firing this! Now which one of you wants to die?' And they put their rifles down. I went away round a little buttress, and I would have been sick if my stomach hadn't have been empty. I was shaking, completely shattered. I later saw this sergeant major lying on a stretcher after another Stuka raid, face down, groaning, with a large chunk of his bottom shot off. I lifted his head up, and I said, 'You said you were bloody well getting out, sergeant major? I'm glad to see you *are* getting out! Good luck!' It wasn't a very Christian thing to do, but that's what I thought of him.

Private Frank Curry
1st Battalion, East Lancashire Regiment

When we got through Bergues, there was a halt at a big château. Captain Andrews told us there was a big meeting and we'd have to await orders. He came back solemn, and said, 'I'm sorry lads, you've drawn the short straw.' They had to have one company back at the Bergues canal. We didn't understand why, but I've learned since that we were being positioned at a point where there was a big road that German tanks could have used to head quickly into Dunkirk. 'I'm sorry,' said Andrews, 'but we're going back to the canal.'

Sergeant John Williams
6th Battalion, Durham Light Infantry

The captain of the West Kent Regiment told the regular engineer officer to go with me and do a patrol to see how far away the enemy were. It wasn't a very arduous patrol. At the start of the patrol, there was a bridge which was mined, and you had to step on the sleepers to get across it, and then lower yourself down into the canal. Before we got to the bridge, the engineer officer said, 'I'll just stay here, and you go up and see how things are, and you can pick me up when you come back.'

He said the same thing for two nights, and the blokes started complaining, so I thought I'd better report it. The next night, I said to the major that I wanted a word with him. I said, 'On behalf of myself and the men, we don't want this officer. He never does the patrols. He's not doing his duty, and it's bad for the morale of the men. I'd rather we just did it ourselves.'

The captain called the engineer officer in, and he said, 'This sergeant tells me that you haven't been doing the patrols. You've been waiting for him, while he does the patrol and gives you a report, and then you've been reporting to me.' The engineer officer suddenly shouted, 'It's suicide! It's suicide! We're all going to die!' and he burst into tears. The captain shouted, 'Shut up, you cunt. You're a bloody disgrace to the army. In front of a sergeant! I'll have you court-martialled when I get back to England!' 'I don't care, I don't care,' said the engineer officer, 'it's bloody suicide, I don't want to die!' I didn't think officers did things like that.

The sequel was rather amusing. The next night, it was just getting towards dusk, and the captain said to the engineer officer, 'Get your kit.' The engineer officer had his batman carrying his kit. 'Come with me,' said the captain, and we all went to a junction in the road, and the captain said, 'If I get back to England, you're going to be court-martialled because you're a disgrace. Now get along that road, and get out.' The engineer officer shot along the road, with his poor batman, and the captain looked at me and said, 'Well, that's that, sergeant.' I said, 'You do know sir, that *that* road leads to the German lines? The *other* road leads to Dunkirk!' 'I know, Sergeant,' said the captain, 'I know…'

Private Frank Curry
1st Battalion, East Lancashire Regiment

We could see hundreds of Germans appearing in front of us. Captain Andrews

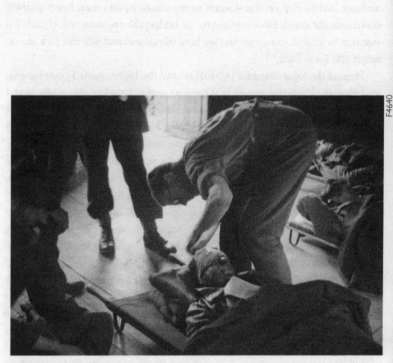

F4640

A British medical officer attends a casualty

shouted, 'Don't fire until they get right down to the canal.' Funnily enough, I wasn't frightened, because Paddy said, 'Don't worry, we'll be prisoners of war.' He convinced me that Captain Andrews would have to surrender. But it went on all day. They'd fire their mortars, and try to come across in little rubber boats. We repulsed them. Simple as that. We were behind the hedges with Bren guns and plenty of ammo, and we just riddled them like stupid. They were like suicide squads. Andrews was on top of a barn, and he could see them coming, and he'd send a runner down to us who'd say, 'Somebody coming on the left-hand hedges!' or 'Enemy troops on the far right!' But then, I could see the Germans stacking up on the hill, hundreds of them, and I thought, 'We can't keep this up. If 100 come at us, and we shoot half of them, some of them are still going to get across.' After that, the barn caught fire, and Andrews came down and said, 'Tell them all, when I blow my whistle, to make a hasty retreat. It'll be every man for himself.'

We got moving, but after about 100 yards, Paddy screamed and fell down. I stopped and looked back, and he was on the ground with his mate Jimmy Johnson bending over him. I believe the bullet hit him in the back and came through his chest, but he had blood coming out of his mouth. He looked at me, this poor old bugger who'd been taking care of me, and he said, 'Get going, son!' Johnson said, 'Get the fucking hell out of here. Go on, lad, run!' For a second, my brain didn't function. Then I threw my helmet on the ground, dropped my rifle, turned, and made an Olympic dash for the hedge a hundred yards away. As I ran, I could feel the bullets flying around me. As I got close to the hedge, lo and behold, how was I going to get over it? It was thick and went over my head. I took a running jump, got on to the top, dragging myself like a madman, and I fell on to the ground on the other side. I kept running until I got to some farmhouses.

Armament Quartermaster Sergeant Frank Hurrell
3rd Army Field Workshop, Royal Army Ordnance Corps

We had come to a bridge over a canal. A voice rang out: 'Halt! Who goes there?' We were rather dumbfounded by hearing an English voice, but I found my voice, and answered, 'Friend!' We were asked to identify ourselves properly, and then we were told to come across the bridge, keeping to the left, as it was mined. On the other side, we were met by a bombardier of the Royal Artillery who escorted us through some trees and foliage into a small clearing where two 18-pounder guns were in position, facing the road we'd just come down. There was a party of about 16 looking after the guns, and they gave us tea and a cigarette, and we found out what had been happening over the last few days. After that, we carried on, and reached Bergues where there were reception people checking us in, and there was a field hospital. The medical officer looked at my leg, and they said they were going to admit me to hospital because my leg and foot had swollen up enormously, but the sergeant at the clearing place said, 'Don't stay here. If you can keep moving, carry on. We're evacuating here tonight. You keep going.' A couple of the others went into Bergues and came back with a walking stick and a pair of slippers they'd found in a bombed shop. I couldn't flex my leg, but I could get by swinging it along.

Private Frank Curry
1st Battalion, East Lancashire Regiment
I got near to this group of farmhouses, and I heard French voices inside. I went in, and a group of Frenchmen came at me. I smiled and said, *'Anglais! Anglais!'* One of the Frenchman – Réné – spoke pidgin English, and he said, 'Where… come…from?' I was in a hell of a state, bleeding all over. I could see British soldiers, officers, French soldiers, all of them seemed to be wounded. An English officer said, 'Get those bloody clothes off. You'll be shot, you stupid bastard!' I went mooching around, and I was given a pair of corduroy trousers which went round me about twice. I tore my tunic off, and put on a woman's blouse. It was lovely next to my skin. And a Frenchman came in, and he had a chicken in his hand. It had just been executed, and the blood was dripping from its neck, and it was wriggling. They poured the blood into jars, and – stupid enough – I had some of the blood because I was starving.

The wounded officers and men were waiting for the Germans to arrive because they couldn't move. But Réné turned to me, and said, 'We move! One hour, we go!' One of the British officers said, 'If I thought you were really going to escape, I'd give you my address…' 'That's out of the odds,' I thought. It got dark, and as we were about to get away, there was a hell of a commotion outside, and in walked three Germans. One of them was an officer, and he was just like in the films – a big, tall, smart-looking fella. He shouted something in French to Réné, and here was me in civilian clothes. Réné pointed to the back room, where all the wounded officers and men were, and said, *'Anglais!'* So the German went in there, and I heard him say, 'You are now prisoners of war! You will accept Geneva rules!' I thought to myself, 'Here's a German officer who speaks French and English!'

When the German officer came out of the back room, he started yelling at Réné in French. And Réné started backing into me, pushing me towards the wall. I felt like saying to him, 'Good Christ, Réné! What are you doing? You're trampling on me!' But this officer must have been saying, 'You Frenchmen get back to the wall!' The officer walked over, jabbering away in French, and he turned his head as if to walk away, but he came back. He pointed at me, and Réné started talking. Réné was still backing into me, almost kicking my shins. Then the officer nodded, waved his stick, and walked away. It was only then that I realised he thought I was French. He went into the other room, and with that, Réné grabbed my arm, and we're through a hole in the wall, and I was on the ground in pig muck and slime, crawling along. I could soil my pants at the thought of it. We started running. I ran like hell.

In the end, we got to a château and there were a lot of Englishmen there. Two sergeants came running over, and they said, 'Get in that room!' I went in, and then an officer came in, and said, 'Who are you?' I said, '3386834, Frank Curry, East Lancashire Regiment.' 'Are you sure?' he said, and he started speaking in German. I couldn't understand what he was saying, and then one of the sergeants said, 'You're a bloody bastard fifth columnist!' And the other sergeant said, 'We're going to shoot you!' 'Fifth columnist?' I said. 'These are my army boots!' They were a couple of real yobbos. One of them said, 'Germans can steal boots off dead men!' I was getting panicky, but the officer said, 'Come with me!' and they led me into another room, where an officer was tearing up papers. He said, 'You say you come from Liverpool?' 'That's right, sir.' 'Can you tell me where you live?' 'Yes, sir. 46 Sutton Street, Tuebrook, Liverpool 11.' 'Now, can we assume that you're at Lime Street station, Curry? How do you get home?' 'You must be joking, sir!' 'How do you get home?' 'I get on an 11 tram, which takes you to Tuebrook, I walk round the corner, and I'm home.' And he turned to the sergeant, and said, 'OK, let him go. But get those civilian clothes off!'

One of the sergeants took me out, and said, 'Get some khaki on!' There were about 60 British soldiers lying dead at the back. I just had to pick one fella. I slid his tunic off. I felt terrible. I said to the sergeant, 'Could you give us a hand getting his trousers off?' 'Do it yourself!' he said. But that's how I changed uniforms, and then I moved off to Dunkirk.

Lorries and transports which have been smashed and burned to render them useless to the pursuing Germans

HU47946

Captain Gilbert White
1/6th Battalion, East Surrey Regiment

We had been manning the perimeter near Furnes until the 31st, then we started withdrawing on that night – and the Germans didn't follow us as we'd
expected them to do. It was just prior to this withdrawal that we had the only
recorded case of an officer who deserted in the face of the enemy. He was a
platoon commander – he wasn't at his post, but he was picked up at brigade
headquarters, which was some four miles to the rear of us, and brought back to
the battalion where he was kept at headquarters. When we got back to
England he was court-martialled, and I as adjutant had to prosecute. The
judge found him guilty and he was cashiered, serving a short prison sentence.
It was very unfortunate, but he just didn't do his duty. We were all frightened,
but he was the only one that gave way.

Sergeant William Knight
No 1 General Base Depot, Royal Engineers

It was just before dawn when we heard this shuffling of feet coming up the
road. We knew that the last of the British troops had ostensibly gone to the
beaches, and we were preparing to pull out ourselves – and then we heard this
shuffling noise. Now, the Germans don't come up with a shuffle of feet, they
come up with a whoosh on motorbikes with sidecars, followed by tanks. So we
knew it had to be the British Army – nobody else would be walking.

After a while a file of absolutely deadbeat, weary chaps came by, led by an
officer with full pack, the same as his men, trying to cheer his men along.
When they got up to us they saw the lorry. I called out to them and said,
'We're just brewing up, sir. Would you like a cup of char?' He said, 'Sergeant,
I'd love a cup of char – but not until my men have had one. Have you got
enough for all my men?' I said, 'I guess we have. The latecomers might not
have any milk, but we've got tea for them, and we've got provisions.'

We got talking to them – and the officer told me that he had had to leave
his wounded behind. His men were so tired that they were absolutely inca-
pable of going any further carrying their wounded comrades, so he'd had to
leave them at a farmhouse. He knew the Germans were right behind and he
was very worried about what would happen to them.

Like a mug, I offered to go back with him. I would take him in the lorry to
the farmhouse. He had a word with his sergeant, and he saw that his men were

all right – they were sitting drinking tea and resting. We got in the lorry and went back down the road for quite a distance, then we heard the sound of action up ahead. I decided if we were going to go to the farm, we'd better go up over the fields and approach from the back. We reached the back of the farmhouse and when we went in, we found his wounded men. Most of them were very badly wounded – and they were engaging the enemy with rifles and hand grenades through the front windows. We managed to get them out the back way, one by one, with others giving covering fire. We got them into the truck and then we went like hell out of there. At first we were shielded by the farmhouse, but as soon as we broke cover and started off across the field, the Germans opened up with everything they'd got. When we got back to where we'd left our men, the truck was a mass of ragged canvas – and it was a good job that most of the men in it were lying down, otherwise they would have got further injuries. In fact, only one bloke did.

We decided things were getting hot, and as Jerry was coming up the road, we thought we'd better get out of there. Since we'd got the wounded on board, we got them right the way down to the casualty clearing station, but by then things were getting very bad. The approaches into La Panne were pretty well blocked, but we managed to push a lot of trucks and personnel carriers off the road and into canals. We unloaded the wounded at the casualty clearing station, then said goodbye to them. Quite a few of these poor devils were pretty much on their last legs. I'll never forget the officer's last words. He said, 'Sergeant, you're one hell of a man,' and I said, 'Sir, so are you.' His men absolutely worshipped him and he stuck with them through thick and thin, getting them right the way down to the beaches.

Lance Sergeant Robert Green
2nd Battalion, Bedfordshire and Hertfordshire Regiment

On Saturday, we got down to just outside La Panne, which apparently in peacetime was a very pretty little town – but it had lost its appeal for me since it was on fire from one end to the other.

Private Albert Dance
Rifle Brigade

I had taken to the open country. I was on my own, and I reached what must have been the last canal around Dunkirk. I walked along the bank until I found a bridge that had been blown in the middle. I slid down it, grabbed the other side and clambered up. I carried on until I could see Dunkirk.

Lance Sergeant Robert Green
2nd Battalion, Bedfordshire and Hertfordshire Regiment

We halted somewhere outside La Panne because there was a whole column moving through it. Away ahead of us a shell pitched right in the middle of the road, and you could see bodies staggering away. One half of me, my hair was standing on end with terror, and the other half was thinking in a very resigned sort of way, 'We've got to go through this, so we might as well make a start.' I remember hearing a voice say, 'Come on, follow me.' I thought, 'Who the devil's that? Oh my God, it's me.' I was so tired I didn't realise it.

Lance Corporal Lawrence Greggain
5th Battalion, Border Regiment

By now, I had got a badly infected wound, scabies, and feet that resembled raw liver. From lying in filth, my uniform was devoid of its khaki colour; it varied from brown, black, grey to dark red blood colour. From the base of my spine down to the back of my legs into my boots was a continuous mass of congealed blood. I had a beard and was dirty beyond description. We were so exhausted that if we stood still for a couple of minutes, we went to sleep on our feet.

2nd Lieutenant Peter Martin
2nd Battalion, Cheshire Regiment

By the time we got to Dunkirk I and my platoon were absolutely shattered. We had been withdrawing as rearguard every night and digging in every day, and we were literally exhausted. The adjutant had told me that as soon as possible I was to try to get the platoon embarked, but we slept in the dunes for about 24 hours solid.

Evacuation

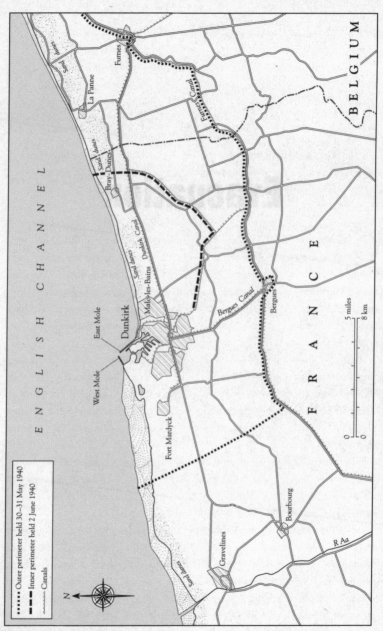

Dunkirk and surrounding area

The dunes were completely covered with men, with long lines coming down to the beach. It was so clearly going to be impossible to get all of that lot off – so that first visit was rather a despairing one.

O peration Dynamo – the most ambitious evacuation in military history – was organised in less than a week. The most direct sea route from Dover to Dunkirk (known as Route Z) became untenable when Calais fell to the Germans, making it vulnerable to German artillery. An alternative route (Route Y) more than doubled the length of the voyage. Admiral Ramsay introduced a third option (Route X) which was *relatively* short and *relatively* safe. The first ships set out on the evening of 26 May.

Initially, these ships were heading for the harbour at Dunkirk, where the inner docks were ablaze from heavy German bombing. On 27 May, Senior Naval Officer Ashore, Captain William Tennant signalled to Admiral Ramsay that every available craft should be sent to the beaches east of Dunkirk – La Panne, Bray–Dunes, and Malo-les-Bains. Tennant also ordered a destroyer to come alongside the east mole, a 1,600 yard-long breakwater in Dunkirk's outer harbour, which became the chief embarkation point of the evacuation. The use of the mole allowed destroyers to pick up troops directly. On 29 May, the armada of 'little ships' began arriving off the beaches.

As the rearguard continued to hold the German advance at bay, British troops tumbled down the corridor into Dunkirk. On 28 May, 17,804 men were rescued. The following day, this number was trebled. Three days later, 68,014 men were evacuated, the highest number for a single day of the operation. By its final day, 4 June, 338,226 Allied soldiers had been brought to safety across the Channel, of whom about 215,000 were British. They had been carried by 222 Royal Navy and Allied ships, and over 800 civilian vessels – including an alleged two-man canoe. Many vessels were sunk or damaged by the almost incessant bombing and shelling. Nine Allied destroyers, nine ferries and 23 trawlers were sunk, as was one hospital ship which clearly sported the Red Cross. There were a large number of casualties sustained as the BEF waited for evacuation, and the army was forced to leave behind huge amounts of vehicles, arms and equipment.

Nevertheless, the success of Operation Dynamo greatly exceeded the expectations of everyone involved, and those of the watching world. It allowed Britain to fight on, and it gave credibility to Winston Churchill's belief that an accommodation with Hitler was to be resisted, despite Belgium's surrender on 28 May, and France's imminent collapse leaving Britain and her empire standing alone against Germany. 'Wars are not won by evacuations,' Churchill told the House of Commons on 4 June. Perhaps not, but a catastrophe had been averted by this one.

Corporal Charles 'Bert' Nash
2nd Bulk Petrol Transport Company, Royal Army Service Corps

I was driving towards Dunkirk, and coming in the opposite direction – fortunately on the other side of the canal – was a German formation consisting of motorbikes and sidecars with light machine guns mounted in them. The road being lower than the canal, we were partly obscured, but one very enthusiastic driver picked up a shovel and waved it in the air at the Jerries with a four-letter expression and some Cockney banter. All of a sudden, Jerry opened up and two or three holes appeared in the blade of the shovel – which he dropped as though he'd been stung by a wasp. He charged up to the end of the canvas cab, parted the little curtain and said, 'Corporal, they're firing at us with real bleeding bullets!' I don't know what I replied, but, after that, he put his foot down and we were going like hammers of steam.

Captain Anthony Rhodes
253 Field Company, Royal Engineers

We arrived at Dunkirk on the night of the 27/28 May, and the first sign we had of the town was in the early hours, looking north-west, where we saw an enormous column of black smoke. A French farmer I talked to as we stopped for a moment said, 'That's Dunkirk. They've already bombed it and they've set the oil tanks alight.' These tanks burned throughout the time I was at Dunkirk and there was this pall of heavy black smoke above half the town.

Private William Ridley
9th Battalion, Durham Light Infantry
Dunkirk had the stink of death. It was the stink of blood and cordite.

Yeoman of Signals Wilfred Walters
Royal Navy – served aboard minesweeper HMS Ross
We were based at North Shields, and on 26 May, we'd been at sea, sweeping. It was a Sunday, and when we'd come in, four or five of us decided we'd have a little run down to Whitley Bay for an evening out. We were waiting for the magic words – 'We're open' – when a policeman came along and said, 'Do you chaps belong to the minesweepers at North Shields?' We said yes, and he said, 'You'd better get back on board at once.' We thought it was an exercise to see how long it would take to get the ship's company back on board in case we suddenly had to go to sea. When we got back, the captain was waiting for us, and he said, 'We're sailing as soon as we're ready. As near as I can tell you, the next stop is Harwich.' We went on to Harwich and the next thing, an officer came on board and asked us how many small boats we could tow across to Dunkirk. The captain asked, 'What's happening?' and the officer said, 'Don't you know?'

Arthur Joscelyne
Civilian – aboard the Thames barge Shannon
I'd come downstairs about seven-thirty, and heard a knock on the door. I found my two brothers there. Vincent said, 'Would you volunteer for a secret mission?' I asked what he meant, and he said he couldn't tell me any more about it – but they wanted people who could sail small boats. He said he was going, and that a lot of the Leigh men were going. I said, 'If you're going, I'll go.' I didn't realise what I was letting myself in for. When we got down to the Royal Terrace, the naval commander asked us if we were volunteering, and we said, 'Yes.' I nearly refused because there was a 16-year-old youngster there who'd signed on. His mother was with him, in tears, saying, 'He's too young to go! I've only got him, because his father's out in France!' The commander was a youngish man and he simply said, 'He's signed up – he's got to go!' So I said, 'If

you insist on that boy going, you can count me out.' There was a bit of an argument, but the boy said he wanted to go, so it was agreed we should both go.

We were told to take the *Renown*, which was a Leigh cockle boat. When we got there, there were two crew on board – and I had a strong feeling that I had to get off that boat. I don't know what it was, but I've had that feeling come over me at other times – and it's always been right. At that moment, three other fellows came down the gangplank, and I asked them who they were. They said they were the skipper and mate, and a naval rating, and they said they'd take over. I was delighted. I said there was no sense in all seven of us going. There was always a very clannish feeling with the Leigh men, a very strong dislike of strangers, so we left it. And when we got back, we found out that the *Renown* had been sunk. The two of us took over a barge – the *Shannon*. The wife had packed us a few sandwiches but we didn't know what we were in for.

Ronald Tomlinson
Civilian fisherman – aboard Tankerton Towers and Tom Tit
Halfway through a film, a flash came on to the screen: 'Anybody in Ramsgate trawlers, please report to the Admiralty office at once.' I took no notice, because our trawler had no water in the boilers and no coal in the bunkers. Somebody nudged me in the back and said, 'Ron, that means you!' 'It can't mean me,' I said, 'because we're blown down.' But after the film, I went down to the Admiralty office, to find out what it was all about. 'What ship are you off?' they said. I told them I was an engineer on the *Tankerton Towers*. 'Could you go round and let the crew know to be down here at half-past five in the morning? Because we need a ship.' They didn't say why they needed it. I didn't know anything about Dunkirk. So I went round and by the time we got aboard at half-past five, there was steam blowing from the boiler, there was coal in the bunkers and there were two lieutenants waiting for us. The navy had done all that during the night. The lieutenants asked, 'What have you got on board?' We said, 'Nothing.' They said, 'We'll have to find something to give the boys a cup of tea when they come on board.' We didn't know what they were talking about.

Seaman Thomas King
Royal Navy – served aboard HMS Sharpshooter
We had been minesweeping near Scapa Flow when we were ordered to Dover. It wasn't until we left there during the hours of darkness, that we learnt that

we were going to take an isolated bunch of soldiers from the beaches alongside Dunkirk. We were totally in the dark about the defeats which were occurring, because the radio wasn't always available. In 1940 there wasn't a lot of media coverage and we were very much in the dark.

Gerald Ashcroft
Civilian Sea Scout – aboard Sundowner

I noticed two naval officers talking to Commander Lightoller aboard the *Sundowner*. When they went, Commander Lightoller said, 'Could you give me a hand with stripping out the *Sundowner*?' I said, 'Certainly – what's it in aid of?' He said, 'The navy wish to commandeer her and go to Dunkirk to bring some British troops back.' I gave him a hand to unrig the boat, and said that if he wanted me to come with him, I'd go. I'd been with the Mortlake Sea Scouts for a number of years. He said, 'I'll warn you – it's not going to be a pleasure cruise, but if you'd like to come with us, we'd be pleased to have you.' We took all the gear out from down below to make as much room as possible, and took out anything likely to cause a fire. We stripped the cabins and filled the bath and water tanks with fresh water. We took the mast down and removed everything from the deck and by the evening, we were ready. We moved out the next morning, and fell in with several yachts on the way down the Thames.

Able Seaman Ian Nethercott
Royal Navy, Anti-Aircraft Rating 3rd Class – served aboard HMS Keith

We had a new captain, Captain Burton, a veteran of the Zeebrugge raid in the First World War. He was a real fighting captain. When we got to Sheerness, he cleared the lower deck and said, 'We're going on a job now, and I very much doubt whether any of us will be coming back.' That cheered us up no end...

Leading Seaman Ernest Frederick Eldred
Royal Navy – served aboard HMS Harvester

On board HMS *Harvester* our immediate assumption was that we were going out on patrol – and the first we knew about the Dunkirk evacuation was when we were across the Channel, lying off the coast of France. We had no prior knowledge that things were so bad – as a matter of fact, I think we were rather surprised that things *were* so bad.

The mouth of Dunkirk harbour. In the foreground are ships of the rescue fleet, while in the background are the burning oil tanks which left a 'pall of heavy black smoke above half the town'

Gerald Ashcroft
Civilian Sea Scout – aboard Sundowner

As we got near to the French coast, we attracted the attention of a Stuka dive-bomber which came down at us. Commander Lightoller stood up in the bow, and I stood alongside the wheelhouse, with Roger at the wheel. Lightoller kept his eye on the Stuka until the last second – then he sung out to me, 'Hard aport!' and I sung out to Roger, and we turned very sharply. The bomb landed on our starboard side. The Stuka came round for another go. Lightoller watched him coming down and said, 'Hard astarboard!' Round we went, and the bomb landed a very short distance away on the port quarter. Water came aboard from the bomb, and we rolled heavily, but the Stuka had had enough and away he flew. Lightoller popped down below, and found we were taking on water from these two near misses. He came flying up again to see another fighter coming at us in a straight line astern. Fortunately he'd been told that when a fighter plane was making an attack, just a second or two before it fired its guns, it lifts its nose in alignment with the guns. He was watching for that moment, and as he thought the plane was about to lift, he sung out to go hard aport, which we did – and the bullets came flying down to the side.

Seaman Thomas King
Royal Navy – served aboard HMS Sharpshooter

On our first crossing the weather wasn't very pleasant – it was what we call 'crinkly' in the navy. We could do 15 knots, so it took us two and a half to three hours to get from Dover to La Panne. We went as a fighting ship, which we always were, and we just didn't know what to expect. We didn't know if we were going to anchor off or just steam around. Eventually we did anchor, but I shall always remember that, on the way in to the beaches, our captain hailed a ship that was coming out with troops and said, 'How many are there?' The reply he got back was, 'There's bloody thousands of them!'

Captain James Moulton
General Staff Officer, Grade 3, Operations Section

Our plan at the beginning was to divide the beach into sectors, one per corps, and we'd give each corps specific embarkation points. The corps would detail the units to be lifted from those points – but that's about as far as we got. We hadn't realised that the mole at Dunkirk would become the main point of embarkation. We were expecting the men to leave from the beaches, and I suppose we were hoping that the navy would arrange some means of picking the men up and taking them out to the boats. I don't think we made any estimate of how many men we could get out per day – that would have been too gloomy altogether. We got into the frame of mind of not thinking too far ahead.

During the night, three sloops arrived on the beaches. They had no idea where the troops were, and all they had to get the men off the beaches were one motor boat and one 27-foot whaler per sloop. I waded out to meet the first whaler in – and a sub-lieutenant RNR in the stern promptly fired a revolver over my head. He thought he was going to be swamped by panic-stricken troops. I managed to calm him down a bit, and I went to speak to the captain. I got them moved up towards one of the corps embarkation points, but after a bit the captain, very reasonably, said that it was very shallow water and he was not going to risk his ships by further movement. He dropped anchor again and got off as many as he could.

I went straight back to La Panne, and spoke to General Adam, salt water and sand dripping off my battledress. I said, 'This is not going to work! I'm sure the navy could do better than this if only someone could tell them what was wanted. Can I go over to Dover and see what I can do?' So I went across in one of the sloops. I got into Admiral Ramsay's underground headquarters in the Dover cliffs. The staff there all seemed mainly concerned with getting together the little ships – they had precious little idea of giving them any firm orders about what to do when they arrived. I saw the Admiral, and I showed him my map with the corps embarkation points on it – but it was obvious I wasn't doing any good at all, so I boarded a destroyer and came back to La Panne.

Armament Quartermaster Sergeant Frank Hurrell
3rd Army Field Workshop, Royal Army Ordnance Corps
As we got to the dock area of Dunkirk, early in the morning, there was a reception committee which checked everybody's identity. They told us to have a rest before going down to the harbourside and then on to the beach. We had a cup of soup and tried to rest, but what with the bombing, the French cruisers and guns in the harbour letting off their pom-poms and anti-aircraft, it was impossible to sleep. You had to be either dead tired or *dead* to sleep with that noise going on. In the morning we moved down into what was left of the harbour –

there were railway trucks bombed, old crane derricks knocked down, there was chaos with boats trying to get in, and ships sunk in the harbour.

Captain Anthony Rhodes
253 Field Company, Royal Engineers

We'd been instructed to go immediately to an office, somewhere in the middle of Dunkirk. There were crowds of people, largely officers, asking 'What are we going to do? Where do we go?' I was told, 'It looks as if transports are coming into the quay today. You'd better find the men you have, find cellars in the town, and you'll be taken off from the quay in the course of the day, with any luck. Keep an eye out for boats coming in.'

Armament Quartermaster Sergeant Frank Hurrell
3rd Army Field Workshop, Royal Army Ordnance Corps

I got on to a boat just after seven that evening, and in the course of loading, an air raid came in. The ship got struck and I found myself blown into the water. There were about 30 of us in the water. I could only doggy paddle because of my wounded leg, but I trod water, and got myself back on to the beach. I'd lost my walking stick on the ship, along with my rifle, and now I had to go back into the harbour area and wait for my chance again.

Captain Anthony Rhodes
253 Field Company, Royal Engineers

We picked our way through the centre of Dunkirk, which was under a pall of smoke, with the stink of burning buildings, and vehicles falling to pieces everywhere. We went to the beach. While we were there, a very efficient little major came round as we were sitting in the dunes. He said, 'There are many men here who've lost their officers. I've got some men here for you – they must have someone to lead them.' He made me get up, and he said to this group of 20 men, 'Look at this officer – recognise his face and stick to him!' He did the same with other officers, giving them each 20 or 30 men who had lost their own officers.

Armament Quartermaster Sergeant Frank Hurrell
3rd Army Field Workshop, Royal Army Ordnance Corps

We were under constant attack from the air, and at one point I took cover behind the wheel of a railway truck. The air raid continued for about 25 minutes, and when the all-clear went and I got out, an officer came up to me and said casually, 'You had a lucky escape there, sergeant.' I asked what he meant and he said, 'That truck's full of explosives – we were unloading them.' The thought of what might have happened was the only time that I felt frightened in the whole episode.

Captain Anthony Rhodes
253 Field Company, Royal Engineers

Towards early morning great queues formed to go to the water's edge where at about four o'clock, out of the darkness, we saw boats coming in. Where they came in, there was a little nucleus of men at the head of the water, and a great queue running from the dunes behind, perhaps a quarter of a mile long. Nobody told us what to do, but it seemed the decent thing to get into the queue and not to try to jump it. At the head of each little nucleus there was a naval officer. There must have been ten or twelve of these queues, and when we were halfway up our queue, the bombing started again. One man ran out of place to the head of the queue when he saw a boat coming. The naval officer turned on him, and I heard him say, 'Go back to the place you've come from, or I'll shoot you!' He said it very loudly for everybody to hear, and that man went back with his tail between his legs.

Signaller Alfred Baldwin
65th Field Regiment, Royal Artillery

These were the wonderful queues that were such a mark of Dunkirk. They were orderly – you had the impression of people standing waiting for a bus. There was no pushing and shoving. In the time that I was on the beach, I never saw any problems with people waiting to get into the boats. They all seemed to accept that they had to wait their turn.

Sapper Harold Tomlin
23 Field Company, Royal Engineers

Our unit was originally all together but then the dive-bombers came in and we separated to the nearest point of safety, anywhere there was a hole in the sand. Bombs fell near enough – I got plastered with sand from the blast. We used to fire our rifles at the dive-bombers as they came down, but that was like trying to knock out an aeroplane with a pea-shooter.

Signaller Alfred Baldwin
65th Field Regiment, Royal Artillery
Every time a plane strafed the beach, all the queues vanished miraculously, then as soon as the strafing finished, they all came up and formed up again where they were before.

Corporal Charles 'Bert' Nash
2nd Bulk Petrol Transport Company, Royal Army Service Corps
So often we'd get near the front of the queue – and near getting aboard one of these wonderful little boats – when Jerry would come over and start strafing the beach, and there was a gigantic dispersal exercise, where we all dropped everything and belted back into the cover of the sand dunes. It was soul-destroying.

Signaller Alfred Baldwin
65th Field Regiment, Royal Artillery
I saw relatively few casualties from strafing. At one time I noticed about a dozen dead sailors, but they'd been pulled out of the sea and laid in a line on the beach. The only other casualties I saw were around a dozen French soldiers who'd taken direct hit from a shell, and they were virtually blown to pieces. There were hundreds of slit trenches all over the beaches – and what I didn't realise then, was that to be shelled and shot at in sand is the best place for it, because the sand absorbs most of the explosion.

Lance Corporal John Wells
6th Battalion, South Staffordshire Regiment – aboard SS Princessa
In some ways, the sand was our saving grace, because the average type of bomb, hitting a hard surface like a roadway, the shrapnel scatters, and you all get it. Going into the sand, there was a thud, and you'd get covered in clods of sand but that was about it. It was still bloody unpleasant.

Private Samuel Love
12th Field Ambulance, Royal Ambulance Medical Corps
A bomb would make a crater and a bloke would fall down in it wounded – and the next bomb would cover him over. Some of the holes were 20 foot deep – so if you fell in and another blast covers you over, you'd get buried alive. I bet there were thousands buried on the beaches that nobody knew anything about.

Captain (Acting) Humphrey 'Bala' Bredin
2nd Battalion, Royal Ulster Rifles

You saw the most extraordinary sights on the beaches. Little groups of British soldiers sitting on the sand as though they were at a holiday resort, playing cards while Messerschmitts flew up and down. You could see the bullets hitting the sand one after the other down the beach, and these soldiers were saying, 'He can't shoot very straight!' when the bullets had missed them by a few yards.

Armament Quartermaster Sergeant Frank Hurrell
3rd Army Field Workshop, Royal Army Ordnance Corps

You had one or two people losing their heads – but the majority were well disciplined. I think this was because practically the whole of the BEF was made up of regular forces, and they had proper discipline. I saw with my own eyes a bloke kneeling in the water, his hands together, praying as the Stukas were coming down. And I saw another fellow, a guardsman, shaving on the beach.

Private Sidney Nuttall
Royal Army Ordnance Corps attached to 1st Battalion, Border Regiment

We were told that no man of the Border Regiment would be evacuated to the UK until he was in possession of a full set of equipment. There was material all over the place – people had thrown stuff away. So we made up our kit with whatever we were short of from what people had thrown away. He then said we had to shave – but there was no fresh water. We had to shave in sea water, which we did – and which was very painful.

Captain Anthony Rhodes
253 Field Company, Royal Engineers

The nearer we got to the front of the queue – the nearer to England – the more intense the bombing became. The Germans wanted to target their bombs on the waterline, where the boats were coming in. So a number of people in these long queues peeled off and went back to the dunes. My sergeant asked me, 'What do you think we should do? Should we hang on here, or go back?' I must say, I was in two minds, because we might get killed up in the front, and if we went back we'd certainly got a better chance of surviving. But we decided to go on, and on the way, you just dug, with your hands, to make little trenches to climb into, because you thought it might save you from the

The destroyer HMS *Venomous* which brought 1,500 British troops to safety on a single night of the evacuation

Some of the 'little ships' that took part in the evacuation being towed up the Thames

splinters. A Messerschmitt came down machine-gunning, and it hit three men 20 yards from me. The last I saw of them, a lot of RAMC people had their stretchers out and were carrying them away.

Signaller Alfred Baldwin
65th Field Regiment, Royal Artillery

I had a great sense of security, because out at sea was this line of destroyers, and they seemed so impenetrable that we must get off all right.

Captain Anthony Rhodes
253 Field Company, Royal Engineers

We got to the head of the queue towards three o'clock in the morning, then just when we were getting there, the bombing got very intense and suddenly word came that we'd all to go back to the harbour; the boats would take us off from there. The people at the front of the queues disappeared, and we found ourselves pretty alone. Everybody seemed to be going back to the town. We were just about to toddle back to the town, when suddenly, out of the darkness loomed a rowing boat with a couple of sailors aboard. They weren't navy – they were chaps from Grimsby. They said, 'We've come from the fishing vessel out there. Scramble aboard!' To get to the rowing boat we had to go in the water, so we took off our clothes. Once we'd been on the fishing boat for an hour, a cry went up – we were all to be transferred to a destroyer. The fishing boat drew alongside it, and we were passed on to the destroyer, which was absolutely packed with people. We were the last that they took, because very shortly an officer came round and said, 'We shall now be sailing for Blighty!'

Arthur Joscelyne
Civilian – aboard the Thames barge Shannon

The soldiers were not used to boats – and they all rushed to get on board. We could have capsized at any moment. An officer stood up in the bows and got his revolver out. He said, 'I'll shoot the first man who makes a move before I give you permission to board – you will do it in an orderly manner!' He stood there with his revolver, while we got about 50 of them on board. They were in such a state that they just lay down anywhere. A couple of them threw their rifles overboard and said, 'We shan't want these any more!'

Lieutenant Commander John McBeath
Royal Navy – Commander, HMS Venomous
Small boats which came from the other side, carrying perhaps only a dozen or
so, could go on to the beaches, and nose into all sorts of little quiet corners.
They were the ones that did a great deal of the carrying back of soldiers.

Seaman Thomas King
Royal Navy – served aboard HMS Sharpshooter
There was no order on the first occasion – it was a free-for-all. Soldiers didn't
know the life-saving capacity of boats and we could only take ten to twelve in
a 22-foot whaler. We kept our distance from the water's edge because it was no
good going right up on the beach; we needed to get seaborne again.

Yeoman of Signals Wilfred Walters
Royal Navy – served aboard HMS Ross
There was a lot of, 'Hurry up – let's get back to England!' from the soldiers.
That was the stock phrase. I took a motor boat in, and there was quite a panic;
everybody pushing and shoving and trying to get in the boat at once. We were
only in three feet of water, and it sunk and stuck on the bottom. We just went
down with the weight of the soldiers.

Leading Seaman Ernest Frederick Eldred
Royal Navy – served aboard HMS Harvester
I saw several small boats capsize, but I don't think it was due to indiscipline. I
just think there weren't enough naval or seafaring personnel to supervise the
operation. Troops were getting into boats probably meant to carry only ten,
and there'd be 15 trying to get in. They'd only have two or three inches' freeboard between the top of the boat and the water. As soon as they started moving, the slightest swell would swamp them. I'm sure that if there had been
more sailors to supervise, no boat would have been overloaded in the first
place. Quite a few men were carrying rifles and some had their packs, tin helmets and such. Equipment shouldn't have been carried. It should have been
personnel or equipment – but not both.

Christopher Dreyer
Royal Navy – Commander, MTB 102
When we first went in, the beaches were absolutely black with chaps. The dunes at the back of the beaches were completely covered with men, with long lines coming down to the beach. It was so clearly going to be impossible to get all of that lot off – so that first visit was a rather despairing one.

Sergeant Leonard Howard
210 Field Company, Royal Engineers
By the time we got into Dunkirk on 30 May, everything seemed to be chaos. The sand was littered with bodies and crowds of chaps all hoping to get off. I was exhausted so I just lay in the sand dunes and slept. The next morning my mate Bill and I went into the water in the hope of getting a boat and being picked up – but there was no hope.

Major William Reeves
3rd Battalion, Royal Tank Regiment
Dunkirk was noise and chaos. There was black smoke blowing over the place, there were aeroplanes coming over and dropping bombs. Huge crowds of people were moving towards the docks, thousands of soldiers were on the beach, people were trying to organise and marshal men to certain areas, and trying to get as many people as possible on to destroyers and other ships that managed to pull into the quayside. Chaos.

Signaller Alfred Baldwin
65th Field Regiment, Royal Artillery
I passed an *estaminet* in the town and it was absolutely crowded with French and British soldiers. The windows were all smashed, and there were lights on. It was absolutely chock-a-block, and these drunk Herberts were spilling out on to the pavement and the road. It stuck out because this was the only light in the area except for the fires.

Sapper Frederick Carter
Artisans Works Company and 135 Excavator Company, Royal Engineers
On the first night in Dunkirk, my two mates and me went out and had a glorious drink of champagne at an *estaminet*, over the top of the beaches. We got

rid of all our cash that way. We'd never had it, but we'd heard so much about this 'champagne' that we thought we'd try it. We had a glorious time with it.

Private William Ridley
9th Battalion, Durham Light Infantry

We were thirsty and we wanted water – so Corporal Davidson and I walked along the front at Dunkirk, and we found an army truck that had been blown through the front part of a shop. It was a water truck with taps on the back, but the front of it was down in the cellar. We couldn't turn the taps on, so I said, 'I'll climb inside – give me your bottle,' I got in the tank and the water was all in the front of the truck. My feet were sticking out the top but I managed to fill the bottles. I called out, 'OK, pull me out Andy!' Not a sound. So I had to pull myself out of the truck. I came out head first, soaking wet, and I looked round for him but there was a Stuka raid on, and he was under the truck.

Next we wanted something to eat, and we saw all these trucks abandoned on the beach. I went into one and found a big tin of margarine. It was opened and all full of sand, but it was all right underneath. Then I found a tin of tomato puree and I'd got some biscuits. Then I heard a voice, 'Come up here, soldier, or I'll shoot you!' I said, 'I'm looking for grub, sir.' 'Come off there!' The truck was derelict and they were leaving it for the Germans – and we'd had nothing to eat. The stupidity of it.

Corporal Charles 'Bert' Nash
2nd Bulk Petrol Transport Company, Royal Army Service Corps

We found food in cans – there were dumps where vehicles had been abandoned which contained cases of army food, including stone jars of rum. Most of us were able to get some of this and take it back to our little nooks and crannies among the sand dunes. But the big problem was drinking water. The water supply had got badly contaminated with foreign material. We were led to believe it was sewage because the sewers and waterworks had been damaged by enemy action, so the only thirst-quenching material we were able to get in any quantity was the liquor out of tinned vegetables – primarily tinned potatoes or carrots – which we laced with a drop of rum.

Lieutenant Wilbur Cocke
Signal Section, 51st Heavy Artillery, Royal Artillery

We were short of food, but we were too tired from lack of sleep to have eaten much. The big problem was water. I was on the lookout for water, but the wells in that area had already been drained. I'd always been a careful soldier, so I still had a little water in my water bottle, and I cautioned my men that they must husband their water. I never came to the end of mine, but it was nasty. I never did find any water – and this was much more worrying than the lack of food.

Signaller Alfred Baldwin
65th Field Regiment, Royal Artillery

I tried to get some treatment for my wounded mate Paddy. I approached a group of officers, and because I was armed with a rifle, I came to attention very smartly, sloped arms and gave them a butt salute – which sounds a bit stupid in the circumstances. I asked if there were any medical facilities, and the senior officer said, 'What's the matter, son?' I said that I had a mate with a smashed foot, and he asked me what I'd done about it. I said I'd soaked two field dressings in seawater and bandaged it up tightly, and he said, 'That's the best thing you could do – now try to get him on a boat.' So I gave him another butt salute and turned about smartly and marched off.

Captain Anthony Rhodes
253 Field Company, Royal Engineers

We found some food in a cellar – but it was largely tins of foie gras and a lot of wine and champagne. This latter wasn't very good for the discipline of the troops because a lot of them got blotto – and some people were sick from eating the foie gras.

Lieutenant Wilbur Cocke
Signal Section, 51st Heavy Artillery, Royal Artillery

Along the esplanade at one place there was a small gypsy encampment of French soldiers, and they very decently held out mess tins to my men. Some of my chaps started to fall out and partake of the food offered by the French. I probably overdid it, but I took their mess tins and turned them upside down, tipped the food out and said, 'There's no permission to halt! You march on!'

HU1530

An exhausted soldier rests and waits on a Dunkirk beach

Signaller Alfred Baldwin
65th Field Regiment, Royal Artillery

Walking on the edge of the beach I saw a little boat bobbing up and down, quite a way out. A naval petty officer was standing there and I said to him, 'What's that out there?' 'It's a boat, mate. If you want it, go and get it.' So I stripped off my gear and left it with my mates, and I swam out. When I got there it was a big old heavy rubber dinghy, and I pulled it back, got it to the shore, and standing there – perhaps watching me all the time, was this naval petty officer. He came into the water, waist-deep, and helped me drag in this dinghy. He said, 'Well done, mate. What are you going to do now?' I said that I'd got a wounded mate back up the beach, and he said, 'Right, you get him, and I'll look after the boat for you' – because it would have been silly to leave it there unattended. I came back with the other two and there was the petty officer, standing with a drawn revolver, with half a dozen people crowding round him, wanting this boat – but he wouldn't let them have it until we got in. We pushed off and paddled it out, because there were all sorts of boats loading up, way out to sea. Rowing boats were plying backwards and forwards from the queues, so we set out, with no real sense of direction. We were just going anywhere, as long as we could get out to a boat.

We'd just got out to sea when over came a really heavy Stuka raid and it sunk a couple of ships – one of them a paddle steamer. We'd spotted this and were rowing out to it – but we were still quite a way from it when it got hit – and it went down very quickly. I think we were so stunned that we just sat there and watched it. I don't recall seeing any survivors in the water, but if there were any, we certainly did nothing to help them. We just sat there in a daze, the next thing I recall, we were back on the beach. I can't for the life of me explain why, but we got out and left this perfectly good boat, which we were quite capable of taking back out to sea again. We just left it on the beach – perhaps it was this overwhelming feeling that we were going to get off anyway. I don't think we had any feeling of impending doom. We would get off some way or another.

Private Matthew Smith
2nd Battalion, Hampshire Regiment

One officer from our regiment got in a rowing boat, and said he was going to row out to see if there was any room on a ship for us. But a lance corporal had different ideas, and got into the water, and tipped the boat up. The officer was deserting. He had to take his turn like everyone else.

Yeoman of Signals Wilfred Walters
Royal Navy – served aboard HMS Ross

Our captain did something that he was quite justified in doing. A skiff came alongside the ship with three army officers, and the captain said, 'I'm not taking you on board this ship. Go back on to the beaches and take charge of your men! That's your place – not trying to get away.' They didn't want to, but the captain said that if they didn't, he'd put a couple of rifle bullets through the skiff and let them get on with it. One of the officers said, 'But I'm a major!' and the captain said, 'I don't care. Get back on the beaches – there are men wanting someone to command them!'

Captain (Acting) Humphrey 'Bala' Bredin
2nd Battalion, Royal Ulster Rifles

There were some unpleasant happenings where boats reserved for the wounded to be taken out to bigger boats were seized by little gangs of people who had lost their nerve a bit.

Major Andrew Marshall Horsburgh-Porter
D Squadron, 12th Lancers

The only ill-discipline I saw was among Belgian staff officers. I was up to my neck in water, trying to get these boats off to the destroyers, and a group of very excited Belgian staff officers came down with a friend of mine, a military policeman, Ken Alexander. He said it was very important to get these fellows to England, but I said they'd have to wait, as we'd got some wounded, and it was difficult to get the boats off as it was a shelving beach and you had to wait for the waves and then get into the boat and shove it off. I explained to these fellows, when we did eventually get them a boat, that they had to get in each side – it was all broken French and gesticulation, but they nodded their heads. I said, 'One lot this side, one lot that side – and then you get in.' All the buggers ran at the boat on one side and capsized it. It was the only time I used my revolver in the war, and I pulled it out and fired into the water and over their heads and told them to bugger off. Ken was laughing and took them off – and I don't know what happened to them after that. Oh God, I was cross with them.

Lance Corporal Albert Adams
East Yorkshire Yeomanry

There were some drunk lads who had come up the side of a queue and were trying to muscle in. The sailors wouldn't let them on the ship, and they told them to get back to the end of the queue.

Corporal Charles 'Bert' Nash
2nd Bulk Petrol Transport Company, Royal Army Service Corps

I saw one naval chap in charge of a lifeboat whack a couple of soldiers across the back of their heads and shoulders with an oar to try to stop them clambering into a vessel that was already full to a dangerous level.

Lieutenant Wilbur Cocke
Signal Section, 51st Heavy Regiment, Royal Artillery

One of our officers was a rather truculent sort of chap, and when certain other groups of soldiers tried to muscle in on our embarkation, he took out his revolver and fired shots across the front of them. I wasn't prepared to do that.

Private Edgar Rabbets
5th Battalion, Northamptonshire Regiment

I saw one case where an officer was out of line – and he was shot by a fellow officer. This man was determined to get on a boat. It was one of the small boats that was carrying people out to the larger ones. I would say he was a man who'd had a rough time somewhere, because he was in a bad way, and he was shouting and waving his revolver around. The other officer got fed up with trying to make him do his job properly, and I suppose he just lost his temper. But this man was obviously suffering. It was beyond panic. It was shell shock.

Sergeant Leonard Howard
210 Field Company, Royal Engineers

I saw British troops shoot other British troops. On one occasion a small boat came in and they piled aboard it to such a degree that it was in danger of capsizing. The chap in charge of this boat decided that unless he took some action it would, so he shot a hanger-on at the back of the boat through the head. It probably saved those chaps on the boat – but I hoped I would never be called upon to do that. I think he did the right thing, but it was awful to see. There was no reaction to this at all. There was such chaos on the beach that this didn't seem to be out of keeping. There were chaps who unfortunately were going round the bend – I saw chaps run into the water screaming because mentally it had all got too much for them. During the two days we were on the beach, at least a couple of dozen men committed suicide by running into the sea. They were under terrific strain, and one couldn't do anything for them.

Private Edgar Rabbets
5th Battalion, Northamptonshire Regiment

The symptoms of shell shock varied – some people went very quiet. One man stood still as soon as the guns started. He couldn't move. He lost all power of movement.

Sergeant Leonard Howard
210 Field Company, Royal Engineers

We spotted a boat called the *Hebe*, which had come aground. Bill Baldry and I waded and swam out to it, and it had scrambling nets out over the side to get us up. We knew that at high tide its crew would sail away, so we climbed aboard. We waited on it for a couple of hours, and suddenly I said to Bill, 'I'm getting off this boat!' He called me all the names he could think of, but he came with me, down the scrambling nets and back on to the beach. That same afternoon the Stukas came down and dropped bombs, and one went straight down the funnel of this ship and blew it apart. I had got off it – and I still can't say why. When I came out of the water, I was bitterly cold. I found a corpse on the beach, and I removed its corporal's overcoat, and put it on to keep warm.

Armament Quartermaster Sergeant Frank Hurrell
3rd Army Field Workshop, Royal Army Ordnance Corps

I knew I was going to get through this – because I'd made up my mind. I had a simple reason – my wife was pregnant and I'd made up my mind I was going to get home. Whether it was by good luck or judgement, even though I had the handicap with my injured leg, I wasn't giving up. I just said to myself, 'I'm going to get there.'

Sergeant Leonard Howard
210 Field Company, Royal Engineers

They landed some beachmasters who were in service dress with red bands on their arms to try to organise the evacuation, and frankly the chaps who'd made it to Dunkirk didn't want chaps in service dress and Sam Brownes and red bands trying to organise them. I remember there was a very flimsy canoe, and two chaps paddled out in it. A Stuka had come down and machine-gunned them and they both leaned the same way and both drowned. The canoe was floating upside down some way off the beach. I knew my mate Bill could swim well, and we were standing together in the water. I was wearing this dead corporal's overcoat, notwithstanding the fact that I was a sergeant and had a sergeant's stripes on my jacket underneath. One of these beach-masters called out to Bill, 'Come out of the water, sergeant major!' We weren't going to come out of the water – after all, we thought there was a chance of getting into this canoe and away. This chap fired his revolver and the bullet slipped into the water very close to us. Bill turned round and went out of the water on to the sand, but I was thinking, 'Well, he hasn't mentioned me,' so I stayed there, watching, to make sure I was going to get that canoe.

Then I heard this chap shouting again, 'Come out of the water, corporal!', and again a revolver bullet slipped into the water very, very close to me. I was livid. I'd got my own revolver in the top of my jacket and I swung round and shouted to this chap, 'I'm not a corporal! You can't judge people by what they're wearing on the beach today!' To my surprise he put his revolver back in his holster and saluted very smartly and said, 'I'm sorry.' I said 'That's all right, sergeant major.' Then I shouted to Bill, 'Get the canoe!' Whereupon Bill swam out to the canoe and pulled it ashore, and we emptied it of water.

We got a couple of spades off an abandoned lorry and used them to paddle out. We undid our fly buttons and took the laces out of our boots so that if we did go into the water we could swim. We went out so far that I said to Bill, 'I know I couldn't make it ashore now.' He said, 'Neither could I.' At that moment HMS *Whitehall* came past us with its anti-aircraft guns blazing away at the Stukas. A fellow with a loudhailer off the stern said, 'We'll pick you up.' But I just thought, 'When the wash of this destroyer hits us, we're going to need picking up!' The *Whitehall* went by us at a terrific rate of knots, and in the end, another sizeable boat threw us a line. As they threw it, it fell across the centre of the canoe. Now, we'd only got about an inch and a half freeboard because we'd shipped an awful lot of the wash of the *Whitehall*, and as the rope hit us, it sank the canoe. We just held on to the rope and they pulled us in towards the ship.

Sapper Harold Tomlin
23 Field Company, Royal Engineers

We built a causeway from the sands, because the boats couldn't come in too close, to allow the chaps to get off. Even then they had to get into the water to get to the boats. We built it with timber and anything that was around – it was a makeshift job, fixed together with nails and botched together, just to make a walkway out over the water.

Major Donald Wilson-Haffenden
HQ – 1st Division

My divisional CRE [Commander Royal Engineers] hit on the idea of building a lorry pier at La Panne by running lorries out, head to tail into the sea, and then building a superstructure on it, which the boats could come alongside. We had a chain of about 25 lorries, and we punctured the tyres so that they wouldn't float. This enabled us to speed up the embarkation tremendously. I remember the CRE sitting on the beach in a deckchair, having built his lorry pier, and when the Germans came over, he took a shot at them every now and again.

Captain (Acting) Humphrey 'Bala' Bredin
2nd Battalion, Royal Ulster Rifles

I still had about 50 of my chaps with me when we got on to the beach at La Panne, and I saw that the engineers had made a pier by driving big trucks into the sea at low tide, putting duckboarding along the top, and using them as platforms for boats to come in and take people off. So we lined up by this pier and waited for a boat to come along. Nothing happened.

Captain Stephen Hollway
Field Park Company, Royal Engineers

As night came on, the tide was going out, and it became quite evident that loading would have to be abandoned because it was impossible for small craft such as dinghies to come up to the beach at La Panne. At this time the phosphorescence of the water was quite the most vivid that I have ever seen, so that all the wet ropes were brilliantly illuminated, and every footstep one took across the wet beach was lit up as if by electricity.

The remains of a makeshift pier, as described by Captain Humphrey 'Bala' Bredin, made by driving trucks into the sea, and placing duckboards along the top

Signaller Alfred Baldwin
65th Field Regiment, Royal Artillery

On the Friday [31 May] morning there was a magnificent show of a section of Guards marching on to the beach, rifles at the slope, quite immaculately dressed. They halted on the beach – right turn, fall out – it was quite a spectacle. There may well have been 50 or 60 of these Guardsmen with four German prisoners. We all looked very closely at these prisoners, as many of us had never seen actual Germans up close before. These prisoners were arrogant – that's the only word for them. I don't know what happened to them, but I noticed that they were very well-built, and very smart – in fact it was a bloody good job the Guards brought them in, because they looked equally smart. Our battledress didn't compare with the Germans' field dress for smartness – but at least these arrogant Germans were in custody of as smart a unit as possible.

Lance Sergeant Robert Green
2nd Battalion, Bedfordshire and Hertfordshire Regiment

At La Panne, shells were dropping all over the damn place, and it was on fire. There were vehicles and bodies everywhere, and we pushed through to the dunes. This was where we went badly wrong – and I'm afraid it was my fault. We came on to the dunes, along with thousands of blokes from all different units, and we came to a little constricted alleyway that we had to go through to get to the dunes on the other side. There was a hell of a crush to get through the alleyway, and two or three of my blokes sat down for a rest. I said, 'Don't be so bloody daft! If you sit down you'll never get going again. Keep going!' I automatically turned through this alley, thinking they were behind me, but just as I did, the shelling came on, and the moment it started, up came everybody and made for this alley. It was just like being carried through the gate of a football crowd – my feet came off the floor and I was carried 20 yards along this thing, and at the far end we spewed out all over the place. I was about 100 yards away from it by the time I got back on my feet, thinking my blokes were behind me. I waited and waited, and they never appeared. So I pressed on, on my own.

Captain Stephen Hollway
Field Park Company, Royal Engineers

I set out walking from La Panne beach, and I came across a signals officer who told me that he had just destroyed the last telephone link with England, and that there was now nobody between us and the German positions. In fact this wasn't quite true, but nevertheless, it gave me a tremendous feeling of insecurity. After walking for quite a long time, the signals officer and I came upon a Royal Navy party who were embarking soldiers from the beach on the rising tide. We hailed them, and they said that they had no more room, but if we cared to swim out to them, they would tow us to a larger craft. By this time, we were both exhausted and tired of walking, so we took off our boots and trousers and swam out, and were towed to a motor yacht which was ferrying troops from La Panne to Dunkirk. As soon as I got aboard this craft, I was so exhausted after a fortnight without any real sleep, that I slept until we got into Dunkirk, where it was proposed that we should be transferred to a larger craft. As soon as we got there, a heavy air raid developed, and there was a shout for anybody who could operate a Bren gun. I volunteered to do this, but unfortunately they had no magazines – so that was another abortive effort to join the fight.

Lance Sergeant Robert Green
2nd Battalion, Bedfordshire and Hertfordshire Regiment
At La Panne, there were four blokes carrying a wounded man on a stretcher. I think the bloke had got a severed clavian artery and a Royal Army Medical Corps bloke was keeping his finger on the pressure point to stop him bleeding, which was a bit awkward, so I gave them a hand carrying the stretcher. We pressed on across the dunes and through a line of trees on to the road, just as some carriers came up, complete with officers. We flagged them down because we didn't know how far we'd got to go, or even where we were. 'Could you pick some wounded up, sir?' He said, 'I'll take the wounded, but nothing else.' So we got this stretcher case on to the back of the carrier and immediately everybody else piled on as well.

I was lying across the top of the carrier, almost immediately behind an officer, and I said, 'Excuse me sir, are you DCLI?' A very irate voice said, 'No we're not. This is the 3rd Battalion, Grenadier Guards.' He simmered down after a bit and said to me, 'Have you come through La Panne?' I said, 'Yes sir.' He said, 'Well, what do you think to it?' So I said, 'I've been in healthier places.'

The truck took us right into Dunkirk and I climbed off and we took the stretcher case off to a dressing station. I stood outside, lit a fag and wondered what to do next. I was on my tod, I'd lost my battalion, lost my company and even lost my ruddy section. Immediately in front of me was a very large and rather ornate entrance to a thing called 'The Casino'. Everything on it was perfect, hardly a scratch, even the glass wasn't broken. I opened the front door, went to step in, and there was a ruddy great hole behind it – an enormous crater. A bomb had blown everything away from the back and left the front wall standing, without even breaking the glass. I decided to find the beach, so I headed down an alleyway to the promenade. Away to the left was a mole with ships coming in and out.

Lieutenant Commander John McBeath
Royal Navy – Commanding Officer, HMS Venomous

In the early days at Dunkirk, when you went in you could go to almost any of the berths. There were a number of ships which had been caught there by events but there was no difficulty about a berth. But after the port had been attacked by air, there were a large number of wrecks and there were very few spaces alongside either the inner or outer harbour for ships such as a destroyer to go in. So much of the embarkation of the army had eventually to be done on the mole, which was really a skeleton concrete breakwater which stuck out on the north side of the harbour entrance. It was never intended for ships to berth alongside, and when there was a strong tide running – as there frequently was – it was very difficult to secure alongside. You had to nose out and then stick wires and ropes through parts of the concrete to secure yourself. The easiest way to go alongside was with a bit of a bump to make sure you got there – and you often got a large chunk of concrete weighing two or three hundredweight arriving on your deck.

Able Seaman Ian Nethercott
Royal Navy, Anti-Aircraft Rating 3rd Class – served aboard HMS Keith

When we first tied up alongside the mole, we went past a troopship at the very end of it which had been sunk. She was lying on the bottom, burnt out. Next, there was a destroyer which was burnt out, and then there was a gap in the mole for about 100 yards. Then there were trawlers and sweepers, also burnt out, leaning against the mole. In the middle section the mole had been shot away and they'd got a load of planks which the troops had to walk over in single file.

Sapper Frederick Carter
135 Excavator Company, Royal Engineers

I'm not a very good water merchant. I don't like water. I thought, 'Well, that's it!' I would have sooner been taken prisoner than gone in the water. Luckily, we marched on to Dunkirk mole, and went off of there.

Lieutenant Colonel Peter Jeffreys
6th Battalion, Durham Light Infantry

About nine or ten o'clock on 31 May, we reached the Dunkirk mole – and the scene was extraordinary. The start of the mole was one mass of troops. I moved forward to find out what we were to do. There was a small body of staff officers at the base of the mole, sending out runners to bring groups forward, who were then sent queuing up the mole. We hoped that at the end of the mole there'd be boats to take us off, and we realised as we shuffled forward, that this was the case. The mole was shelled spasmodically, but I never saw a shell hit it. One or two men had been killed close to the mole and you could see them lying there, but on the whole, casualties on the mole seemed light. Finally we got to the head of the queue – and there was no boat. But about 50 yards out, in the gloom, I could see a boat approaching, and sure enough, a Royal Navy minesweeper eventually drew up alongside, threw down a gangplank, and on we marched.

Lieutenant Wilbur Cocke
Signal Section, 51st Heavy Regiment, Royal Artillery

We formed up very near the mole, and it really did work according to the plan. We were called forward and a destroyer – HMS *Scimitar* – came in, stern first, alongside this ruined mole, and with great difficulty we scrambled aboard. We were terribly lucky.

Gerald Ashcroft
Civilian Sea Scout – aboard Sundowner

The harbour mole leading down to the destroyer was jam-packed with soldiers so tightly they couldn't move. There were no British aircraft at all, and only the destroyer's anti-aircraft fire to depend on. The German air force was having a field day – and the fighters were coming straight along the mole, machine-gunning all the way. The troops just had to stand there. I felt very sorry indeed for them.

Lance Sergeant Robert Green
2nd Battalion, Bedfordshire and Hertfordshire Regiment

All down one side of the mole were British odds and ends, and on the other side was a more or less complete French regiment, waiting to embark. Some of the French had bicycles and attaché cases – but not a weapon between any of them. On the other side were British – half of them half naked, but every man had something with which to fight.

Ronald Tomlinson
Civilian fisherman – aboard Tankerton Towers and Tom Tit

I was concentrating on going into the pier. I didn't even moor up, I just kept the engine running and let them jump aboard. As soon as I got a boatload, I went out to the nearest ship, dropped them, and came back in. I just kept filling up. I had them sitting in the cockpit and on the deck. I couldn't say how many – 40, maybe 50. One poor lad could hardly walk, so we took him down to our cabin and I thought he might as well have my bunk. But when I looked round, the cabin was absolutely full – everybody had followed me down. An officer said to this lad, 'Come on, get out of that bunk! I'm an officer!' So I said, 'There's no such thing as officers in these circumstances!'

2nd Lieutenant Allan Elton Younger
61 Chemical Warfare Company, Royal Engineers

We decided to round up our men, who must be somewhere on the beach, so we started at one end. We gradually collected our two sections and they formed a group of some 70 men. I then did some reconnoitring and found that groups were being evacuated from the mole by British destroyers. I decided to join the queue there. This was being organised by an officer who sat in a little slit trench, surrounded by groups of men, each of which had been given a number, and as room on the mole became available, he would call the numbers to move up to the mole in order. This was quite under control and disciplined, with everybody patiently waiting their turn.

We joined the queue, but then the organising officer got up and joined what I suppose was his unit, and marched off. Nothing happened for a bit, so I moved forward and took his place. I felt that somebody had to do it. I was only a second lieutenant, but I had my gas cape on, so there was no way anyone

HMS *Vivacious* sits alongside the Dunkirk mole. A direct hit from a German bomb has just sunk the trawler in the foreground

could tell my rank. As other groups came up, I allocated them numbers and told them where to sit.

Destroyers were coming and going, and the groups gradually moved forward. Eventually the time came for our group to move forward so I – as my predecessor had done – got up from my little trench, rejoined my group, and marched forward. We got on to the mole – and soon after that the shelling became worse, and some shells landed on the mole in the middle of one of the parties. The mole wasn't straight – there was an angle in it, and there had been an officer at that angle, directing the groups on to the boats as they arrived – and he became a casualty. Again I went forward, and took the job of the man directing units on to the boats, shouting to them to get moving at the double when there was a boat in, and telling them to lie low when the boat had pulled out. I did this for a bit, until again, my unit got to the front and I joined them on a destroyer which took us back to England.

Sergeant Robert Coupland
East Riding Yeomanry

The controllers down on the lower level of the mole were getting the wounded aboard the *Royal Daffodil*. They seemed to come to an end of the walking wounded and stretcher cases, and this navy captain came along. He took charge and he was on the higher level. He put his hand out and said, 'Those to the right of my hand move up on to the top and get aboard the ship, and God help anybody who's on the wrong side of that hand who moves.' He gave the order, up we went, and one man moved out of line. He just said to the two matelots that were with him, 'Get him and bring him up here.' It did the trick. He threatened him. He said, 'Personally I shall see that you are the last man to leave here!' We got on to the *Royal Daffodil* and we finished up at Margate.

Lance Corporal John Wells
6th Battalion, South Staffordshire Regiment – aboard SS Princessa

A Royal Navy destroyer was taking on some French troops. A French officer started to rush up the gangway, and the young naval lieutenant on the bridge told him to stop. This bloke wasn't standing for it – he carried on running up. So the lieutenant drew his pistol and shot the Frenchman dead. It was a very sobering thing to watch. But I realised – right then – the importance of discipline. After that, they came up one at a time. I admired that young lieutenant. He was right.

Private Victor Burton
1st Battalion, East Lancashire Regiment
We got on the long jetty and we were told to march along. There were shell holes in it, and every now and then – it was dark now – there were people falling through the holes. You'd hear a splash, and you couldn't help them because you couldn't see what was happening.

Lieutenant D'Arcy McCloughin
9 Field Company, Royal Engineers
I was halfway down the mole, when a small motorboat stopped just below me. A lieutenant commander RN in civilian clothes shouted up, 'Room for three more!' This was no time to work things out, so I hastily pointed to two chaps on either side of me and said, 'You two and me.' They jumped, and I jumped. That made up the complement. It was a 28-foot motor boat and there must have been about 30 of us on board besides the skipper, so we didn't make much headway. We cleared the mole and the troopships, but then we realised that we were getting dangerously close to the shore and not making very good speed against the tide, and were likely to go on close to the shoreline until we got to the next town, which I suppose was Calais.

Ordinary Seaman Stanley Allen
Royal Navy – aboard HMS Windsor
When we got alongside at Dunkirk, a file of Scottish soldiers, who were wearing khaki aprons over their kilts, came along, led by an officer who'd got his arm in a sling. He called out to the bridge, 'What part of France are you taking us to?' One of our officers called back, 'We're taking you back to Dover.' And he said, 'Well, we're not bloody well coming!' They turned round and went back to continue their war with the Germans on their own. It was something remarkable.

Robert Newborough
Civilian in command of Fleet Air Arm motorboat
We brought some foreign troops back, but I tried to pick the British ones, because I felt they should be the first home. Maybe it wasn't the right thing to do, but I felt it was my duty. Sometimes one got a bit ruthless and said, 'British only!' One felt after all that we were going there to rescue our own chaps, and the French had their own country to get back to.

Able Seaman Ian Nethercott
Royal Navy, Anti-Aircraft Rating 3rd Class – served aboard HMS Keith

When the troops arrived alongside us it was very sad – a lot of them had got dogs with them that they'd picked up. But as the men arrived with their dogs, the military police were shooting them and throwing them in the harbour. Every time they did this, there was a great 'Boo!' from the sailors on the ships loading up the men. We couldn't see any reason why these dogs shouldn't be taken back to Britain.

Lieutenant Commander John McBeath
Royal Navy – Commanding Officer, HMS Venomous

The men's morale was most impressive, because one rather expected to find a dejected beaten army, but it was far from that. They were very tired, but they had their tails right up. They'd been asked to bring their rifles back, so they would slide down the poles or ladders to get on board, and then they'd just chuck these rifles down on to the deck. The fact that many of these rifles were fully loaded and without the safety catch on was not their headache…

Engine Room Artificer Andrew Begg
Royal Navy, served aboard HMS Icarus

We had a couple of dozen men down in the engine-room – who were in severe shock, shivering like hell. We put them in there because they needed some heat and it was warm there. They fell asleep – because they felt they were safe because they were on board a ship, but we had to go through the bombing to get out, and there was bombing for a good three-quarters of an hour. After that, the bombers would give up and go back – because there were plenty of nearer targets for them.

Able Seaman Ian Nethercott
Royal Navy, Anti-Aircraft Rating 3rd Class – served aboard HMS Keith

It's very difficult to remember the evacuation in any sort of sequence, because the whole time I was there I was closed up at action stations on a gun, firing at German aircraft and shore targets. On one occasion, I'd only been firing for a few minutes when all of a sudden the gun went off target. I couldn't make out what had happened. I looked across the gun, and the gun-layer had been completely decapitated. Something had hit him and taken the whole of his head and half his shoulder off. He was just lying in the harness, spouting blood everywhere. I shouted to the ammunition numbers to change round – which means you all move up one, so I had to take the gun-layer's position. As I went round, the deck was swimming in blood, so I shouted out to the loading numbers to chuck the sand down. We dragged the gun-layer off the seat and put him up against the lockers and resumed firing. We kept firing for about half an hour at everything and anything.

Engine Room Artificer Andrew Begg
Royal Navy – served aboard HMS Icarus
There was no thought for safety. The skipper sat with his leg over the bridge yelling, 'Come on! Hurry up! Get a move on!' We got our complement, and they cut the couple of ropes and went out astern, and as we went out to sea, two destroyers came in past us. We had just set off when we rammed a tug loaded with soldiers and sunk it. It must have been a hell of a loss of life, because we cut it in two. All the poor soldiers must have been drowned – but we couldn't stop.

Able Seaman Reginald Heron
Royal Navy – served aboard HMS Keith
I was in the wireless office of HMS *Keith* and there was a hell of a crash and everything shook like hell. We knew we'd been hit because we were more or less expecting it. I mean, we'd been there four days – it was a wonder we hadn't been hit before. A bomb from a Stuka went down the funnel, and blew out the whole of the underpart of the ship. We grabbed the codebooks, and put them in a specially weighted bag and we threw it over the side. Then someone shouted, 'Abandon ship! Throw everything floatable overboard!' So I threw a dan-buoy overboard. A dan-buoy's a long thing, a bit like a jousting lance with a big cork float at the end. I jumped in behind it and started swimming with one arm. I swam over to a tug a few hundred yards away and grabbed hold of a rubber tyre on the side. Then the tug actually started up and it got quite speedy and I was getting dragged through the water at a rate of knots. There was somebody above me, hanging on to the edge of the tug and a stupid sailor was shouting at me to push him up. So with one hand I was hanging on to the rubber tyre, and with the other I was trying to push this guy up so the sailor could haul him aboard. After all this palaver, we got aboard eventually, and headed back to Dover.

Able Seaman Ian Nethercott
Royal Navy, Anti-Aircraft Rating 3rd Class – served aboard HMS Keith
We swam away from the *Keith* towards a motor lighter. We slowed down a lot because they were bombing us in the water, and the impact kept punching you right in the stomach and making you sick. What's more, we were in a big patch of oil and we kept getting it in our mouths and eyes – you couldn't get rid of it. A boat called the *Cervia* came round and round, time and again, and eventually picked up all those who were alive – although there were a lot of dead in the water. I crawled aboard and got under the gunwales and went to sleep, and didn't think any more of it. I thought, 'There's nothing more.'

Lance Sergeant Robert Green
2nd Battalion, Bedfordshire and Hertfordshire Regiment
While we were standing on the mole, a German aircraft turned and headed straight down towards us. Having been shot at from every conceivable angle by aircraft over the past fortnight, when anybody did that, you instinctively went to earth. Down the side of the mole there was a big solid stone wall and I heard a terrific clatter above my head, and lots of swearing. I thought the machine-gun fire must be hitting the top of the wall I was lying under, but I looked up and it was anything but. It was a bloke in the Northumberland Fusiliers with a Bren gun, firing at this aircraft, swearing his head off.

Before I got to the end of the mole, I saw one of the most tragic sights I've ever seen. 'Make way! Make way!' We made way, and an RAMC bloke was leading another bloke. He must have been about six foot six, he had nothing on other than his shirt, trousers and a pair of boots. You've seen zombies described where a man's eyes are absolutely opaque – the only thing that was moving was his feet, as the RAMC bloke was leading him by the arm. Everything else in that bloke was dead – I don't know whether it was shell shock or what. If he hadn't been so big and finely built you wouldn't have noticed it so much.

2nd Lieutenant Peter Martin
2nd Battalion, Cheshire Regiment
I saw something that harrowed me for the rest of my life: a French soldier with one eye hanging out down his face, screaming for help. He was running round like some demented hen – it was absolutely awful and I was powerless to do anything about it.

HMS *Vanquisher* picks up troops from the Dunkirk mole. It is low tide so the soldiers are using ladders to embark

Private Edgar Rabbets
5th Battalion, Northamptonshire Regiment
There were quite a lot of wounded, but they were not all being looked after well – as you would expect under the circumstances. The RAMC people were trying to do their best under very trying conditions. They'd established themselves in odd corners where they were reasonably sheltered, and the wounded were being taken in to them, and getting as much treatment as they could give. At least they got their wounds bandaged up – and those that were too bad were put on stretchers and moved when possible. A few of us got together to carry these wounded chappies down to the hospital ship when it came in, and then we went back to the beach.

Signaller Alfred Baldwin
65th Field Regiment, Royal Artillery
Some people came along in the evening, shouting, '65th Field, 65th Field!' so we joined them. We walked along the beach with them, pushing Paddy on the bike, until we reached the foot of the mole. By this time the air raids had stopped, but artillery fire was coming in pretty heavily, and there was lots of machine-gun fire from the west end of the town. At the bottom of the land end of the mole, there were lots of rocks and boulders, so we couldn't push the bike any further. I got Paddy in a fireman's lift across my shoulder and clambered over the rocks. He was moaning like buggery – not about the pain – but because I insisted on carrying a rifle that I'd found. I was determined I wasn't going to let it go, and he was moaning like mad about this. I was telling him to effing well shut up.

We clambered on to the land end of the mole and there were shells dropping all around. A couple of boats were burning out at sea and there were fires all over town, with smoke and shouting. The noise was horrendous. We sat on the end of the mole and, looking out to sea on the right-hand side was a very low wall, and we crouched down behind this. Somebody lit a fag and as the match flared out there was a great shout, 'Put that light out!' – which they did. Very shortly after that, the mole itself was hit by a shell. Then a shout went up, 'Wounded and injured first!' I thought we qualified for that, so I picked old Paddy up, slung him over my shoulder again, and went off along the mole. It was a very black night and there was all this noise and confusion around, yet I never felt any sense of fear. I don't think I was even registering what was happening.

217

We came to a gap in the mole which might have been ten feet across, and over it were laid a couple of planks. There was a naval chap standing at the land end of these planks, and he said, 'Take a run at it, mate.' So I went back a few steps and ran at these planks. With the weight of one man they might well have been all right, but with two they were sagging pretty badly by the time I got into the middle. I think I would have fallen off had it not been for a couple of navy blokes on the far end, who just grabbed hold of me and dragged me on by my battledress. I remember them shouting to me, 'Not much farther now!' I staggered on, still with Paddy on my back, and I think I'd have gone right off the end of the mole, but there were two officers there who stopped me, took Paddy off my shoulder, and I went up the gangway on to the ship. They carried Paddy up and sat us down on the deck – which was pretty crowded. They wanted us to go down below, but I said I wanted to stay up on the deck. I felt instinctively that if we were going to be bombed or shot at, I would stand a better chance on the deck, so we tucked ourselves into a corner, out of the way. I must have gone to sleep, because I don't remember the boat leaving the dock, but I do remember dawn the next morning that we woke up and could see the coastline of England on our left-hand side.

Corporal Charles 'Bert' Nash
2nd Bulk Petrol Transport Company, Royal Army Service Corps
Some medical bloke came along and said, 'We urgently need fit people to help get the wounded aboard hospital ships. Any of you lads who'd like to help out, come on!' Me and another three fellows joined them – the other two in our group stayed behind. We volunteered for stretcher-bearing, and we spent 12 hours, going backwards and forwards with walking wounded and stretcher cases, ferrying these poor fellows along what was left of the mole. All of a sudden, out of the blue, a redcap shouted, 'Here! We've got room for a few more! Who'd like to come aboard?' I clambered aboard what turned out to be a little fishing smack. There were about 100 of us aboard, and we started back to England. I found out afterwards that the two who didn't volunteer never made it back. They were killed after they took refuge in a house on the waterfront which was dive-bombed.

Private Sidney Nuttall
Royal Army Ordnance Corps attached to 1st Battalion, Border Regiment

We had the job – which was not very nice – of carrying the wounded. We had to get them down to the beach on to boats. It was quite a walk, four of you carrying a loaded stretcher. We couldn't do much for the wounded because we had no medical equipment, apart from our field dressings. We used to take the stretcher cases down, wade into the sea, with water up to our chests. Then you had to pass the bloke into the boat, and they took them away. We did this for two or three nights. When we came out I had a tide mark of salt on my uniform across my chest.

Captain Stephen Hollway
Field Park Company, Royal Engineers

During a heavy bombing raid, I went down flat on the beach to escape the missiles. Eventually I came to, having either been knocked out by a blast, or just collapsed from sheer exhaustion. I came to as dawn was breaking, and there was not a soul in sight on the beach. I realised that I had been left for dead.

Private Harry Dennis
1st Battalion, East Surrey Regiment

I arrived on to the beach – and the next thing I knew, I was waking up, and over my head was a white substance. It was the ceiling of a ship's cabin. I asked, 'Where am I?' and they said I was on the *Albany* – a minesweeper – on my way back to Blighty. But I've no recollections at all.

Lance Corporal John Wells
6th Battalion, South Staffordshire Regiment – aboard SS Princessa

We entered Dunkirk harbour on the *Princessa*. We were in the middle of the main channel, and there were two ships on either side and we were dive-bombed. Both of the other ships got hit at the same time and they both exploded. It transpired that they were ammunition ships. The poor little *Princessa* went down straight away. She was only a tiddly little ferry boat. The next thing I knew, I was lying on the cobblestone quayside. I was rather intrigued because I was one of half a dozen corpses that had been pulled out the sea and dumped there. The others were all in grey uniform. They were the first ruddy Germans I'd seen! And the souvenir hunters had all got their knives out and cut out the swastikas and badges from the Germans' uniforms. I felt for my Staffordshire brass knots – yes, I'd still got my buttons and emblems. I was very wet, but it was a nice, sunny day and I dried out fairly quickly.

2nd Lieutenant Arthur Curtis
7th Field Company, Royal Engineers

Because we were wounded, we had been placed in a hotel on the seafront, which had been converted into a temporary hospital. Sitting in the hallway was a senior Royal Army Medical Corps colonel, and he looked absolutely dead beat. There was an orderly holding him up, but his job was to sort the sheep from the goats, deciding who could wait and who was urgent. I was taken up to one of the bedrooms, which had a double bed and a double mattress on the floor. I shared the double mattress with an RAMC driver, who'd also been shot in the side. We were quite chummy. On the double bed was a much more seriously wounded chap who'd had both his ankles smashed, and he was in great pain.

The nurses came round and gave us tea, but I don't think we had anything to eat – I don't think we even thought about it. The next day, a message came round saying anyone who could walk should report to the lounge, so we went down and were formed up in pairs – a more lightly wounded chap with a more seriously wounded one. I was put in charge of a padre who'd had his jaw blown off. His head was completely swathed, you could barely see through the gap in the bandages, and he couldn't see where he was going. I helped him down the steps and we went up across the esplanade, and down on to the beach. There was a shed in which, in happier times, they had kept the lilos and pedalos. They had all been kicked out, and the glass roof had been smashed to prevent flying glass, and we settled down on the broken glass on the concrete floor. I discovered that if glass has been properly smashed up, it is surprisingly comfortable to sleep on.

We lay down there for a few hours, then before dawn, we got up and formed into our crocodile again. The tide was out, there was a long stretch of wet sand, and there were these famous queues of people, all waiting to go forward. The wounded were given priority, so we didn't have to hang about. We went straight down to the water's edge, and in the early morning hot sun and mist we could see the outline of a vessel. My father had been in the coastal artillery, and we'd spent a lot of time looking out to sea, and we'd always had *Jane's*

Fighting Ships by the front window so we could identify ships. So when some-body said, 'What's that?' I said, 'It's a French battleship, it's probably the Strasbourg.' It turned out to be a paddle steamer from Bournemouth. We were loaded into a boat, and we were rowed out to where the water was deep enough for this paddle steamer, then hoisted aboard. I found a nice little corner on the skylight over the passenger saloon. I didn't fancy going below, as I think if a ship's going to sink I'd rather be on deck than below. But a sailor came round and said, captain's orders, all the wounded were to go to the saloon. This was a shame, because you couldn't really see out from there – there was just one port-hole, but that meant having to get up and look, and we were a bit tired.

Corporal George Ledger
8th Battalion, Durham Light Infantry

When we got to Dunkirk on Saturday, there was just a feeling of dejection – and we were that tired and filthy dirty We were picked up in lorries on the outskirts and taken the last few miles, to drive through the people who were guarding the perimeter, you couldn't just walk through. They were fighting a rearguard action, keeping the perimeter open for us. When we got through, we got out of our lorries and started walking through Dunkirk. It was one horrific sight – machines, lorries, guns, armaments, strewn both sides of the road – in fact it was that bad in places that it wasn't a case of marching like a disciplined troop, we were straggling through in different sections to get past the debris.

2nd Lieutenant Peter Martin
2nd Battalion, Cheshire Regiment

We managed to secure a lift out towards the destroyers in what I'd call a whaler, manned by four soldiers of the Royal Engineers who were doing the rowing, and I got the platoon of 30 men into this boat with another ten, including an army padre I'd never seen before who sat in the middle of the boat. We set off in the gathering dusk, and we were about 400 yards away from a destroyer when suddenly it up-anchored, swung round and started off towards England. The padre leapt to his feet and shouted, 'Lord, Lord, why hast thou forsaken us?' We were so overloaded that with every stroke of the oars, water lapped gently over the sides, but when the padre leapt to his feet, the boat rocked, and water poured in. With one accord everyone yelled, 'Sit down!' That great sound echoed across the water to the destroyer which turned round and came and picked us up.

Corporal George Ledger
8th Battalion, Durham Light Infantry

I walked halfway along the beach and there were rows and rows of troops, five or six deep, right up to the water's edge, and there was an officer standing at the head of each one. As I walked up to the front, towards the officers, a lorry came up and started unloading collapsible boats. They started putting these together as I approached, so I went to give them a hand. I didn't go to join the queue – and after we got about ten of them set up, and pushed out into the sea, I decided to get into one. They pushed me off, and I went before my turn because there were 500 or 600 people waiting – but nobody said anything. When I got out so far, a motor boat came round, and it got hold of me with a big hook, and towed me away to a transport ship. I still had my rifle as I got on the ship, but the first thing they did when they got me on board was to take my gun off me. And then they sent me down below. As soon as I got down, there was hot tea. It was a feeling of satisfaction that I could sit and rest – but it wasn't a case of feeling safe yet, because there was still bombing going on.

Lieutenant D'Arcy McCloughin
9 Field Company, Royal Engineers

The Luftwaffe was very active. They were dive-bombing any worthwhile target, such as the mole and the ships out to sea. During the course of an afternoon I counted up to 180 bombs unloaded by Stuka attacks on a ship about two miles out which, I discovered, had already been sunk two days before.

Lieutenant Harold Dibbens
102 Provost Company, Royal Corps of Military Police

Jerry was flying down and machine-gunning us. Dozens of men were lying injured from being hit by machine-gun bullets. One plane came down towards me and I jumped into a bomb hole. He missed me but the hole I chose had been used as a latrine by other soldiers.

Part of the rescue fleet photographed from an RAF aircraft

C1719

Gerhard Schöpfel
German Messerschmitt 109 pilot

We flew against the British troops who were being rescued by little boats. We were trying to halt the boats going back to England. I tried to shoot at them. Our main thing was to go against the English.

Sergeant Major Martin McLane
2nd Battalion, Durham Light Infantry

The RAF did a very poor job of defending us. The Germans were working in close cooperation with their aircraft. When they wanted support, they called in their dive-bombers and their fighters who strafed and bombed us to clear the way of us. And what support did we have? We had no damn thing at all. Not a bloody thing. We were just left to God and good neighbours.

Flying Officer Harold Bird-Wilson
17 Squadron, RAF

I know that the army had a very rough time of being bombed and strafed, and they accused the fighter squadrons and the RAF of failing to support them. They said they never saw the RAF fighters over Dunkirk, which surprised us greatly, because we had two patrols over Dunkirk, per squadron per day from dawn to dusk, whether we were actually over the town or inland, trying to intercept the enemy. We protected the beaches considerably, making continuous patrols throughout the hours of daylight.

Pilot Officer Tony Bartley
92 Squadron, RAF

Frankly if it hadn't have been for the RAF, the troops would never have got off. Because the German Air Force quit the beaches. We turned them back. I'm damned sure that Fighter Command had a hell of a lot to do with it.

Sergeant Richard Mitchell
229 Squadron, RAF

We'd set off from Biggin Hill just as it was getting light and we'd do three trips to Dunkirk by ten o'clock in the morning. There were just four of us and we weren't battle-hardened at all and I think it was the worst period of the war. We had a little field telephone and when it rang, we all thought that they must be sending us back to base but when he put the phone down, the CO said, 'Come on chaps, we've got to go again.' Most of the time, we didn't reach Dunkirk. We attacked bombers or we were attacked on the way there.

Flying Officer Harold Bird-Wilson
17 *Squadron*, RAF

Every time we took off we went into the unknown, just hoping to intercept the enemy. We had quite a few raw pilots at the time – people with only ten hours on Hurricanes. Although I was only 19 or 20, it was up to us more experienced pilots who had been through the battle over northern France to try to look after these young chaps, but we didn't have time to give them any lessons, because on every sortie we were going into a fight. The only lessons we could teach were verbal, telling them to throttle back, that their aircraft wouldn't stall and that they shouldn't be frightened. These lads didn't have much chance of surviving, really. This was where we took most of our casualties. They hadn't learnt to turn their aircraft tightly enough and they were just raw meat for the more experienced German pilots. But the Germans had casualties too, and we picked out many of their less-experienced pilots and shot them down, so it was 50–50, I suppose.

Flight Lieutenant Alan Deere
54 *Squadron*, RAF

I was the first Spitfire pilot to have combat with a Messerschmitt 109, and that was over Calais Marck. But I regret to say, I was shot down by the rear gunner of a Dornier bomber, which eventually came down itself. It was fairly cloudy and this Dornier appeared. I got on to his tail and fired a burst. Suddenly, I could see return fire from his rear gunner. I felt a juddering. A bullet had gone into my glycol tank, so that was my coolant system gone. That meant I was hors de combat, and I had to come down. I crash-landed on the beach between Dunkirk and Ostend and the Dornier came down smoking over the top of me and glided away to come down somewhere inland. I wasn't injured until I landed, when I hit my head on the front of the cockpit. I was knocked out momentarily. I landed wheels up, so to make certain, I landed right on the edge of the water. The tide appeared to be coming in. I was only out for a short time, then when I came to I scrambled out, got my parachute and walked up the beach towards a café. By that time the tide was gradually

CHI 4694

Flying Officer Harold Bird-Wilson – photographed as a wing commander in 1945 alongside his Mustang Mark III

coming over the Spitfire. It was never recovered, so I imagine it sunk into the sand in the course of time.

Flight Lieutenant Gerald Edge
605 Squadron, RAF

I fired at a Messerschmitt 109 as he came towards me over Dunkirk. I could see a lot of my tracer and bullets hitting around his cockpit but he kept on coming. I gave him another burst, thinking that must stop him but it didn't. At that moment, there was a flash and a terrific bang in my cockpit. I thought he must have blown my tail away. I tried my controls. They still worked but I flew the thing home as though it were a newborn baby. When I got back to my aerodrome, I asked the airman if there was anything left of the tail. 'Yes, sir. There's no mark on it.' I got out of the aircraft and went back to report in when the airman came running over, saying, 'Can you come, sir, quick?' 'Why?' I asked. 'You wait and see, sir.' As we got to the aircraft, he said, 'You know you said there was a big bang in the aircraft? Come and look at this, sir! On the outside of the cockpit, just above your hand, there's a black line and there's a tiny splintering on the inside. And there's a little mark on the top of your throttle lever. We'd like to look at what you're wearing, sir.' What had happened was that a cannon shell had gone through the side of my aircraft, nicked the top of the throttle lever, gone through my glove, nicked the rip cord part of my parachute, edged the aluminium seat and hit the armour plating where it had blown up. The seat had caught all the shrapnel and the back of my parachute had stopped me feeling it. If anything had happened differently, I would have been killed.

Pilot Officer Tony Bartley
92 Squadron, RAF

A fighter pilot I knew was shot down at Dunkirk and went in the sea. He swam out to a boat and he got on board and the navy chap said, 'Get back! We're not picking you up, you bastards! We're only picking up the soldiers!'

Pilot Officer Hugh Dundas
616 Squadron, RAF

When we came back to Britain army people used to say, 'Where the hell were you lot?' Nobody tried to knock my block off, but there was hostility and criticism, and we took it rather hard because we had our losses and we certainly were there.

Lance Corporal John Wells
6th Battalion, South Staffordshire Regiment – aboard SS Princessa

Firing Bren guns at the Stukas from the beaches was rather a dead loss because they were armour-plated underneath. So I said, 'What we want is an armour-piercing gun.' We had an anti-tank gun with a bloody great cartridge at the back of it and a stupid little magazine with five rounds in it. So we got ourselves downwind of the ring and we managed to scrounge a railway sleeper and we dug it into the sand. We made up a three-man team, two men wedging the anti-tank gun on to the sleeper and the third one firing. We had a more or less end-on target as the aircraft dived – and it worked like a charm! That brought the buggers down! We brought two or three down like that. It's a mystery to me why it never really caught on.

2nd Lieutenant Ian English
8th Battalion, Durham Light Infantry

On Saturday, we were told we must be ready to do a counter-attack. We waited for orders, but by the evening the idea was abandoned and we were to march along the beach to Dunkirk. There was a lot of confusion when we first got there – a lot of troops milling around and no order as far as we could see. Then we got orders to go out that night to the mole. It was very dark, apart from the fires from the burning oil tanks. We went out on to the mole, and we filed out and waited. French troops were also coming out and they were very anxious that they got on ships as well, and they kept shouting, 'Anglais à la droit!' so we kept to the right of the gangway. Very soon a destroyer came in and we were told to jump aboard – which everybody did. Within a few minutes the ship was full and off we went.

Robert Newborough
Civilian in command of Fleet Air Arm motorboat

I think the 'Dunkirk spirit' was absolutely true – there was a great spirit and everybody possible who had a boat, went. One trip as we were coming back, I saw a fellow going the other way in a canoe. I shouted, 'What the hell are you doing?' and he shouted back, 'I can take one other!'

Lieutenant Commander John McBeath
Royal Navy – Commanding Officer, HMS Venomous

In *Venomous* we made eight or nine trips to Dunkirk, and although we were not supposed to take more than 900, we brought back many more, and on one trip we brought back 1,400 in error.

Leading Seaman Ernest Frederick Eldred
Royal Navy – served aboard HMS Harvester

I don't think destroyers have ever carried as many men as we did. It must have been hundreds, crammed in every space you could think of. We just set them down anywhere we possibly could and gave them drinks and cigarettes. The sick-bay staff were going round the ship looking after the injured – but there were men everywhere – down the stokehole, in the engine room, mess decks, upper deck. The only place we couldn't have them was round the guns – we had to leave space so our gunnery people could operate.

Lieutenant Commander John McBeath
Royal Navy – Commanding Officer, HMS Venomous

In the first instance we went in day and night, but we were suffering too many casualties from air attacks, and they decided latterly only to do night operations. We used to sail just before dark from Dover and a whole heap of ships would go in and sit off Dunkirk in a big crescent formation, waiting to go in. Then, if you saw a hole that somebody had just come out of, you'd rush in. I, being a relatively junior officer, was liable to be left to the end, so many times we resorted to little tricks – sending a signal saying, 'Make way, we've got Rear Admiral Dover on board' – and quite often it worked. We'd get in, get our load and get out again. The idea was not to be the tail-end Charlie of the party, because that meant coming back in almost daylight and you'd perhaps get a bit of a dusting.

Yeoman of Signals Wilfred Walters
Royal Navy – served aboard HMS Ross

Quite a lot of soldiers were using the inner tubes from lorry tyres, inflated, and the rifles as paddles to come to the ship the best way they could. Just as one soldier came alongside, his inner tube suddenly deflated. One of our stokers was a navy champion swimmer, and he went straight over the side, and the soldier was his own brother! And they hadn't met for over four years.

Seaman Thomas King
Royal Navy – served aboard HMS Sharpshooter

On the third trip over, we heard a shout and we stopped. We were a couple of miles out, and we saw a chappie in the sea without a stitch on. I went and picked him up. He might have come off the beach or maybe he'd come off another ship that had been sunk. We covered him up and he wasn't too bad for his ordeal. He was lucky.

Lieutenant Commander John McBeath
Royal Navy – Commanding Officer, HMS Venomous

One came across lots of these small boats with a dozen or so soldiers on board, heading resolutely back for England. One quite often offered to take their crews of soldiers off them so that they could go back for another load, and they said, 'No fear! We've got our 12 pongos, and we're going back to England with them! You go and get your own!'

Gerald Ashcroft
Civilian Sea Scout – aboard Sundowner

The destroyers and cross-Channel boats used in the evacuation were coming past us at full speed, and presenting us with very high washes. In order to weather these, we had to be able to get round head first and ease down into the wash. If we'd taken any broadside, she would have turned right over. Occasionally we did get caught broadside in a swell and Lightoller, who was standing on the bow all the time giving directions for steering and evading aircraft, resorted to what he'd done when he had been standing on an upturned lifeboat throughout the night, off the *Titanic*. When a swell had built up there, he'd waved his arm to whoever was standing on the upturned boat, to lean to the left or right, according to the direction of the swell – and that was what he did now with the troops on deck. Commander Lightoller had been the second officer and senior surviving officer of the *Titanic* when she struck the iceberg and sank in 1912.

Arthur Joscelyne
Civilian – aboard the Thames barge Shannon

We saw a ship's boat full of soldiers, and they were resting on their oars. In the front of it there was a smaller dinghy, with about a dozen dark-skinned fellows in – who hardly spoke any English at all. They were part of a Spanish labour corps, and they had attached themselves to this ship's boat full of soldiers, and they were doing all the work, rowing like mad, while these soldiers were sitting back and letting them pull it. We got alongside and got them on board. One of these Spaniards had a small suitcase and he held on to it as if his life depended on it. I'd love to have known what was in it.

Richard Helyer
Auxiliary Fireman, Fireboat Massey Shaw, London Fire Brigade
We heard a terrific explosion. Down in the engine room you seemed to hear it ten times louder than anywhere else, and I nipped up to the upper deck and all I could see was a cloud of smoke. A French ship loaded with troops had struck a mine, and within a minute or two she'd gone completely. We were close, and we steamed in and picked up about 40 survivors. We had a real job collecting them. They were covered with oil, so when you pulled them out, they just slipped through your hands. It was a terrible business; there were people with their legs hanging off. In fact, all but one were injured, and we had these poor devils lying all over the deck. We had to put them in the galley and the toilet.

Francis Codd
Auxiliary Fireman, Fireboat Massey Shaw, London Fire Brigade
We were on the scene in five minutes. The ship had sunk completely and the sea was full of screaming men and dead bodies. We sailed into the middle of this terrible scene and dropped anchor – we thought they could perhaps edge themselves towards us, so we put out our long bargepole so they could grab it. We got some in like that, but others couldn't reach it, so we changed our position slightly. One poor man had both his legs broken – to get him in, I had to lean right over to drag him on board. I remember the effort required, and the pain the poor devil was in. We took in as many as we could of these wretched Frenchmen, and we went full steam ahead for Ramsgate to get these chaps medical attention.

Ordinary Seaman Stanley Allen
Royal Navy – served aboard HMS Windsor
The *Crested Eagle* – the old London pleasure-boat which used to go between Tower Bridge and Clacton – had become a hospital ship, painted up with Red Crosses. She'd been bombed and had settled in the water, but the German air-

Dunkirk shortly after the evacuation

HU83524

craft were still machine-gunning her – and that wasn't cricket. That wasn't the right way to win a war, having a go at wounded people.

Private William Ridley
9th Battalion, Durham Light Infantry

A rumour went round that we were going to have to go back into action, but that proved not to be true. We marched at DLI pace along the promenade and came to the mole and it seemed about 200 Frenchmen came running towards us – panicking. They ran into us and pushed us out of the road. I remember stepping over dead Guardsmen on the mole, and the mole itself had holes in it with planks across. The ship at the end was the *Prague*, which had brought us across. I was utterly and bitterly ashamed. I was. I don't know about anyone else.

Captain James Hill
2nd Battalion, Royal Fusiliers

On my section there was one infantry brigade and we were gradually getting them off. Finally brigade headquarters went, and the old brigade commander was a splendid old boy with grey hair – rather a Poona type. They all got on this lifeboat, but they were too heavy, so the lifeboat went down – bang. He said, 'Come on boys, get off. We'll give her a shove.' He jumped off with a number of others, and they gave her a shove, and away the lifeboat went – and they all waved goodbye. They just left him there. I've never seen a brigade commander so angry in my life. My next job was to get him safely away – but you couldn't help laughing.

Private Sidney Nuttall
Royal Army Ordnance Corps attached to 1st Battalion, Border Regiment

We were getting shot up on the beaches at Bray-Dunes, but luckily, most of the dive-bombing was done on the ships. I did see a dive-bomber shot down, by infantry, using rifles. The pilot made a mistake, and instead of diving from the stern of the destroyer to the nose, and carrying on up the coast, he arrived from the sea and finished up over the coast, coming very low over Bray-Dunes. There were thousands of men, lying in the dunes, and everybody started firing their rifles. We saw a piece of the plane come off, and it veered off and went into the ground, well behind the town, then we saw the smoke coming up where it crashed.

Lieutenant Colonel Eric Griffith-Williams
27th Field Regiment, Royal Artillery

We walked down to the beach at Bray-Dunes. Towards the docks, we came across battalions of French walking across our paths, heading for a destroyer. I met a chap I knew, General Percival, who said, 'I'm afraid that's the last ship, you'll have to go down to the beach and see if you can find anything afloat that you can get into.' We found a barge, sitting on the sand, so we got on board. We waited for the tide to rise, but before we were afloat, other troops arrived and asked if they could come on board, and so we ended up with lots of Royal Army Service Corps and others. My adjutant, who thought he knew something about engines, went down below, and suddenly there was a chug, chug of the engine. At the last minute, just as the water was almost up to their necks, a group of six guardsmen came up, and I squeezed them on. Then there was the question of getting the sail up, as none of us knew anything about it. I shouted out, 'Does anyone know anything about sails?' and by the grace of God, there was a man, a private, who said he'd worked on a Thames barge, and he very kindly got the sail up.

Major Donald Wilson-Haffenden
HQ – 1st Division

I said to General Alexander, 'Sir, if you will give me permission, I will move the wounded to the end of the mole, so that we can get them off first before the last troops come on tonight.' We reckoned that this was to be our last night of the evacuation. He said, 'Haffie, no casualty is to be moved on to the mole until the last of the fighting troops are away, because the country needs fighting troops now, and the casualties will be protected by the Geneva Convention.' I'm afraid that, on that occasion I just burst into tears. I'd hardly slept for eight days, and he said, 'Don't be a fool, Haffie. You've got to realise that we're custodians for the whole of Britain and we've got to get the fighting troops back!' I saluted smartly and said, 'Yes, sir.'

Captain (Acting) Humphrey 'Bala' Bredin
2nd Battalion, Royal Ulster Rifles

When we got down to the mole at Dunkirk, the commanding officer said that he understood that there was a boat there that could take all of us. We saw an Isle of Man paddle steamer moored alongside the mole, which was rocking to

The bodies of British soldiers and abandoned vehicles litter the seafront

and fro because of the bombs dropping in the harbour, and we started getting on board. There was dead man lying across the gangplank, and we stepped over him fairly gingerly. I gradually managed to get my company into little corners, and reasonably comfortable, and then I sat down myself. After a little time, I saw a man in a white coat walking about and stepping over myriad people laying sitting and lying around. I wondered, 'Is this by any chance a steward?' I beckoned him, and I said, 'Excuse me, are you a steward?' 'Yes sir,' he said, 'can I do anything for you?' I said, 'Well, would it be possible to produce a glass of beer for me? Or if you can't, a glass of water…' 'Yes sir,' he said, 'by all means. But you do know the rules, sir? I can't supply you with any alcohol 'til we're three miles out…' How could we lose the war with people like this around? He was as good as his word and by this time I'd remembered myself, and I made sure the soldiers got something as well.

Private Albert Dance
Rifle Brigade

When I arrived on the beach, the order came along that there wouldn't be any more boats. Chaps were just sitting there, waiting to be picked up by the Germans. I headed north-east towards La Panne. When I got up there, I noticed a wooden jetty running out into the sea. It had been hit by a couple of shells but it went out quite a way. I clambered on to it and got out to the end and fell asleep. When I woke, it was dark and a boat was banging into the jetty. I heard English voices and I looked up and saw a little sailing yacht with two men aboard. One of them said, 'There's no one here! We've got to get back!' so I shouted out. I leapt down on to the yacht and I hit my head on the deck. I still had my steel helmet on and I must have banged myself in the back of my head and knocked myself right out. The next thing I remember was someone saying, 'Come on chum! Have a cup of tea!' I had a mouthful of tea and then he said, 'Do you want to see the white cliffs of Dover?' And there they were, coming up.

Coming Home

A survivor from a sunk vessel is pulled aboard HMS *Sandown* on 28 May

> *When we saw the white cliffs looming up,*
> *I was down in the little wardroom with the other officers.*
> *I think we were too tired for either sorrow, jubilation or any feeling.*

The Admiralty had hoped that 45,000 troops would be rescued from Dunkirk. In the end, seven and a half times that number were evacuated. As they arrived home, many of these soldiers were astonished to find themselves greeted as heroes – rather than as the remnants of a trampled army.

Captain Anthony Rhodes
253 Field Company, Royal Engineers
I went down into the hold where I was given a hammock, because I was dead tired. I'd been asleep for about a quarter of an hour when somebody came in and said, 'We understand there's an officer here.' I'd lost all my insignia, but I didn't want to be recognised as an officer – I wanted to go to sleep – but they insisted 'a naval officer wants to see him'. I had to climb out of the hammock and go up with them to the wardroom. I talked to some naval officers – who were splendid. They had a huge bottle of gin, and said, 'What this chap needs is a good portion of gin,' so I was given a large glass of gin, and then I went to sleep in one of the officers' cabins.

Leading Seaman Ernest Frederick Eldred
Royal Navy – served aboard HMS Harvester
With regard to morale, the men were in good shape – but some had been travelling for days and were absolutely fatigued. All the same, the officers supervising

them seemed to be doing their job, and the men themselves were magnificent.

Leon Wilson
French gunner – served with 229 Heavy Artillery Regiment

The captain of the destroyer was the finest gentleman you could wish to meet. The way he said, 'Come on Frogs. Sit down and have something to eat!' It was a good joke! We sat down and ate bacon, cheese, everything normal. I don't think the Savoy could have given us such a meal. We didn't finish eating until we arrived at Dover.

Ordinary Seaman Stanley Allen
Royal Navy – served aboard HMS Windsor

There was a little dog – a terrier-type mongrel – that came on board with some of the soldiers. He only understood French, which rather tickled some of the soldiers. After I spoke to him he wouldn't leave me, and that little dog came back with us on the other two trips we made. One of our sub-lieutenants felt that Kirk, as we called him, should not be destroyed to comply with the necessary anti-rabies laws, so after the evacuation was over, Kirk was collected by a PDSA van to go into quarantine for six months before, as the sub-lieutenant put it, 'being taken on the staff' of the parish where his father was vicar.

Lieutenant Commander John McBeath
Royal Navy – Commanding Officer, HMS Venomous

There were several amusing cases when people got on board and went to sleep in some out of the way place, having had no sleep for a long time. We'd arrive back in England, discharge everybody and get back to the beaches again, and then the soldier would suddenly appear – he'd made the trip back to Dunkirk again without knowing it.

Lieutenant D'Arcy McCloughin
9 Field Company, Royal Engineers

An unmanned motor torpedo boat quite close to us was going round in circles. It appeared that there was no one on board, but there was a very fine-looking anti-aircraft gun on the forecastle. We got in its way and stormed aboard it. In that melee, one of the hot-headed chaps who got on board before me shot himself in the wrist and had to be hastily carted back into the motor boat. We tried to take the gun to pieces to take it off, but it was beyond us. We had no

A French dog anticipates a new life in England

tools. The boat had been bombed or attacked because the steering was shot and the engine was still running, so it was useless to us with no means of making any repairs – so we filed back on to our motor boat and carried on.

Arthur Joscelyne
Civilian – aboard the Thames barge Shannon

As it got lighter, we could hear the roar of planes, and all of a sudden, out of the mist we saw five Stukas. They came over us and circled, and I thought, 'Now we've really had it. We're really in trouble.' But the mist came up again and about 500 yards further on there was a destroyer, and they changed their minds. Instead of going for us, they went for the destroyer. I saw them roaring down and the bombs dropped out of them, and the thing disappeared with a huge mass of bubbles all round it. But when it all calmed down, the ship was still there! It was amazing that they could have dropped these bombs all round, and the water must have absorbed the shock. I said to my brother, 'Look, it must be a shoal of mackerel over there.' He said, 'Don't be silly – that's shrapnel!'

Stoker Charles Maggs
Royal Navy – served aboard HMS Shearwater

I saw a chap who was wounded – obviously bleeding from a wound in his arm, and his greatcoat was stained with blood. I was speaking with the French liaison officer, and I said we'd better take a look at this chap. I got permission to go to the mess and get some instruments. I'd trained as a biologist, and I'd still got my dissecting kit. I came back and ripped his coat off and had a look. They'd put a tourniquet on his arm, but he had a partially severed brachial artery, and the French officer and I poured brandy on it, sliced it open and put a couple of artery clamps on his arm. I had no gut to tie the artery with, so I just bandaged it up, closed it, and put a label on it telling the medics what I'd done. It was do as can be done.

Able Seaman Ian Nethercott
Royal Navy, Anti-Aircraft Rating 3rd Class – served aboard HMS Keith

The wounded had all types of injuries – trench burn, trench mortar wounds, men with half their face blown away, shoulders blown away, and bad stomach wounds. Some chaps were kicking and screaming, and a lot of the quiet ones were slowly bleeding to death. Quite a few died during the crossing and we helped to unload them alongside the jetty at Dover. The army doctors pulled blankets over their faces and carried them ashore.

Lieutenant Wilbur Cocke
Signal Section, 51st Heavy Regiment, Royal Artillery
We embarked on the HMS *Scimitar* and although the officers were put down in the wardroom, I preferred to go on deck. The troops were lying about and falling asleep immediately, all over the superstructure. I believe there were minefields out to sea, so we started out parallel to the coast, and when we got near the heights of Calais, we were fired on by German field guns – which meant a lot of water spouts popping up round us. We put on a terrific turn of speed – I'm used to boats, but the stern wave was about 12 feet high, curling over the stern. We really did move.

When we saw the white cliffs looming up, I was down in the little wardroom with the other officers. I think we were all too tired for either sorrow, jubilation or any feeling. We disembarked and were taken to a train where ladies brought us tea in mugs – which we were delighted to have. We were told the train was bound for London, which suited me because I'm a Londoner, but as soon as it set off, all of us went straight to sleep, and I woke up in Dorset.

Bosun John Chrisp
Royal Navy – served aboard HMS Jasper
We heard a cry from someone on a small ship, saying he was in trouble, would someone come and help him? We went back four or five miles to where we thought he was, and there was nothing there but wreckage.

2nd Lieutenant Arthur Curtis
7th Field Company, Royal Engineers
When we got underway I looked out – and it was a sight I've never forgotten. Beside our little paddle steamer was a K-class destroyer – the most modern ship they had at that time. There we were, dirty, unshaven, covered in blood, and there was this immaculate ship, gleaming white, red and blue, as if it had come straight out of the laundry, with a battle ensign flying on top. She was going flat out and zigzagging because the Stukas were coming down, and her Bofors were going bump, bump, bump. It was a marvellous sight. She wasn't

Able Seaman Reginald Heron later in the war

22385

hit, and I suppose she might have been diverting the Stukas from hitting us. There's a deep channel that runs fairly close in, and then banks further over, where at low tide there's not really enough water for a big ship to cross safely, but the paddle steamer could, so we were able to go straight out northwards, and then turn left into Margate. The destroyers were laden with people, and they had to go along the coast, which meant they were also subject to getting shot by artillery further down the coast by Gravelines. We had an uneventful trip after that and we came off at Margate. They told us to hand in our weapons, so I handed in my revolver.

Private Sidney Nuttall
Royal Army Ordnance Corps attached to 1st Battalion, Border Regiment
I'd no idea what day it was, or even what time it was, because in those days, I didn't have a watch. The officers did, but the other ranks didn't. I understand we came out on a Sunday morning – I believe it was the penultimate day. We came out in the dark, and got on to one of the destroyers, HMS *Icarus*. They were trying to get off before first light, before the Stukas came down, but they hadn't managed it, and they had to stay. The gunner told me they'd no anti-aircraft shells left, so they were firing common shell – anything to keep the planes higher up. They'd no chance of hitting them, they'd have needed to hit them point blank – but at least it kept them up. There was a 16-year-old boy on the *Icarus*, the ship's boy, and he'd been on that destroyer for quite a long time. I didn't realise that people that age went into action, but certainly the navy boys were there. He was kept busy making us cocoa – *kai*, they called it. We needed something, because we were very dehydrated. They also fed us bully beef sandwiches, about an inch thick, which went down very well, because we hadn't had anything to eat in three or four days. We pulled out at first light, and sailed for Dover, and as we landed at the jetty, we were told to throw our ammunition in one pile, and rifles in the other. We were then sent straight up into the station, alongside the jetty, more or less, and there were trains on every platform. They said, 'Any platform, any train,' and they were pushing us aboard. I ended up in Halifax.

Lieutenant Colonel Eric Griffith-Williams
27th Field Regiment, Royal Artillery
When we started sailing, we couldn't get the boom round, and my adjutant had

found a school atlas in the cockpit – damned if I know what it was doing there – so I tried to point the thing where I thought it ought to point, then the Boche started bombing the ships. I'm not sure if they hit any. But within about three hours, there wasn't a ship in sight. They'd all sailed out of our sight.

I'd taken the tiller, and everyone else was asleep by then. The shore had disappeared and all the other ships had disappeared, and we were all alone. A sergeant major woke up and there was a commotion. He appeared, and he said, 'I'm afraid we've got a lot of petrol on board, sir.' Just as they'd started bombing, they found all these petrol cans down below, and so then a panic started. We thought we'd better chuck these cans overboard. So they started doing that, but I couldn't smell any petrol, and I said, 'Let's open one of those cans.' And we found out that it wasn't petrol – it was drinking water that had been brought out from England with the rations. So that panic was over. Then this sergeant major said that there were lots of rations down below, so the troops got a damned good meal. The shelling had stopped by then, and everyone went to sleep.

I carried on, trying to steer in the right direction. Then out of the blue, I saw a motor boat approaching, and it went round and round, getting closer and closer, and eventually it came alongside, and an awfully nice chap, a lieutenant, spoke to me. I asked him how he was getting on, and he said, 'If you continue on this course, you'll be in Germany very soon.' But he very kindly put a boy on our barge, and they managed to get the boom out where it ought to be, and he left the boy on board. He was marvellous, and he sailed us back. I took a sleep then, and we got to Dover in the dark. It was dark when we were approaching our own coast, and out came a motor tug and tied us alongside and took us into the harbour.

Lance Sergeant Robert Green
2nd Battalion, Bedfordshire and Hertfordshire Regiment

Our destroyer left Dunkirk mole about eight in the morning. The commander said, 'Chuck your arms down here,' and there was a great pile of rifles on the foredeck. I made my way under the break of the forecastle and went down a deck, and after a while we cast off. We headed out to sea going flat out, zigzagging. Every now and again there were near misses, and you could feel the whole ship lift – but the thing which I had to admire was the sheer sangfroid. There was an old naval pensioner there, collecting up empty tea dixies. After a particularly unpleasant near miss somebody said to him, 'It would take more than one bomb to sink us, wouldn't it?' He said, 'Oh no – one will be enough. We've only light decks over the boilers in these ships. Any more dixies there?' Just as if he was on a bank holiday excursion. I thought I'd never had a more hairy hour and a half in my life. You sat there trying to look unconcerned, and lighting a fag. It was absolutely nerve-racking. I developed a wholesale admiration for the black gang in the navy – the engine room and stokers. The tension really began to build up – there was a very young soldier who really went bonkers for a minute or two. He made a dive to get up on deck, and that was a relief because we could actually do something. Everybody piled on to him and said, 'Sit down, silly bugger,' and that was a relief. The next thing was, 'Right, come up on deck.' The engines stopped and we got up there. There were three destroyers moored alongside in Dover harbour, right along the quay. I've never seen a more beautiful sight in all my life. It was a lovely day.

Private George Lambert
9th Battalion, Durham Light Infantry

I came off the pier and jumped on to a boat from there. I came off on one of the last boats, on 2 June. We didn't come off as a platoon, it was every Tom, Dick and Harry. I was with one lad from our platoon – Bill Bell – and we came off together. We weren't sure we were going to get off, we prayed. I hadn't had anything to eat for two days. The last thing I had before I left France was a tin of sardines and a spoonful of jam, and that didn't go down very well. All I can remember on the boat, when we got settled down and it moved, there was a French lad, and two of us laid one way, and the French lad lay in the middle, we put a greatcoat over us and we just slept. The next thing we knew, this lad had woken up and he pointed and said, *'Douvre'* – and it was Dover – and he opened a bottle of crème de menthe that he'd been carrying. It just burnt my stomach because I hadn't had anything to eat. I vowed I'd never drink it again.

Private William Ridley
9th Battalion, Durham Light Infantry

A ship was waiting for us – we got on, and I looked up and there was a sailor lad, Merchant Navy. He said, 'Are you hungry?' I said, 'I'm starving!' and he throws a bar of chocolate. I caught it – and that's the last I remember. I can't remember eating it, or lying down or going to sleep. The next time they woke

Rescued troops arrive in England on the deck of an Isle of Man steamer

us up they said we were just off Dover. I looked up and saw Dover harbour, and we were pulling in – and then the boat turns round. I thought, 'God, we're going back!' And the tears come in my eyes. I didn't know the boat had to turn round to get into the harbour. I was relieved I wasn't going back.

Corporal Charles 'Bert' Nash
2nd Bulk Petrol Transport Company, Royal Army Service Corps
We had a couple of near misses as we got away from the shore. Jerry chose that moment to come over and start strafing, and I remember being down in the net locker and hearing Jerry coming over very low, and the metallic clatter of bullets striking the superstructure of the vessel, but the top and bottom of it was that we managed to get out to sea. It seemed a very, very long journey – the best part of 24 hours to get to Ramsgate. One of the milestones of the journey was the issuing of good old 'nautical navy cocoa'. If you can visualise the sensation of having lived on chalky water out of tinned potatoes for the best part of ten days, and having the delicious experience of drinking hot, sweet, milky cocoa – out of a galvanised bucket, made in the good old nautical fashion.

Arthur Joscelyne
Civilian – aboard the Thames barge Shannon
After the third night without any sleep, we rounded a big buoy and started to head home. I was sitting on the cabin hatch, and as the barges went through the water, all the phosphorescence of their wake was trailing behind them. I looked over the side, and about three feet to the side of us there was this round object – a mine. It was just the distance of the wash of the barge that kept it away from the boat. I looked at Harold and he looked at me and he said, 'Oh my God – that was a mine!' My heart was thudding and I began to wonder where the next one was going to come from.

Bosun John Chrisp
Royal Navy – served aboard HMS Jasper
A little drifter came alongside us with a lot of soldiers packed up to the funnel. A Scots chap said, 'Can you tell me the way to Dover? I'm afraid I've lost my way.' So we gave him a course and he went off with all the soldiers cheering. 'We'll have a pint with you when we get in,' he said.

Private Samuel Love
12th Field Ambulance, Royal Army Medical Corps
The boat we got on, the *Hird*, had taken a hit, but was still able to sail. As we backed out of the harbour, Jerry was after us all the while. I was on deck. I wasn't going below. I was going to be where I could jump into the drink. I don't think the ship had any anti-aircraft weapons – but if a German plane showed its nose under the big pall of smoke, nearly everybody that had a rifle flung something up at it – even if it was only spit.

We hadn't gone above four or five miles when we lost three ships in 20 minutes. When the first bang went off, the captain of the *Hird* said, 'It isn't us. One of our destroyers has just run into a minefield.' It was the *Wakeful*, but in fact, it was torpedoed by an E-boat. Then two more were sunk – and the last one was sunk by one of our own destroyers. Weren't we clever? There were all these soldiers on deck – 640 of them – and our destroyer thought it was a E-boat, and cut it clean in half. The commander of the *Wakeful* that was sunk first, he got picked up the one sunk by our destroyer, and then he was picked up by the *Hird*.

It was the next night that we arrived in Dover. We had to go round what they call the 'Y' route – the long way. We'd got no drinking water all the time we were on board, and no food – they just had enough for the crew. So it was seven days since we'd had anything to eat or drink.

Robert Newborough
Civilian in command of Fleet Air Arm motorboat
I remember one chap singing 'We're going to hang out the washing on the Siegfried Line'. 'It's a bit late to do that…' I thought.

Able Seaman Reginald Heron
Royal Navy – served aboard HMS Keith
All the way back to Dover, we were being strafed by German fighters. We were all crowded on the deck of this thing – completely exposed. There was an officer in his pyjamas for some weird reason – standing up, waving his arms over his head and shouting, 'Survivor! Survivor!' at the fighters and then he started making engine noises. I tried to ignore him.

Sapper Frederick Carter
135 Excavator Company, Royal Engineers
I had seen an officer dead by the water's edge, and I took his revolver off him. I thought I could trade it for something else. On the way back on HMS *Calcutta*, I fired it into the water, and it was going, and I gave it to an officer. He said, 'They won't let you in England with that. You might as well let me have it.' And he gave me a souvenir off the boat – an anti-aircraft shell case. But I didn't mind. I kept that shell case for years until I mislaid it somewhere.

Yeoman of Signals Wilfred Walters
Royal Navy – served aboard HMS Ross
After the evacuation we got to the basin at Sheerness, and someone gave orders that the ship was not to be disturbed at all for 24 hours, so that the whole ship's company could have unbroken sleep. We slept for 24 hours without moving.

Richard Helyer
Auxiliary Fireman, Fireboat Massey Shaw, London Fire Brigade
As we were waiting for the *Massey* to come back on the third day, they brought in a load of German prisoners to land, but the feeling was so high, that they decided to land them somewhere else, because the soldiers in the harbour would have murdered them if they'd got their hands on them.

Ronald Tomlinson
Civilian fisherman – aboard Tankerton Towers and Tom Tit
We got back into Ramsgate harbour at about 9.30 on the Saturday morning. We went ashore, and I went through the fish market. As I was walking, a voice says, 'Ron!' I said, 'Hello Mrs Oliver, how are you, pet?' She says, 'Have you seen anything of Dave over there?' I said, 'No, love, it'd be a chance in a million to find him. No, I'm sorry.'

Richard Helyer
Auxiliary Fireman, Fireboat Massey Shaw, London Fire Brigade
We had been sitting having a cup of tea at three in the afternoon, and within a few hours we were taking part in what was one of the greatest events in British history. When I look back, I'm amazed. The miracle of Dunkirk is really an understatement; just the problems of getting the men off the beach are

hard to appreciate, especially when you've got a surf running, because those little boats were so easily pushed over.

Ordinary Seaman Stanley Allen
Royal Navy – aboard HMS Windsor

We saw all the soldiers coming back without their equipment, and we began to think this was the end of our way of life. We didn't know how long we'd be able to hold Jerry off in England. We knew we had the navy, and that we would fight – but we didn't know what the soldiers would be able to do if Jerry landed – because they had nothing.

Mounds of rifles on the quayside at Dover

The Fight Goes On

H1778

The evacuation from Dunkirk was barely completed before a second BEF was sent to France to fight alongside the remaining French forces. As the band of the Royal Marines plays, British troops board a ship on 15 June, 1940, the day *after* German troops entered Paris

The sky seemed to be black with bombers and all seemed to be dropping bombs on Dunkirk harbour. In that direction there was nothing but a pile of dust and smoke and flying debris. It seemed absolutely hopeless trying to get through.

Operation Dynamo did not bring home the entire BEF. More than 140,000 British troops remained in France, some of whom had failed to reach Dunkirk, whilst others had never even known of the evacuation. The 51st (Highland) Division, south of the river Somme, had been cut off from the remainder of the BEF by the sudden German advance. It continued fighting after Operation Dynamo against a strengthened enemy which could concentrate all its efforts on the remaining Allied resistance.

In the meantime, Churchill was so keen for France to stay in the war, that he was promising the arrival of a second BEF that would fight alongside the French in Normandy. The 51st (Highland) Division was intended to be part of this new BEF – but it was forced to surrender on 12 June when it was surrounded at St Valéry-en-Caux after attempting to retake the Abbeville bridgehead.

Sir Alan Brooke, the proposed commander of the new BEF, was firm in his belief that France was about to surrender, yet British and Canadian troops continued to be shipped across the Channel. The British government retained an unrealistic hope that the second BEF could help the French resist the Germans. But once German troops entered Paris on 14 June, it became abundantly clear that France was beaten, and the order was given that the newly arrived BEF should be evacuated from Cherbourg, St Malo, Brest and other ports. At St Nazaire, the huge Cunard liner *Lancastria*, bringing home more than 6,000 soldiers, civilians and crew, was sunk by German aircraft on 17 June. More than

3,500 people were killed. It remains the worst maritime disaster in British history.

France signed an armistice on 22 June. In all, over 191,000 Allied troops were evacuated to Britain after the end of Operation Dynamo.

Captain Paul Hawkins
7th Battalion, Royal Norfolk Regiment

We were some 15 miles behind the River Somme. The Germans were not doing any attacking over the Somme because this was the time when the evacuation of Dunkirk was going on – or so I learnt afterwards. One of my sergeants had a wireless set and he had it on. We heard the BBC saying that the 51st Division had taken up a very strong defensive position on an almost impregnable river, the River Bresle, that had machine-gun emplacements all along it. That made him so cross that he kicked the wireless set into the little stream that the River Bresle was.

Captain Derek Lang
4th Battalion, Cameron Highlanders

When we arrived on the Somme, we were expected to take part in another major attack. It was under Charles de Gaulle, and it was to try to pinch out a German bridgehead west of the Somme. On 4 June, we went into the attack in the most gallant fashion. We started it with 600 men, and in the course of three hours, we were down to 250. It was absolutely disastrous, the whole thing. The other two companies on our left had a roughly similar fate. I was back at the château which was our headquarters, and the sight had to be seen to be believed when all these casualties were being brought in. Our doctor and two or three others were stripped to the waist, working flat out, trying to deal with the casualties. The attack went on the whole day, but late in the afternoon, we got the order to withdraw. And for the following eight days until we were captured, we went back slowly but surely.

Captain Paul Hawkins
7th Battalion, Royal Norfolk Regiment

We gradually withdrew back to St Valéry. We got orders direct from Churchill, brought by a man acting as his envoy, that while the French army was still fighting, we were not to surrender. We were to remain with the French army. So we gradually withdrew into St Valéry, and we understood that there were plans for the navy to take us off. I was sent down one evening to the port of St Valéry to see what it was like. I met a naval officer, and saw the port, and I realised that it was impossible to get any large vessels into this cramped fishing port.

The next thing we found was that some of Rommel's tanks and armour had gone straight through the French army, and he'd turned a certain proportion of them back towards us at St Valéry. When I next went down to the port area, I could see on the bluff of the cliff, overlooking the port, some German tanks who'd got along the coastline. It seemed to me that there was not much hope of getting away.

General Fortune had several demands from a German commander that he was to surrender. They were very gentlemanly about it. They never tried to blot us out. The answer always came from General Fortune that he was not going to surrender until he was given the orders by his superior officer – the army commander of the French on our right. And about a day later, the Germans brought the French army commander in an old taxi, and he told General Fortune that he had surrendered with his army, and that it was likely that the French government was going to surrender.

General Fortune told me to tell all units that I could get in touch with that they were to destroy any weapons they had, and that it was a case of every man trying to get away if he humanly could, as we were surrendering. One of my platoons got down to a beach a little to the north and found two boats and managed to get their platoon on board. They rowed out to some of our ships that were lying off the coast in the mist. They got away – but the irony was that they were put into the 18th Division which was sent out to Singapore. They were all captured there – and many of them never came home.

Captain Derek Lang
4th Battalion, Cameron Highlanders

We had hoped that we were going to be pulled off from St Valéry, in orderly fashion, by the navy. But by this time, St Valéry was an inferno of fire from incendiary shells. The whole place was really in the most dreadful state. As a battalion, we pulled away out of our perimeter fences down the little lanes, down into St Valéry, where complete chaos reigned. We pulled back into the middle of all this. Later in the evening, we were instructed to destroy our vehicles. We were still hoping to be evacuated into the wide open arms of the Royal Navy. But things went wrong. The weather was against us. The tide was against us. They simply couldn't get in to take us off.

That night was terrifying and come the dawn it was a question of seeing what we could possibly do to break away on our own. One or two of us looked around to see which direction in which to go. We saw a couple of ships five miles away to the east, opposite a little place called Veules-les-Roses. So myself and a number of Jocks made our way along the beach towards these ships. It was a terrifying sight, because there were a number of bodies lying at the foot of the cliffs. We were being fired at by cannon and machine gun as we went – not aimed specifically at us, but aimed along the beach. When we got to Veules-les-Roses, there were a large number of British troops already there, and quite a lot of French, too.

There was a British boat there, a large trawler-type fishing boat, aground on the sand. We climbed aboard – and it was a seething mass of human beings all waiting for the tide to come in and float the boat. Then the Germans began to close in on us along the top of the cliffs. My last moments before capture were spent firing a Lewis gun – which was fixed on to the side of this boat – at these tanks. Quite a forlorn hope, of course.

Then they began to fire their own guns down at us, and they made enough holes in the boat that even had it floated, it would have sunk again straight away. I was mildly wounded in the face by shrapnel – and that was the end of it. Soon afterwards, the Germans came on to the beach and captured us all. The Germans were very arrogant, very excitable and quite delighted to have caught us all.

Captain Paul Hawkins
7th Battalion, Royal Norfolk Regiment

The surrender at St Valéry was extremely orderly. Except for the odd person, there was little chance of getting away. We had been marching backwards, we had had very little rest, very little chance to have proper meals. People were dead tired by the time we surrendered. The thing that impressed me: we were captured by the SS, and their discipline was marvellous. They treated us extremely well; they were very punctilious in saluting superior officers and so forth. And they were terribly surprised at the amount of people they captured.

British and French soldiers marching away from St Valéry-en-Caux in German captivity

Sergeant William Knight
No 1 General Base Depot, Royal Engineers

On 1 June, my men were in a defensive position, waiting for the Germans to come up the road. It was then we discovered that as well as running up and down, supplying people with what they needed, ferrying the wounded and all the other things we'd been doing, we were actually part of the perimeter defence line.

We could hear the noise of panzers coming up, and my men were waiting with their rifles and they'd also put out booby traps. They hadn't wanted to leave because I hadn't come back, so they just dug themselves in and prepared themselves for whatever was going to happen. So we went into action, and lined ourselves up in the bushes and trees on either side of the road. The first to come along were the German motorcyclists, with machine guns mounted on the sidecars. We picked off the first three quite easily, and the motorcycles went haywire – that caused quite a lot of chaos. Then the booby traps that the chaps had laid in the road went off. They put them at 20-yard intervals – which was the interval at which the German tanks used to travel – but unfortunately the lance corporal who was detailed to let them off didn't wait until the first tank got on the furthest mine. So out of all the mines they put down, the majority of them were expended uselessly. I got my own back on him later – I got him transferred to the Orkneys.

That was our first taste of action. As soon as the Germans started poking the muzzles of their tanks in our direction and ripping off with machine guns, we departed. After all's said and done, we knew that rifles were no match for the armament they had – especially in view of the fact that very few of our men had ever fired them before.

We retreated a bit further and gradually got assimilated into the overall defence of the perimeter. Eventually, on 3 June we found ourselves at Rosendael. We dug in there, but we got chased out by the Germans and went on the run. Five of us dived down into the cellar of a demolished house and stayed there, with fighting going on all round us. That area had been pretty much demolished, so we stayed with our heads down, waiting for it to ease up.

By then I'd more or less given up, because I didn't know where we would get any support from. There didn't seem to be any British behind us or in front of us. We thought we were isolated, so it was a question of being captured, surrendering, or being killed. I was in two minds about it, but I didn't want the men to see that I was perplexed – they looked to me for everything and seemed to have implicit faith in me. But I was extremely worried.

Early in the morning I went up the steps from the cellar to the landing, and looked out over the top. The sky seemed to be black with bombers and all seemed to be dropping bombs on Dunkirk harbour. In that direction, there was nothing but a pile of dust and smoke and flying bricks and debris. It seemed absolutely hopeless trying to get through. I stood on that landing and for the first time in my life, I was really frightened. Up to then, I'd had the feeling that nothing was going to touch me, then I realised that only an act of God would get us out of there. Things were that desperate.

We had no communications. We'd long since lost our wireless sets, which we dumped to take on ammunition. I was at my lowest ebb. Then I heard a scurry of feet, and two civilians covered in muck and dust practically fell on top of me. They took cover in the cellar as well. They turned out to be two locals. One could speak English quite well and the other had a smattering – so I listened to what they had to say. They said that as soon as it got dark, provided we hadn't been caught in the meantime, they thought we could get away by taking back lanes and going across certain smallholdings and byroads. I said, 'We've got a lorry stashed just a little way away – do you think you can guide the lorry out?' They said they didn't think they could do that, but with a bit of effort I managed to persuade them. So on the night of 3 June they guided us out from Rosendael and down the back paths. At one point we went over a canal on the top of lorries which had been pushed into the water. They got us clear of the Dunkirk perimeter – I'd previously reasoned that the front-line German troops had gone past us and were lined up between us and the harbour, so I would only have the lines of communication and the secondary troops to go through if I went that way. The following morning we found our lorry and drove it out. We had transport again.

These two Frenchmen became quite cock-a-hoop. They said that we could take a byroad practically all the way down to Hesdin, which was a considerable way down towards the Somme – and that was where they would be leaving us. Come the night of 4 June, we found a wood and because I felt it wasn't safe to travel by night – you couldn't see what you were running into – we backed up and prepared to bivouac. But before we'd got out of the truck, we heard motor engines coming down the road. We looked out and could just see the slit headlamps of a procession of lorries coming in our direction. As they went past, we saw that quite a lot of them were French camions and British 3-ton Bedfords and some smaller British wagons – but they were all driven by Germans, so I assumed they must all have been captured. They were going our way, and although there was a motorcyclist at the front, there wasn't one at the back, so we quickly started our engine and got out on the road and chased after them. We joined up as the last member of the convoy.

We went for quite a distance like that and it helped us on our way considerably. It was just getting towards dawn and I estimated that we'd covered 30 or 40 miles, when I saw the light of the motorcycle coming back towards us. We'd been running without lights, so we cut the engine and coasted to a stop. The motorcyclist came up and fell in behind the last one of the convoy, and they continued on their way. If the driver of the last vehicle had looked, he'd have seen us – but they didn't see us. He obviously didn't consult his rear-view mirror. Even then he wouldn't have seen us, because it was dark and we were running without lights. He probably wouldn't have thought that we were British – I don't suppose he would have expected anybody would have been so darned silly as to follow them up – but being so darned silly was the name of the game.

There was a lot of sweat and fear – you could almost smell the fear at times because you just didn't know what was round the next corner. We took that lorry cross country and I remember felling trees and filling in ditches with timber so as to take the lorry across. We barged into and knocked down some quite stout hedges – but we had to get through. This proved our downfall eventually, and we got captured.

We got down as far as Poix – fighting, running and hiding all day. We'd passed through the British lines by this time and the Germans were chasing us all the time – they seemed to be all over the place. On one occasion we rounded a corner and there were some tanks with Germans grouped round them. There didn't seem to be anybody in them – they were having a break. So we took advantage of the fact that we'd caught them unawares and we got as close to them as we possibly could and gave them a barrage of hand grenades – which seemed to more or less put paid to them all. By then we'd accumulated Brens and all sorts of kit, and we managed to keep the Germans down long enough for one of our chaps to clamber up and drop a grenade into the turrets of the tanks to deal with anybody left inside. We retreated again before the noise attracted more Germans. We ended up taking three prisoners with us and handed them over to some French officers. When we arrived they were having a meal – tablecloth, wine, all laid out – and they were enjoying themselves. They were extremely disgruntled when we brought the three German prisoners up and handed them over. One of the men was wounded and he managed to shake his arm and spatter blood all over their nice fresh tablecloth. He was most unpopular.

On 7 June we were going across country between Forge les Eaux and Buchy, down the Rouen road. I knew the countryside fairly well and we looked down from the top of a hill on to the Rouen–Buchy road. It seemed clear, so we left our cover and went down the lane, which had steep banks either side of it. As we came out on to the Rouen–Buchy road, we saw a German personnel-carrier on one side of the road and two motorcyclists on the other, with their machine guns trained on us. They'd spotted us coming down the lane and were lying in wait for us – so we were caught and captured. They made us get out of the lorry and sit on the banks. I was separated from the men and sat on the bank on the left side. The other chaps were made to sit in a line on the other side, and we all had to sit with our hands on our heads. After a while of sitting there the personnel carrier left and we were left with just the motorcyclists who posted guards either end of the lane, sandwiching us in between.

Eventually, the other motorcycle disappeared, leaving the one motorcycle and sidecar and two men guarding us. They both had automatic weapons slung across their chests and they were making jokes at our expense. I decided I wasn't going to let them get away with that, so I started talking to the blokes over on the opposite bank, vilifying the Germans in every way I could, calling them names. As they didn't take umbrage, I gathered they didn't understand English. I decided to risk it and said to Eddie my driver, 'You'll have to be prepared – presently I might make a break. If I go for one of the guards, for God's sake all the rest of you get hold of the other guard as quick as you can, before he can unsling that damn gun.' Eddie said, 'OK,' and we looked at the Germans. They obviously hadn't understood the exchange, but they started to wig us about talking.

In a very conciliatory manner I reached for my breast pocket and immediately was threatened by automatic rifle. I said, '*Zigaretten. Zigaretten,*' and the guard consulted with the other one and gave me permission. I took out my cigarette case and took out a cigarette – and I offered it to the guard, hoping to get him near me – but he wouldn't come near. I lit the cigarette and put it in my mouth, thinking, 'So far so good.'

We'd been sitting there for quite a considerable time, and I said to the guard that I wanted to relieve myself. He said that was all right, so I stood up and started to climb the bank. He immediately shouted at me, 'Nein!' I said, 'But I must.' I pointed to a bush and started to undo my trousers. He understood and indicated that I could get behind the bush. I went up and got behind the bush, watching him all the time. He came walking down a few steps nearer to make sure everything was all right, and I just slipped my braces off my arms and made a motion as though to pull my trousers down. He looked around at the other guard and said something to him. As soon as his attention was off me I just went through the air and managed, more by luck than judgement, to grip him by the throat. He hadn't time to bring his weapon into play, and the other guard was so taken aback that he hesitated for a second, not knowing what to do. He obviously couldn't shoot me for fear of shooting his mate – that was his undoing, because all the other boys hit him at the same time, and he went down.

I was very unlucky because this guard had a trench knife in his boot, which he managed to pull. I was muffling his automatic weapon by the weight on top of him and my hands round his throat, but he managed to reach for this knife and he brought it up. I saw it coming and put my hand in the way, so he sawed right through the joint of my hand and into my chin. I was very pleased the moment I found his jugular and he went limp – otherwise he would have cut my throat.

He was out, but I was bleeding profusely. The other guard had been battered to death, so we were free – it was as simple as that. We all piled into the lorry and didn't wait to move the motorcycle out of the way. We just knocked it aside and we were off. It was such a relief – and although I was bleeding a lot, we managed to get a field dressing on to my head, wrapped round as if I had toothache, and another around my hand – very untidy, but effective.

All the way to Rouen there were signs of Germans. They were already in the northern part of the town, but we hit the bridge at the bottom of the Rue Jeanne d'Arc and went across – and we found all the way along the south parapet of the Seine were British troops, all drawn up. On the right as we went down there were British and Scottish troops and on the left were French,

Belgians, Moroccans, and even some Poles, and they were preparing the bridge for demolition.

A group of officers who'd been standing there came rushing up and said, 'Thank God you're here. We've been waiting for you for hours.' I said, 'If you'll excuse me, I want to go to a dressing station.' 'But aren't you here to blow up the bridge?' 'No, we've just escaped from the Germans up the road. They're at Buchy.' The officer said he was awaiting for someone to come and blow the bridge, so I said, 'If you don't mind, while you're waiting, I'll go and get attended to – and if when I come back nobody has turned up to blow your bridge, I've sufficient explosives aboard – I might be able to damage it, at least.'

I got myself doctored up with a bandage round my head and one round my hand and I went back. Just as I got back there, they said, 'It's all right – the chap has arrived,' and he was already underneath, wiring up the buttresses.

After the bridge was blown, the consultation was that, now we were all on the south side of the river, what should we do? I heard that the 51st Highland Division was making for St Valéry, but I'd had previous experience of making for sea ports and getting cut off, so I didn't think I'd do that. In a very naive fashion I decided that I'd make for Switzerland – it was a neutral country, while France was practically overrun. So we started off in the opposite direction to the 51st Highland Division. We learned subsequently that they were all captured at St Valéry. We headed for Beauvais, but just before we got there, we heard that the Germans had taken it, so we decided the best thing was to go further south.

That was on 8 June, and the ninth was a Sunday. We diverted from Beauvais to Compiègne, but before we got there we were told that Jerry was not only in the town, but in most of the forest round about. Our lorry broke down at Senlis on the 10th. There was fighting going on all around. We used the last of our explosives to help some French and Belgians who were holding the Germans off, but were running out of ammunition. The French officer in charge told me that he was frightened that the Germans would creep up behind them, using a cottage and two houses as vantage points. I said I thought we could help him out, and with the aid of the last of our explosives we demolished the cottage and the houses, thereby earning a debt of gratitude from the French and a load of French wine – which was extremely nasty and sour. Nevertheless, they kept pressing it upon us and calling us comrades – so we decided to stay and assist them in the defence of Senlis.

I discovered that Senlis was not very far north of Paris – we'd really wandered across the country since leaving Rouen. We helped them set up machine-gun points and stayed with them until after Jerry attacked, but then we found we'd run out of ammunition ourselves and French ammunition wouldn't fit the .303. There was no point in staying because the only thing we had left to fight with was our bayonets.

It was coming up to 12 June, and we set out on the Paris road. We couldn't possibly get through to Switzerland – that was off because the Germans had cut down there and had very nearly taken Paris. We were being pushed back all the time, so we decided to make for Paris and see if we could find a British command there – after all, where the fleshpots are is usually where you find most of the senior officers.

Corporal Donald Draycott
98 Squadron, RAF

We were practically the last to embark on the *Lancastria*. She was a single-funnel thing, and looked like an old ship. She was only complemented, I think, for trooping a few hundred, and there was between 6,000 and 7,000 troops and air force on board. We were assigned to paliasses right on the bottom of the hold. It was pretty grim down there, and having a strong sense of preservation, I thought, if we got attacked by submarines or we hit a mine on the way home, we wouldn't have a chance down there, because of the difficulty of getting out, particularly if the lights have all gone. So I decided to stay on the top deck.

At about midday, the first action stations sounded, and the order came over the tannoy, 'All people other than gunners to get below decks!' but I was just under the first deck, and stood by the deck entrance. I saw a German aircraft swoop over the top of us, and make for the next liner, the *Oranse*, which was about a mile away. I saw the aircraft come down quite low and then pull up. His bomb doors opened, and either two or four light series bombs left the aircraft and hit the *Oranse* on the bridge. Everything on the boats round the destroyers opened up, anti-aircraft fire and rifle fire. But the aircraft climbed away into the cloud, and he got away with it. Most likely, the wireless op would be ringing his base and giving the information that we were transports at anchor off St Nazaire.

At approximately three o'clock, the action stations went again, ordering everybody down below except the gunners. I went down and stood just away from the deck door by number one hold. I stood there, holding the railings, and the first salvo that came down was a near miss. The ship jumped, the lights all flickered, but everything settled all right. And then within half a minute, I heard another aircraft scream down. There was an almighty crash and from the hold, there was a flash and smell and I could see cordite smoke. All the lights went out. There was smoke everywhere but I noticed the smoke was swirling out through the doorway that I'd come in. So I dashed for that, accompanied by other people and I arrived on the deck. The deck was a scene of confusion, and already, the ship had taken on a decided list.

There was no panic where I was, and although the hit had been so close to us, none of us had been hit by any debris or bomb fragments. We all managed to get out on to the deck. I remember seeing people lying on the deck, looking as though they'd been blown up from the engine room. There was an army sergeant shouting, 'Come on lads! Roll out the fire hose!' And I remember saying to him, 'You've had it chum! You're wasting your time!' I went with one of the armourers to the bow to have a look back – and she was sinking slowly in the water. So I said to this chap, 'Well, I'm a swimmer… I'm over the side…' I looked down, and there was a 30-foot drop. I wasn't worried so much about the jump, but previously when I'd been looking over the side, there were Portuguese men o'war in the water; big jellyfish that can give you a nasty sting. The only thing I thought, I wasn't bothered about the Luftwaffe, I was thinking about these jellyfish. I took my tin helmet off, my uniform, my boots, I clutched my paybook and my French francs, and I jumped feet first over the side.

When I broke the surface, I was right up against the ship's plates, so I decided to strike out away from her. I swam about a hundred yards, and came across a plank which looked as if it had been blown off one of the hatches. I sat on that, and the thing that surprised me was how calm I felt. I thought, 'Well, I'll sit on this, and I'll get a grandstand view. I'll never see anything like this again.' So I sat on this hatch cover and turned and looked back at the ship.

By this time, she'd got a heavy list on, and they were trying to launch the lifeboats. I saw one of the lifeboats, as it was being lowered, the falls at one side were hung up. Somebody got a hatchet and severed the rope, and the lifeboat dropped vertically into the sea with all the people in it. That was the only lifeboat I saw attempting to get away. There were people trying to get through the portholes, but they had a cork lifejacket on, and they couldn't make it – so what they did, they pulled back, took the lifejacket off, pushed the lifejacket through the porthole, and came through it. By that time, people in the water without lifejackets had grabbed hold of them to support themselves.

I never saw any bad behaviour. I saw an army chappie jump off the side in full kit, and when she was going down at the front, so the propellors were out of the water at the back, I saw another army chappie jump off the stern and drop across the props. He didn't allow for them, and I presume he was killed.

There was nobody close to me in the water. I could hear some of the chaps shouting that they hadn't got lifebelts as they were going down, shouting, 'Oh my God!' and things like that. I heard singing. People on the ship were singing 'Roll out the barrel' and some odd ones in the water took it up.

I would say that the majority must have been able to swim. There would be non-swimmers amongst them but one of the bad things was that being built for trooping an average of a few hundred and having thousands on, there was a shortage of lifebelts. There wasn't lifebelts for the majority of people that were on the transport. The destroyer, the *Havelock*, put a dinghy out with two sailors in, pushed Carley floats over the side, and put scrambling nets out for people in the water to get on. But just then, a Luftwaffe aircraft came over and made a pass at the *Havelock*, and she promptly disappeared full steam ahead.

As the Luftwaffe was making its bombing runs, the front gunners and rear gunners on the aircraft were firing at the troops in the water. One thing I noticed was that when some RAF Hurricanes suddenly appeared, as they flew over low, I could see some of their pilots removing their Mae West flotation gear and pitching it over the side for people in the water. And I heard one or two faint cheers when the Hurricanes appeared, because the Luftwaffe beat it.

The *Lancastria* went down by the bows first, and started to tilt. Then, as she took water in, she went down by the stern, and began to list at an angle of about 45 degrees. The last look I had of her from a distance, she was practically on her side with people that had stayed on 'til the end jumping into the sea. Of about 200 members of 150 Squadron that I was with, the people that stayed in the hold, we lost about 100. About 50 per cent of the squadron personnel.

I was in the water about an hour before I finally got picked up and put on to the *Havelock*, and I wasn't even cold; it was a lovely June day with just a little floating cloud and my teeth weren't even chattering. I've an idea that I was picked out of the water by a dinghy with two sailors. One of the seamen on the *Havelock* fitted me up with a pair of slacks and a shirt, and gave me a tot of

The view from a rescue boat as the *Lancastria* sinks

rum, and a hot drink. And we started circling round, putting more floats out, and picking up more survivors.

Eventually, they transferred us to the *Oranse*. They put a 'Jacob's ladder' over the side, a rope ladder, because the deck of the French lighter was slightly lower than the deck of the *Havelock*. We were standing shoulder to shoulder on the deck of the *Oranse*, and we couldn't move. If I remember rightly, I spent the night on the deck with a blanket over me.

Sergeant William Knight
No 1 General Base Depot, Royal Engineers

They put us on a barge and sent us out to join a ship which was lying in the searoads just outside St Nazaire – about three miles out. We were taken on board the old troopship, the *Lancastria*. I put all my men up on the foc'sle – I'd had some previous experience in the Merchant Navy and I knew that if the boat was hit, if she was torpedoed on one side, she'd list that way, and the boats would be in the water before you knew it, whereas the boats on the other side would be up on top of the hull. I told my men, 'You won't be on board long before you get to England – 48 hours at the most. The best thing to do is to bivouac up on the foc'sle head where those big square Carley floats are. It doesn't matter what angle the ship goes down, the Carley floats always float up and they always float square and you can get on them. A lifeboat will sink – but a Carley float won't.' So they made a bivouac in the lee of the Carley floats using their rain capes. I went to see what provisions could be found to feed the troops, and while I was away from them, somewhere amidships, the bomb struck. It went right down the funnel and the ship more or less broke in two. Luckily I was on the right end.

I dashed up forward as best I could, among all the shrieking and jostling and fighting, to get to my own people. I cast a look over the side and could see oil flooding out into the water. There were people already in the water and being covered in oil – and some of this oil had caught fire. All around us, bigger boats were putting their lifeboats into the water and coming towards us. I managed to get down to the forewell deck where there were very few people, and I got there just as it went under. I went under with it, but mercifully I was clear of the oil. When I came to the surface I struck out. I saw my chaps shouting and gesticulating from the Carley float, and I swam across. They hauled me aboard and we sat and watched the last of the *Lancastria*. We also watched the oil gradually coming closer and closer to us – and once again, I felt really frightened. But then a lifeboat came over and took us aboard. Subsequently a French fishing boat pulled alongside and they took us aboard with a lot more of our troops who had been picked up.

Corporal Donald Draycott
98 Squadron, RAF

We weren't blaming anyone for the disaster, but I could hear people saying, and I was inclined to agree with them, that they couldn't understand why the *Lancastria* had been at anchor from half-past six in the morning until we were hit at three in the afternoon. If she'd been underway, she probably wouldn't have been hit.

We came into Plymouth, and we were unloaded on to the quayside, and there was RAF and army police, army and air force officers, sitting at tables, and you were supposed to go up and give your rank, name and unit. There were NAAFI canteens there, and they supplied us with sandwiches and hot drinks, and then we were asked, because we were RAF, rather than going to an army or naval unit, whether we would hang on for a few more hours to be transported to an RAF aerodrome. So we marched through Plymouth to the station, and they laid on a special train, and we were on it practically all night, before finally finishing up at RAF Yatesbury in Wiltshire. The thing that amazed me was that as the coaches brought us from Yatesbury Station to the guardroom, the policeman on the gate said, 'Has anybody got any duty chargeable stuff?' We all told him where to get off! I'd lost everything! Even the paybook with the French francs that I'd clutched as I went over the side.

Trooper Ernest Cheeseman
5th Battalion, Royal Tank Regiment

We joined a whacking great stream of refugees and tried to get ahead of them. There was more courtesy on the roads then than there is these days, but it was a very slow business. That afternoon there was another dive-bombing. I immediately found myself in the ditch at the side of the road in the foetal position, my hands over the back of my head, and umpteen bodies on top of me. We were lucky and so were the refugees, but one of the refugees had a cart and horse with their belongings on, and that wasn't so lucky. The horse was killed and the suitcases were scattered all over the road. When we got back into the lorry, this was in front of us. My sergeant went ahead to guide me over the debris without going into the ditch at the side of the road. I remember distinctly that he was urging me on like a father – then his voice suddenly changed. 'For God's sake, bloody drive over its bloody legs – the horse is dead! It will not feel anything!' But I felt this revulsion at driving over a dead horse. More was to come – another air raid. 'Get your wagon up the road as fast as you bloody well can!' While he was shouting, lads were getting off the wagon and running to the ditch and up the road, and I think I heard the scream of a bomb, but I couldn't believe what was happening. My sergeant was killed, but I didn't go over to him. Instead of going to the spot where he ought to have been and seeing if he was alive, I just jammed my foot on the accelerator, over the crater, and I had to get my bloody vehicle safe, because without that we were dead. That's my excuse. But I should have stopped to see if he was OK. The warrant officer tank commander told me later that I did the right thing in saving the vehicle, but even now I feel guilty. I was a coward, I suppose.

The sergeant had had a fair idea where we were going – but he was gone and the information was gone as well. The next day we stumbled on a column of absolutely every different type of British army vehicle you can imagine – about 18 vehicles and all like us, loaded to the gunwales with stragglers who represented just about every single regiment in the BEF. There was an officer in charge of organising this – he gave us as much petrol as possible, as we were getting low, and he organised a meal for us, a few biscuits and some chocolate. It was this officer who started talking about a place I'd never ever heard of before – Dunkirk. Where on earth was that? We'd passed through many of these French villages, but he wasn't speaking of them, and if I remember rightly he was talking about it in the past tense. We were heading south-west, away from Dunkirk. Dunkirk was already over. So we were in France for quite a while after the evacuation from Dunkirk had finished, and so were an awful lot of other soldiers.

The tanks didn't move with us – we'd lost those altogether. I believe my battalion saved about half a squadron of tanks – they came out of Cherbourg, where we'd landed. But we'd forgotten we were in the tanks. We were just part of the BEF, trying to get out of France. The tanks didn't even come into my mind until after we'd joined this officer. I said, 'Hello, we're getting out of France!' That was the one big light at the end of what we hoped was not too long a tunnel.

At nights we pulled in wherever there was a road with trees. We wouldn't stand on the road because of aircraft, we only stopped under cover of trees. We got petrol from siphoning it out of abandoned vehicles that had full tanks. We'd used up all our reserves. We were carrying cans of petrol – 12 gallons, which for a lorry was about 30 miles. But the officer was working it out; he'd got this amount of petrol and this amount of food, and you require that, and he was sharing it out. I've no doubt some people went to French petrol stations, but we managed without it.

We made it to Brest, where, astonishingly, field upon field upon field alongside the road were filled with British lorries. We were told not to set fire to them, but to sabotage our vehicles. On our lorry we were carrying spare guns and ammunition for the tanks, and also a Bren. We were told to leave all personal stuff there except our paybooks, because we were loaded down with weapons and ammunition. My load was a Bren gun and a tin of Bren gun magazines. Another chap had a tripod and what-have-you. About ten or twelve kilometres from Brest, we force-marched, as good as any infantry. You can imagine the exhausted state we were in, goodness knows when we'd last had a night's rest, what with the dive-bombing, and our emotions being torn to bits. I remember getting to the dockside in Brest – and it was cobbled – and just dropping down on the cobbles while we were waiting our turn to get on board. And I've never seen such a dilapidated ship in all my life.

When we were lying on the ground exhausted, resting, a few of the French dockers showed us a bit of mercy. They'd broken into a crate full of punnets of strawberries, and we all had a punnet of strawberries each.

Lieutenant John Redfern
2/6th Battalion, East Surrey Regiment

On 7 June, a lot of armed Frenchmen arrived, and when I asked them what they were doing, they said they were counter-attacking. I asked what they were counter-attacking, and they said the enemy was just in front of us – I didn't know the enemy were anywhere near us. I went and spoke to their colonel, and he asked who I was. I told him, and explained that I had four anti-tank guns that I was covering. He said, 'You've got a line!' I said, 'No, I've got a few blokes covering an area by fire only. All I've got is one Bren per section, rifles and bayonets!' He told me that the enemy had broken through from the north-east, and he'd been ordered to counter-attack. I said, 'Good!' He said, 'No, I'm going to countermand the order!' I said, 'Why? I'll join you!' He said,

'No. I didn't know you had a line here!' I said, 'I haven't got a line! You can't countermand the order! You have artillery! Make your position here!' He said, 'I'm going back to the woods. If you're in trouble, come back to me there.' So he left me on my own.

At about three o'clock in the afternoon, I saw struggling down the road two people dressed in French tank uniform. They came halfway down, looked about, and then turned back. Then two vehicles with troops came down the road, and when they were halfway down, I asked the two-pounder to open up. He did and he did a lot of damage. We opened fire, and then two of my blokes were rushing towards me, shouting, 'The Germans are here! They took us by surprise!' I told them to get to the rear and look after our rear for us. Then there was deathly hush. Some refugees were put on the top of the hump in front of a gun position – the Germans were using them as shields. From my right, I heard a German saying, 'Englander! You are in a difficult position! You will surrender!' I said to the blokes, 'I think the answer to that is "No!" because we don't know what troops are here. They have killed a lot of prisoners, and I think we'll stay here!' They all agreed, so we hung on. The German said, 'Englander, I will ask you three times to surrender!' He did it three times, and we said no. I told the blokes, 'Fix your ruddy bayonets!' And then the Germans charged – but for some unknown reason, they stopped and went back. They threw grenades which destroyed my two-pounder gun. But they never came after us. I don't know why...

So they left us there, and darkness fell. I went to see what our casualties were. I found that I only had four blokes left out of my eight. The German grenades had done quite a bit of damage. So I decided to evacuate, to see if we could get back to the headquarters. The sergeant had been wounded in the chest and stomach, and I said, 'I honestly can't move you; I daren't move you. If I come across anybody at all, I'll get medical aid to you.' He agreed. So I left as much food and water as I had with him, and I left the position.

We went by the edge of the wood, and as we approached a bend, there were shots fired. There was obviously a German standing patrol, using the wood as a resting place for the night. I told my blokes not to make a sound. The next thing I heard was, 'Don't shoot! We're English!' and suddenly all hell was let loose. A hand grenade was thrown at me, and landed next to me. I heard it fizzing away, but I couldn't see it, so I couldn't put my tin hat over the ruddy thing. I made the sign of the cross, and it went off, and went into my leg. I told my runner that I would crawl back 100 yards, and I told him to get the other blokes to come back to me. I waited half an hour, but nobody came back. I decided to get on to the main road, and I was getting very tired, and I decided to have a kip in a ditch. When it got a bit light, I carried on down the main road, and I came to a village. My leg had stopped bleeding, and it didn't look too bad. I went through some woods, and about 200 yards down, I saw a wagon. Some French troops came from the back of it. They were the troops who had been meant to counter-attack the day before. I went up to the colonel who said I'd better be evacuated to a hospital. He said, 'Can I go and look for your men?' I said, 'If you do I'm coming with you, but I don't see any point, because I've no doubt the Germans have now taken the position.' He put me into an ambulance with eight French, and ordered it to go to Rouen.

I was put on board the Red Cross ship, *Shropshire*, and they X-rayed my leg and decided to operate. I must have woken up while I was on the operating table, because I saw the masked people in front, and the surgeon had a scalpel in his hand, and he was saying, 'I'm going to cut...' I was trying to say, 'For God's sake, don't! I've woken up! I can see you! I can hear you!' But, of course, nothing came out. I heard the surgeon say that he couldn't operate for some reason, and the next thing I knew I'd woken up back in my berth.

Robert Sheppard
Part-British, part-French civilian in France

I saw the arrival of the Germans in France like a sort of dream. I didn't see the horror of an occupation immediately. I saw the Germans arriving, putting machine guns at each corner of the streets, driving fast down the roads. They were showing they were present. My father was arrested by the Germans in late June 1940. My father was British and my mother was French, so he was arrested as an English subject. I had my first encounter with the Germans when they knocked at the door. My mother was frightened, and I opened the door, and three Germans asked for my father. One of them was speaking a little French, and I said my father was out. 'All right! In that case, you come with us!' They explained to my mother that I was being arrested until my father joined the prison in exchange for my liberation. Which, of course, he did immediately he arrived home. I saw my father arriving at the prison, practically shouting, 'Where is my son?' And we sort of exchanged position. This was my first contact with what would be the misery of the occupation by the Nazis.

July 1940 was the real start of a clandestine life for me. At this point, many members of the British Army were in hiding, trying to find a place to embark, and Nantes was an important harbour. So, in June, July, August, we had quite a lot hiding in the area. Without instruction, we set up a friendly chain to help the British Army members to escape from France. It was a very difficult task, because we had to find people to hide members of the British Army! They were mostly in civvies, hiding in farms, and we had to pick up these English-looking officers and men who themselves were in doubt about us. It was a very interesting part of the Resistance to convince these men that we were true friends, and really wanted to help them get back to their own country. This was my first action – walking through the streets of Nantes, riding a bicycle through the country, to help the British Army members who were lost. I was very young and we were extremely careful with what we were doing. Personally, I picked up about ten, perhaps a few more, members of different regiments. Until the German invasion, we had a lot of British Army in the area, and my father being an ex-member of the British Army, we were very friendly with the British, and we had many at our home for lunch, for dinner, and for drinks. So, it was easy for me to spot the types, and to give them confidence.

Henry Metelmann
German soldier – served with 22nd Panzer Division
We were part of the occupation army in France, and we had the weapons – so civilians just had to obey, but they hated us. You could sense it. They hated the guts of us. I remember going to a football match. I loved football; I played it myself at school and in the Hitler Youth. It was an open ground, and people stood round it, and wherever I went on the touchline, the French people just moved away. I went to another place and the same happened. I stood there on my own. And somehow I did not like it because I really wanted to go there and be friendly, watch a football match – and they cut me. And there were some children playing football at the back on the grass, and the ball somehow came to me, and I picked the ball up and knocked it about a little bit and kicked it back to them. They picked the ball up and walked away. And somehow that hurt me. I didn't like it. I left the pitch. Left the football ground.

I remember something which rather shocked me. There was a beautiful large house, a drive leading up to it, and big wrought-iron gates, and a French industrialist lived there. And this industrialist gave a party, and the German

officers were invited, and I was a guard there. For two hours I stood there, presenting arms. And I saw all the French civilians going in there, and the
German officers and women, and I couldn't tie it up because I felt that *we*
were the masters of France, so why were *they* inviting us here? And then, later,
I saw the goings on when the German officers came out, drunk, falling down
the stairs, and prostitutes were being brought in. As a young Hitler soldier, it
shocked me! It spoiled my image of the German Reich idea. We had beaten
the French, we were the masters, and now we were going to a party with these
second-rate French people. I was shocked.

Back in Blighty

A drink and a smoke on return

HI 636

It was not, at that time, considered to be a defeat, purely because I think
the British Army was not used to having defeats. It was only later that it
bore on one's mind that in fact it had been a complete and utter defeat.

The evacuation of the British Expeditionary Force from Dunkirk can-
not be considered a victory for Britain. For the British people, it set
the scene for a period of terrible dark, underpinned by stubborn hope. An
invasion seemed imminent. Church bells were silenced across the country,
to be rung only as a warning of the arrival of the German invaders. Yet,
even during these bleak times, as first Fighter Command of the Royal Air
Force, and then the people of Britain's cities, resisted the Luftwaffe, the
nation drew self-belief born from Operation Dynamo, from the 'miracle of
deliverance, achieved by valour'.

It is sometimes suggested that the fabled 'Dunkirk Spirit' is a construction
of hindsight. Yet it is clear from the accounts that follow that many of the
soldiers who returned home, trampled and dispirited, were astonished by
the reception they received: they were welcomed as heroes. Such optimism in
the face of grim reality was skilfully fostered by Winston Churchill. If the
essence of leadership in bleak times is the ability to dull the rational faculty
and to substitute enthusiasm for it, then Churchill was a leader of true
genius. His attitude of determined calm would rally the nation across the
darkest days, as Britain's immediate future was determined in her skies.

When, four years later, British troops returned to France, they came as
part of a more formidable fighting force that had learned many lessons. They
were better equipped and more effectively led. Subsequent fighting in North
Africa and Italy had instilled them with confidence. But they had never
forgotten that, during the despairing days of May 1940 – when the future of

the British Expeditionary Force had seemed hopeless – the seemingly inexorable enemy had been resisted, and could, perhaps, be beaten.

Captain Anthony Rhodes
253 Field Company, Royal Engineers

At Dover, we got on a train heading for London with civilians who were going to their offices in London. So the train was full of soldiers, but sitting next to you there might be a man on his way to his bank. One very nice man pressed two half-crowns into my hand, which was rather nice. These people in the train were very sympathetic to us. They wanted to know what had happened. They could see that we all had about three days' growth of beard. They could see that our clothing was falling to pieces and that we'd had an unpleasant time.

2nd Lieutenant Ian English
8th Battalion, Durham Light Infantry

In England, the reception was amazing. We were put on a train, and wherever we stopped, people came up with coffee and cigarettes. We had evidence from this tremendous euphoria – quite unfounded – that we were some sort of heroes and had won some sort of victory. It was obvious that we had been thoroughly beaten.

Captain (Acting) Humphrey 'Bala' Bredin
2nd Battalion, Royal Ulster Rifles

We arrived at Dover, and the only thing I remember after that was waking up in a train at a place called Headcorn in Kent where the women almost gave us a party. They invaded the train with tea, coffee and buns. It was as if we were a victorious army, and it rather embarrassed us. We felt, damn it, we'd run away. But they made us feel as if things were more or less normal again. And the next time I woke up was at Tweseldown Racecourse near Aldershot, where I was told that I'd slept for 16 hours.

Lance Corporal Albert Adams
East Yorkshire Yeomanry

We arrived at Margate on the *Royal Daffodil*. By the pier where we got off, there was a soldier with a big bag. He told us to drop all our ammunition into the bag. One man dropped a couple of hand grenades, and the soldier ran off. They had their pins in but he didn't know that.

Corporal George Andow
4th Battalion, Royal Tank Regiment

When we got into Dover, we came off the boat and were sorted out. The Red Cross people were there with mugs of hot tea and sandwiches, then we got on board a train and finished up in our own barracks in Farnborough. They got us all lined up on the square and tried to do a roll-call to see who was missing. You'd give what information you could about your comrades, but there were not very many of us on the square – maybe 100. Near enough 30 died on the boat.

Captain Peter Barclay
2nd Battalion, Royal Norfolk Regiment

We were met in the early hours of the morning at Newhaven and it was the most extraordinary anticlimax that I've ever experienced. There had been the appalling din – which one became pretty well accustomed to – and now there was dead silence except for the odd seagull.

I would pay tribute to the morale that we had in the battalion. It was the most thrilling feeling to experience the spirit of the chaps who are with you. It's intangible, but it's a most exhilarating and potent influence, a wonderful reviver. You can never feel tired or depressed when you've got a spirit round you like that. The whole thing was treated as a jolly well worthwhile job that had to be done.

Leon Wilson
French gunner – served with 229 Heavy Artillery Regiment

When we arrived at Dover, they were shouting, 'British one side! French other side!' and the British went somewhere else. We gathered all together, and a train took us into London about two hours later. When we arrived in London, we were transported to White City Stadium, which they'd already prepared for the French forces. That was our headquarters, because de Gaulle was already here.

Captain Gilbert White
1/6th Battalion, East Surrey Regiment

The reception was tremendous – when we arrived at Dover quay there were a hell of a lot of ships, destroyers unloading wounded. It was organised chaos.

The whole thing was done extremely well, and there was a great deal of activity and movement. We were entrained after a couple of hours, and on the platform there were a lot of WVS with tea and buns, welcoming us home. 'Jolly good job!', 'Well done you!' It was all rather fictitious considering we were a defeated army, but they were delighted to see us back, and I was asked if I would like to send a telegram to my wife, who hadn't heard from me for some days. I said, 'No,' as I thought the receipt of a telegram might worry her. I said I'd wait and get in touch with her as soon as we'd landed at our camp.

Corporal Charles 'Bert' Nash
2nd Bulk Petrol Transport Company, Royal Army Service Corps

Eventually we arrived at Ramsgate and we climbed up the harbour steps. The regimental sergeant major-type in control said, 'Now then lads, you're back in the UK. We've got a job of work still to do. What I want to do is make sure you get to your units as soon as possible. All you people who live in the south of England – I'd like you to get over there. Let's say everybody from the south of Luton onwards, over to the left, and all you chaps that live up north – that's north of Luton and Bedfordshire, I want you to move to the right.' So we were divided into two squads, and the crunch was this: I was in the squad who lived in the south of England and we were quickly put on a train designated Chester up in the north, and I'm led to believe that all those poor blighters who lived in the north were stationed in Aldershot or Chichester. At the time I was a bit angry, but afterwards, this professional soldier business began to creep into me, and I understood that if they'd allowed me to get anywhere near my family in the state I was in, I would have had half of Fulham very badly demoralised. The object of the exercise, I'm quite certain, was to take us away from where we lived, whip us into shape, and make soldiers of us again.

Major Donald Wilson-Haffenden
HQ – 1st Division

Everyone was dead tired. I hadn't slept for about eight days and I was really at the end of my tether. We were wonderfully received in England. I went right up to London. I don't remember much about the journey because I slept all the way – and my wife was waiting for me at a hotel in Camberley. I discovered through her bank where she was, so I went straight on to Camberley and went directly to bed. Shortly afterwards my wife came and shook me awake. 'There's an air raid on. You'll have to get up and go down to the cellar.' I said, 'Look, I've been bombed all the way back. I'm not going to any cellar. I'm just going to sleep.'

Eileen Livett
British Red Cross Nurse

I remember those young men and how they suffered. They were young, and when some of them first arrived on the ward, they were so muscle-bound, they couldn't lie on the beds. Hospital beds are notoriously hard, but even these were too soft for them, so they used to lie on the floor by the side of their beds. They just couldn't relax on the bed. They wanted to lie on the floor, but hospitals in those days were almost regimental – they had to be just so. In the morning, you went round straightening beds, and if the sheets weren't absolutely straight and in line, you were reprimanded. They couldn't tolerate these boys lying on the floor, and the sister had fits. She said, 'Nurse, we can't have this. The matron will be round any minute; we have to get them into bed!' The boys wouldn't move – even though we begged and cajoled them.

Lance Corporal Lawrence Greggain
5th Battalion, Border Regiment

I was taken to St Mary's Hospital in Sidcup. For three days, I hardly knew what went on. They treated my wound, which had turned rather nasty, and they helped me to get rid of scabies and what-have-you. I was partially blind – which gave me an excellent excuse for putting my hand up the back of the nurse's skirt. I was horribly undernourished, and later they told me I slept for 36 hours.

Private Victor Burton
1st Battalion, East Lancashire Regiment

I still had my rifle and cigs, and still had my bandoliers – so I got in this corner of the boat with my rifle between my knees, and just sat there. I was fast asleep, and it only seemed a few minutes later there was a civilian tapping me on the shoulder. He had a big white pot of tea and some lovely corned beef on white bread. Ooh, I enjoyed it. I said to him, 'Where are we?' and he said, 'We're just going into Ramsgate.' I couldn't believe it, because I thought we were going back into France. I was still with another mate of mine, Tommy Kelly, so we went across the pier at Ramsgate off the promenade, and there was a military policeman there, and he sent Tommy one side and me the other. I went on a train that went up to Pontefract, Tommy went on one that went to Ashton Barracks. Later on, when we met up again, he said he went home that night. I said I was damned glad I didn't go home because we were all lousy. The whole street would have been lousy.

When we arrived it was a lovely day and we sat in the grass and had these lovely boiling hot showers. We had all clean underwear. When I came back, we shaved, and I thought I'd go and have another bath – and I had about half a dozen good baths before I put the clean clothes on. Then we only had one problem – between a few of us we only had a few francs, and we wanted to buy a pint, so I thought I'd sell one of my two pistols. We went into this pub and I sold a pistol to get some beer money for the lads. I got £6 for it, which was a lot of money then – but we had a lot of beer out of it.

When we met up again at the battalion, we heard that Captain Ervine Andrews, company commander of B Company, had been awarded the Victoria Cross. He was a crack shot and he'd been on top of a barn picking them off right, left and centre. Because we were in his company, and we were attached to it, we were right pleased – we had put a good show up.

Private William Ridley
9th Battalion, Durham Light Infantry

We got on the train, and sat on the floor, and we were utterly ashamed of what had happened. It wasn't until we were passing stations, and there were oranges coming through the windows and cigarettes and all sorts that I lifted my head up. And there was this big warehouse, and written on the slates in white was, 'Welcome to the Dunkirk heroes.' But I was utterly ashamed. And it took me many years to get over it.

Eileen Livett
British Red Cross Nurse

After the Dunkirk evacuation, we had a lot of the casualties, and we had a lot of nurses who were still receiving their training. There were Germans among them who had not been interned, and one day I saw one of these German nurses with a beautiful bouquet, and said to her, 'What beautiful flowers! Who gave you those? You've got an ardent suitor!' She just smiled and walked away. These Dunkirk casualties were in the main wards, but the side wards were taken up with the officers, two beds to a side ward. In one side ward we had a young Highland lieutenant who just kept talking all the time. In the other bed was a major, an older man, who didn't say anything at all. Well, we concluded that the boy kept talking from a shock reaction, and the other, not saying anything, could equally be a shock reaction. It was a week later, fortnight maybe, I went off duty, and when I came back after the weekend off, the major's bed was empty. I asked one of the nurses I was friendly with, 'Where's the major?' She said, 'He's gone.' I said, 'Gone? But he wasn't ready to be discharged.' She said, 'No, I know, come into the sluice and I'll tell you.' The sluice was where we had our little gossips, where we emptied bedpans, and sister never came in to see what we were doing. She told me very hurriedly that two plain-clothes detectives had arrived, spoken to sister, gone into the side ward, and then they'd gone off with the major. She didn't know why. The next day, I popped home to visit my people, and there was an item in the stop press column of the newspaper, 'German Spy Arrested in North London Hospital', so we concluded that our major was the spy. I wondered whether the bouquet that the girl had was a signal for her that he was arriving, to get in touch. But in two or three days, all the German nurses had gone, they'd been interned.

Private George Lambert
9th Battalion, Durham Light Infantry
People were lined up when we landed, and they were dishing out cups of tea for us. I felt defeated. They took us to a camp, but I was so fagged out. Everybody got a razor blade, but we had to share the razor with three people, and consequently, by the time we got back to the battalion proper at Lyme Regis, I had adapted to what they called a 'dirty shirt' – scabs all over your face.

Lance Corporal Kenneth Carver
5th Motor Ambulance Convoy, Royal Army Service Corps
I arrived back in England with a pair of French gumboots, my battledress trousers, an anti-gas cape, my jacket, and a French beret I'd got from a house somewhere. I remember getting on to a train, but I don't remember getting off it. I was told, three days later, that I was in Hampshire, where I woke up in a tent with my head in a nurse's lap. I was crying my eyes out and was absolutely bewildered as to why I was doing this. She said, 'Keep crying, corporal. Keep crying.' Apparently it was exhaustion, and it was a good thing I did, because I would have had a breakdown otherwise. From then on I regained my senses and strength.

Eileen Livett
British Red Cross Nurse

There was one young boy whose case I found very distressing – his injuries were terrible, but he was so brave, he never once whimpered. After he'd been in a couple of days, the matron appeared on the ward. The matron in those days was always a person apart, venerated, terribly strict, completely in charge of the hospital. Even the young doctors were terribly careful how they spoke to matron. She appeared when the staff and I were doing this boy's dressings, and she stood at the foot of the bed, and asked, 'How is he?' Staff said, 'He's doing quite well, matron.' She said, 'I've brought him some strawberries. The first strawberries out of my garden.' This boy had his eyes bandaged up, so he couldn't see but he could hear. So she turned to me, and said, 'Nurse, go and get him some cream to go with them.' I said, 'Cream, matron?' because this was wartime, and cream was unheard of. 'I said *cream*, nurse! Go on, hurry up!' I said, 'Where do I get cream, matron?' 'Nurse! Take the tops off all the bottles on the landing!' Each ward had its own fridge, so I had to take the cream off about eight milk bottles. I took it back, dipped a strawberry in the cream, and put it into his mouth. And I can see his face now, it lit up. Suddenly I realised, our matron *is* human, Very human, to think to do that for this poor boy.

Private Edgar Rabbets
5th Battalion, Northamptonshire Regiment

In Dover, ladies were there with cups of tea and bars of chocolate and cake. I got tea and a cake, got on the train and we went off to Camberley. I think people in Britain knew what had happened by this time, because this was towards the end of the evacuation and they must have seen a lot of people come before we arrived – probably gave them a shock. Overall, I think the morale of the troops was pretty good – which might have inspired people a bit.

Signaller Alfred Baldwin
65th Field Regiment, Royal Artillery

We landed in England on Friday 31st, and I remember helping to carry Paddy across the other boats, because we were lashed up alongside other boats in the harbour. Paddy was picked up and taken away in an ambulance, and I never saw him after that. We were shepherded off very rapidly into trains, which pulled out as soon as they were filled up. On the way we stopped somewhere around Redhill, at a small village station, and all the village ladies came out. They gave us each a postcard, on which we wrote our home address, and they posted them for us. In fact the postcards were all delivered by the post office, free of charge. It just let our parents know that we were in England again. Back at home I think they realised that we'd been beaten, and we'd had a real hammering, but nevertheless, they treated us as heroes. You'd have thought we'd won a battle instead of lost one. All the houses that backed on to the railway lines had banners outside, 'Welcome home, boys! Well done!' You really felt something like a hero.

Eileen Livett
British Red Cross Nurse

The young lad with shell shock used to ramble – he'd say they were advancing up a field, and that he saw the Jerries advancing up all around him. These lads were so young. There was one I remember most, the one I was most touched by. I went on duty one morning, and sister said, 'We've a bad case on the ward, nurse, how many hours' duty have you had?' I showed her my passbook and she told me to go to the staff nurse on the end bed, and assist her with the dressings. Normally you had the clean nurse who was hygienic, scrubbed-up with her gloves on, and the dirty nurse, unscrubbed, taking away the dressings and doing the dirty side of things. If you were scrubbed-up with your gloves on, you didn't touch anything that could be infected. I was usually dirty nurse. This lad was quite conscious – only about 18 or 19. We started to take the dressing off his thighs, and he must have been in marvellous condition before the war, very healthy, because he had got these third-degree burns right through his flesh, the size of a soup plate on his thighs and it was already healing. His eyes were bandaged right over, so he couldn't see us, but we could talk to him. I took the forceps to take off the bandage around his head, and his ear came away with the dressing. It was terribly charred. I heard from one of the other nurses, he'd been trapped in a burning tank. He was very badly charred. I was off duty for 24 hours, and when I came back, he'd gone, and when I asked where he was, they said he'd died. Apparently when the nurse took the bandages off his eyes, he realised he was blind, and although he was healing so beautifully, the shock was just enough to finish him. When I went back on duty, his mother was still sitting there. She was just sitting at the foot of the bed.

Sergeant Leonard Howard
210 Field Company, Royal Engineers

When we got back to Ramsgate the WVS and the local organisations were extremely kind to us. We were dead tired, but I remember they gave us tea and buns, then put us on a train. To my surprise, there were military guards on the train to prevent us from getting off. I suppose it was the right thing to do, because I would have been one who would have got off the train if I'd known that I could get home. We finished up at Shrivenham, which was then an artillery Officer Cadet Training Unit. The officer cadets filled palliasses with straw for us. We hadn't slept really for a week or two, and we slept. At 21 years old I suppose one gets over exhaustion fairly quickly. We were fit, and while we wouldn't have relished the idea, we would have been fit to scrap again in seven days. We were expected to be soldiering as soon as we recovered from our sleep. In my unit we lost at least 65 taken prisoner and had some 12 or 14 killed.

Gerald Ashcroft
Civilian Sea Scout – aboard Sundowner

When we arrived at Ramsgate harbour we were told to wait for orders to enter, so we sung out that we'd got 130 troops aboard, and could they have ambulances standing by. They replied that we should enter immediately. So as we went through the harbour entrance, the *Sundowner* suddenly gave a terrific lurch as those down below started struggling up. She nearly turned over. Commander Lightoller sung out to everyone below to stay down, and she came up to rights. We started unloading the troops off the deck. When the last troops were gone from the deck, Roger in the wheelhouse sung out for them to come up from down below and they started trooping up. We had counted 129 troops aboard – but when they were all gone, we had only counted 128. There must have been another one somewhere, and Lightoller went down again. There, sitting on the loo, fast asleep, was one nearly unconscious Tommy. He woke up – 'Come on lad! Time to go home!' Up he staggered.

Christopher Dreyer
Royal Navy – Commander, MTB 102

We were jolly tired at the end, but one was very resilient in those days, and three of us went and had a jolly good dinner in Dover and the next morning we drove our boats in company back to Portsmouth. We were perfectly all right, but we got a week's leave after it, which we did need. It had been quite tough. I suppose we had eight or nine days continuously operating, and it was quite tiring.

Arthur Joscelyne
Civilian – aboard the Thames barge Shannon

When we got in, I looked at myself in the mirror, and by gum, my face was caked with soot from the old tug chimney – because we were in direct line with the smoke. I'd got about five days' growth of beard and I was in the clothes I'd been living in for five days with all the dirt from the barges. We all looked like tramps. It had been a very unpleasant experience.

I don't suppose you'd have got the same weather and sea conditions again in 50 years – and to get those conditions at that particular time was incredible. Nobody will ever convince me that it wasn't some sort of divine intervention. I'm not a particularly religious man, but it was only the fact that conditions were so good and so calm – and the Channel is very rarely smooth at that time of year – that it was possible. I'm convinced that it was an act of God.

My brother Vincent told me his story – we'd never spoken about it between us before. Vincent reacted in a totally different manner from us, and he was proud of it. He was happy to tell people about it. Vincent went down earlier than us and he, by a strange coincidence, was also sent to the Renown, and he found they'd got too many crew and didn't want him. He saw another of the Leigh cockleboats – the Resolute – and they only had two on board, so he went with them. There were six of these cockleboats, the Renown, the Resolute, Reliance, the Defender, the Endeavour and the Letitia. They set off under the command of a naval officer as a little flotilla. He ordered them to go ashore, and the Leigh men refused – they said it was madness, because if they got on shore with the tide going out, the boats would have been weighted down with soldiers and they would have been stuck. They refused to go ashore to the beaches to pick up the soldiers, so they went alongside the mole instead, where they loaded up with all the men they could find. He said that all the soldiers they picked up were officers – I asked him how that could be, but he was certain they were. Afterwards, I found out that they were not in command of troops but in administration.

Aircraftman Leslie Haines
Forward Air Ammunition Park, RAF

The Falmouth ladies were wonderful to us. They gave us sandwiches and pasties and things. Eventually, we were told that they would arrange a special train to take us all up to London to be dispersed. While we were at the station, I saw a railway inspector that I knew. 'Oh my God! Les Haines!' he said. 'Your father thinks you're dead! God! You're here!' He got on the telephone to my father in Plymouth as we got on the train. After a while, the guard came along and said, 'Is one of you Les Haines?' 'Yeah. Me.' 'Right,' he said, 'I've got news for you. This train is stopping in Plymouth station. Look out! Your father and mother's gonna be there!' The train stopped with all these dozens of soldiers inside and there on the platform were my parents. You can imagine the scenes. They thought I was dead and gone.

2nd Lieutenant Arthur Curtis
7th Field Company, Royal Engineers

We were all waiting on the front at Margate and I began to feel a bit hungry so I thought, 'I'll go and see if I can cash a cheque.' There was a Lloyd's bank across the road, so I went in and formed up in a queue of people who were doing their business. They looked up and saw this chap queuing up in a red greatcoat, bloody and unshaven. I asked the cashier if I could cash a cheque, and he very apologetically said he didn't think he could do that. I only wanted a fiver…

Lance Corporal John Wells
6th Battalion, South Staffordshire Regiment – aboard SS Princessa

We were entrained on to a place called Burton, where the breweries are. It was a transit camp. About two o'clock in the morning, air raid sirens went and we got woken up from this deep sleep, and I really got the abdabs. It really affected me – the timbre of that siren going, it caused some nerve to go. Some time later I was in the air force on leave, and a siren went on the radio and I just burst into tears!

I still suffer to this day, bursting into tears for no reason. I mean, I can't tell you why, it sounds terrible, 70 years old, but still happens. I'm not trying to dramatise it, it's just one of those things. I can only quote what a particular neurosurgeon said to me. He said, you're bloody lucky to be alive! What are you complaining about? Which of course is true.

Eileen Livett
British Red Cross Nurse

They had built about four big wooden emergency wards in the grounds of the hospital, and one of them was full of French. They were very different to our boys; they were much more free and easy in their manner. There was a centre table which was normally sister's table, where she had her vases of flowers or whatever. It was definitely sister's preserve. *They* took it over as their table to play cards on, those that could get up. Sitting in the middle of the ward – *gambling*! Very different to our boys who were very quiet, 'Yes nurse, no nurse.' Polite. More regimented.

There was one amusing incident – although I didn't find it amusing at the time. One of these boys on the ward had a blockage so that he couldn't pass urine, and I was on duty, and all of a sudden he yells, 'Nurse! Nurse! I want a bottle! I want a bottle!' So I went and got him a bottle. I pulled back the screen and asked, 'Do you want a bedpan?' He said no, he wanted the bottle. So I gave him the bottle, and after a few minutes, I went back. 'I've done it! I've done it!' he said, and he was bouncing up and down in the bed. I told him to be careful, as I had to get the bottle out. So I lifted back the sheets, and went to get the bottle and he was bouncing up and down – he was absolutely in seventh heaven, because he'd been able to pass urine, and the bottle slipped and hit the floor. I said, 'Oh dear, now look what you've done!' I bent down very gingerly to pick it up, and it was all right, but there was a big crack in it, so I went into the sluice to empty it. When I put it under the sluice to wash it, the force of the water broke a chunk off and it went down and blocked the sluice hole. I looked round behind me, and there were about six other nurses with their bedpans and bottles waiting to come forward. I said, 'I'm sorry, you can't come for a moment, a piece of this bottle's broken and gone down the sluice hole.' One of them said, 'Come on, hurry up and get it out!' I said, 'I can't get it out!' 'Why can't you get it out?' 'I can't put my hand in there!' 'Well, you've got to, we're queuing up here. And it's nearly time for doctor's rounds, we can't be in here with bedpans when it's doctor's rounds.' So I had to put my hand in…

Private Albert Dance
Rifle Brigade

I was in a pretty poor physical condition when I got back. I'd had very little sleep and I'd not had my boots off for a week. When I eventually got them off,

I was amazed. I had a ring of sock above my ankle and nothing on the foot. Underneath the arch of my foot was all the wool packed together and congealed with blood. My feet were bloodied and blisters had burst. I could only wear slippers for a while.

I got off the train at Woolwich, which was where my sweetheart Maisie worked. I went up to the place she was working and saw the foreman and he said, 'I know all about you! I'll tell her you're here!' and she came running out with all the other girls looking on and we embraced.

What was left of the battalion reformed at a tented encampment at Okehampton. The amazing thing was that the RSM put me on a charge because my boots were dirty. I was brought in front of the colonel and I told him that I had no cleaning gear and no money because I'd handed my paybook to the RSM when he'd sent me out on patrol in Hazebrouck. At first the RSM denied any knowledge of this but eventually the adjutant said that he'd seen some paybooks handed in. After that the colonel was pretty good and I got some money and cleaned up my boots.

Corporal Charles 'Bert' Nash
2nd Bulk Petrol Transport Company, Royal Army Service Corps

There was one incident on our way to Chester. I looked out the window and saw the power station at Battersea – which was literally at the bottom of my front garden. They wouldn't let us out, so there was nothing I could do about it. Then a little miracle came along. A chap strolled along the train platform – an auxiliary fireman – and I looked at him and thought, 'I know your face' – and the penny dropped. He lived halfway down my street. I said, 'Hey, are you George Brown?' He looked at me and said, 'Yes,' and he came over and, underneath my ten days' growth of beard, he spotted who I was. He said, 'God almighty – you're Bert Nash! You're dead!' I said, 'I'm here! I wonder if you could get a message to my parents and my wife to tell them I'm safe?' He said, 'Bloody hell – by all means.' So I wrote a little message on an empty Woodbine packet. That turned out to be one of the greatest things that could have happened, because my unit as a whole had left France ten days before me, and the commanding officer had reported me as adrift and missing. Unfortunately, being right on the job, the War Department had notified my wife that I was missing. That was confirmed by many of the members of my unit that were home on leave, calling in and seeing my parents and wife, who naturally asked,

'Where's our Bert?' and they said, 'Oh, I don't know, Mr Nash. We had to leave him behind. The last time I saw him was so and so…' So it left our house in Fulham a very, very sad home. Then to receive a message, an actual confirmation of a sighting of me by a neighbour, saying he'd seen me at Chelsea station, supported by a little letter on a Woodbine packet – I can imagine what must have taken place in my house.

Aircraftwoman 2nd Class Edith Heap
Women's Auxiliary Air Force

Dunkirk didn't seem like a disaster. Once Dunkirk was lost, the feeling was, 'Oh good, now we're on our own, we'll manage.' Which of course was probably very stupid, but that was our feeling – elation, because we were by ourselves and we could do our own thing.

Captain Peter Barclay
2nd Battalion, Royal Norfolk Regiment

I think we had been shockingly badly equipped. Some of the equipment we had, we'd not trained with. There was a shortage of ammunition. We'd had very good commanding officers who had trained us remarkably well in the more orthodox forms of warfare, but we hadn't done enough movement at night by transport. Nor had we done enough actual warfare training at night. The commanders were terribly rigid in their attitude, and there was a lack of learning about the enemy's techniques. I know this because I had previously commanded Battle School and we used to base our teachings, as much as we could, on the German training manuals and we learnt an awful lot from them.

It was not, at that time, considered to be a defeat, purely because I think the British Army wasn't used to having defeats. It was only later that it bore on one's mind that in fact it had been a complete and utter defeat – but it wasn't as though our morale was low. In my unit all the things we'd been asked to do we'd done – we'd blown up all our bridges on time, and our casualties had not been excessive.

Leon Wilson
French gunner – served with 229 Heavy Artillery Regiment

Ten years later, after the war, I said to my wife that I wanted to see the village where I stopped outside Dunkirk, but I couldn't remember its name. After travelling for half an hour, I recognised the church from a distance, and I had to stop. When I got there, it was exactly the same. I could see where we were sitting, and I could see the shop on the right-hand side with bicycles. But to be honest – I was a coward. I couldn't go in to say that I was sorry for pinching some of their bicycles. But I was very upset for seeing the place that saved our lives.

Corporal Charles 'Bert' Nash
2nd Bulk Petrol Transport Company, Royal Army Service Corps

I was allowed home for a fortnight's leave. Now, my father had retired as a police officer, and he'd acquired a nice little general store in Fulham. Rationing had started, but he still had a reasonable supply of food and when I got in, my mother said to me, 'Now, my boy, you must be starving. What would you like?' I said that I'd like a nice omelette. While she was looking at me and talking to me, she cracked about 11 eggs into the frying pan – so I had the biggest omelette I'd ever had. She didn't do it intentionally, but she was so absorbed looking at me, she just kept cracking eggs, and the blasted omelette was so big it was more like a Christmas cake.

Stephane Hessel
Served with French Army

I had the feeling that the ones who betrayed the alliance were the French. I never felt that the British did anything that they shouldn't have done. We know that some people were critical of the way the evacuation was made, and there were critical attitudes expressed in the French press. But as far as I am concerned – and the people with whom I had contact – they felt right from June 1940, that the British were our only hope, and what they did was the best they could do. I never had any feeling of lack of solidarity with Great Britain over this whole period.

Lance Corporal Lawrence Greggain
5th Battalion, Border Regiment

Immediately I got home, I had nightmares about people attacking me, and if unexpectedly woken up in the night, I would quite often take up a fighting position instinctively. It went on for three or four years, but it doesn't happen now.

Corporal Charles 'Bert' Nash
2nd Bulk Petrol Transport Company, Royal Army Service Corps
It took about ten days for my morale to increase. I felt very dejected when I arrived. But once the danger had gone, I appreciated what had happened, and how lucky I was. I had a damn good weep, I don't mind admitting it.

Lance Corporal Lawrence Greggain
5th Battalion, Border Regiment
I think the war hardened me. It made me more callous, I suppose. Putting not too fine a word on things – it made me more brutal. When there is brutality, you become almost half-consciously infected by it yourself.

Eileen Livett
British Red Cross Nurse
We saw these evacuated men as heroes, because we all realised how tight the situation had been. From the little information we got over the wireless, we knew they were fighting a retreat, and it was really touch and go. We were very much aware of the miracle of them being saved.

A wounded French soldier comes ashore at Dover

Index of Contributors

Entries in **bold** type indicate photographs

Adams, Lance Corporal Albert [21129] 200, 284–5

Allen, Ordinary Seaman Stanley [6825] 212, 231, 233, 240, 252

Andow, Corporal George [7196] 285

Andrews, Captain Harold Ervine [12209] 135, 166, 167, 169, 288

Annand, 2nd Lieutenant Richard [10416] 6, 10, 17, 25–6, 47

Ashcroft, Gerald [10086] 183, 185, 208, 230, 292

Baldwin, Signaller Alfred [6491] 126, 128, 136–7, 188, 189, 192, 194, 196, 198, 205, 217–18, 290–1

Barclay, Captain Peter [8192] 12–13, 15, 34, **35**, 37, 45–7, 48, 53, 61, 63, 65–6, 78, 79, 81, 82, 83–4, 285, 297

Bartley, Pilot Officer Tony [11086] 224, 227

Beamont, Flying Officer Roland [19128] 73, 91–2

Beaton, Sapper Percy [6322] 6, 7, 8, 19, 21, 29, 30, 32, 36, 71, 72, 76, 78, 86

Begg, Engine Room Artificer Andrew [10782] 213, 214

Bird-Wilson, Flying Officer Harold [10782] 73, 224, 225, **226**

Bredin, Captain (Acting) Humphrey 'Bala' [12139] vii, 48, 49–51, 60, 66–7, 129, 162, 190, 199, 203, **204**, 234, 236, 284

Brown, Private Robert [10393] 71, 153–5

Burton, Private Victor [18204] 36, 134, 183, 212, 287–8

Butland, Sister Catherine Mary [6811] 110

Carter, Sapper Frederick [6488] 4, 6, 7, 10

Carter, Captain (Acting) Stewart [7039] 77–8

Carver, Lance-Corporal Kenneth [6493] 68, 72, 88, 129, 289

Cheeseman, Trooper Ernest [18516] vii, 129–30, 273–5

Chrisp, Bosun John [16843] 243, 249

Cocke, Lieutenant Wilbur [6378] 196, 200, 208, 243

Codd, Francis [9341] 231

Coupland, Sergeant Robert [17746] 211

Curry, Private Frank [19770] 134, 140, 145, **164**, 165, 166, 167, 169, 170–1

Curtis, 2nd Lieutenant Arthur [16268] 220–1, 243, 245, 294

Dance, Private Albert [18258] 60, 128, 129, 174–5, 236, 295–6

Deere, Flight Lieutenant Alan [10478] 225, 227

Dennis, Private Harry [6371] 12, 20, 60–1, 63–4, 85–6, 125, 219

Dibbens, Lieutenant Harold [6388] 222

Doe, Lance Corporal Edward [7329] 118–20, 122, 124

Draycott, Corporal Donald [8214] 268–70, 272, 273

Dreyer, Christopher [8984] 194, 292–3

Dundas, Pilot Officer Hugh [10159] 227

Edge, Flight Lieutenant Gerald [12674] 227

Eldred, Leading Seaman Ernest Frederick [6901] 183, 193, 229, 239

Elliott, Private David [16706] 26–7, 64, 101, 109, 110–11

English, Second Lieutenant Ian [6413] 91, 93–5, 97, 133, 228, 284

Evans, Private Bert [10730] 146, 149–50, 151, 152, 153

Fahey, Gunner Brian [10433] 147–9, 150–3

Fox-Pitt, Brigadier William [7038] 102

Frederick, Sergeant Alexander 'Sandy' [19804] 28

Green, Lance Sergeant Robert [6226] 90, 111, 113, 125, 135, 139–40, 174, 175, 205, 206–7, 209, 215, 246–7

Greggain, Lance Corporal Lawrence [24615] vii, 6–7, 24, 25, 289, 298, 299

Griffith-Williams, Lieutenant Colonel Eric [4517] 234, 245–6

Haines, Aircraftman Leslie [20523] 294

Harding, Lance Bombardier William [6323] 7–8, 10, 11, 24, 27, 29–30, 34

Hawkins, Captain Paul [6931] 258–9, 260

Heap, Aircraftwoman 2nd Class Edith [13927] 297

Helyer, Richard [9394] 231, 251–2

Heron, Able Seaman Reginald [22385] 214, **244**, 250

Hessel, Stephane [10731] 65, 86, 298

Hill, Captain James [6348] 43, 51, 53, 86, 90, 91, 113, 114, 233

Hollway, Captain Stephen [6359] 58, 64–5, 76, 77, 203, 205–6, 219

Horsburgh-Porter, Major Andrew [905] 199

Houlton-Hart, 2nd Lieutenant Darby [15355] 133

Howard, Sergeant Leonard [6837] 42, 140, 161, 163, 194, 200–2, 292

Hurrell, Armament Quartermaster Sergeant Frank [6677] 102, 104, 169–70, 186–8, 190, 201

Jeffreys, Lieutenant Colonel Peter [9237] 92, 131, 133, 208

Joscelyne, Arthur [9768] 181–2, 192, 230–1, 242, 249, 293

King, Seaman Thomas [6973] 182–3, 185, 193, 230

Knight, Sergeant William [6627] vii, 118, 173–4, 262–8, 272–3

Lambert, Private George [16723] 64, 247, 289

Lang, Captain Derek [7167] 258, 259–60

Ledger, Corporal George [16722] 163, 221, 222

Leggett, Private Ernest [17761] 12, 13, 43, 45–6, 66, 67, 68, 73–4, 78, 79, 81–3, 84–5

Livett, Eileen [12514] 287, 288–9, 290, 291, 295, 299

Love, Private Samuel [6728] 124–5, 137, 139, 163, 189, 250

Maggs, Stoker Charles [9377] 242

Martin, 2nd Lieutenant Peter [12669] viii, 47, 48–9, 126, 175, 215, 221–2

Matthews, Flying Officer Peter [10451] 73

McBeath, Lieutenant Commander John [2808] 193, 207, 213, 229, 230, 240

McCloughin, Lieutenant D'Arcy [6442] 16, 25, 45, 49, 61, 101, 162, 163, 165, 212, 222, 240, 242

McLane, Sergeant Major Martin [10165] 224

Metelmann, Henry [8171] 278–9

Mitchell, Sergeant Richard [11364] 224–5

Morgan, Colonel William [3948] 16

Moulton, Captain James [6818] 59–60, 131, 185–6

Myers, Corporal Thomas [10166] 165

Nash, Corporal Charles [6464] 126, 162, 180, 189, 195, 200, 218, 249, 286, 296–7, 298, 299
Nethercott, Able Seaman Ian [7186] 183, 207, 213–14, 215, 242–3
Newborough, Robert [9721] 212, 228, 250
Nuttall, Private Sidney [21116] **69**, 71–2, 78, 190, 219, 233, 245

Pardoe, 2nd Lieutenant Philip [6465] 32, 119, 120–1, 123–4
Priest, Private Stanley [10695] 155–7

Rabbets, Private Edgar [6552] 67–8, 70, 87, 88, 90–1, 107, 108, 111, 113, 200, 201, 217, 290
Redfern, Lieutenant John [20972] 275–7
Reeves, Major William [6626] 102, 104–7, 194
Rhodes, Captain Anthony [6703] 15, 37, 41–2, 46, 59, 60, 114, 180–1, 187, 188, 190, 192, 196, 239, 284
Ridley, Private William [16729] 72, 91, 111, 130, 131, 135–6, 181, 195, 233, 247, 249, 288
Roell, Werner [12563] 74
Russ, Private Thomas [14979] 8

Scarborough, Reverend Cyril [4820] 10, 140–1
Schöpfel, Gerhard [14770] 224
Sheppard, Robert [10445] 277–8
Smith, Private Matthew [6325] 198–9

Taylor, Aircraftman 2nd Class Arthur [7336] 43, 46
Taylor, Captain Anthony [8993] 70
Tombs, Private Alfred [10725] **144**, 146–7, 149, 150
Tomlin, Sapper Harold [16606] 188, 203
Tomlinson, Ronald [9728] 182, 209, 251

Vaux, 2nd Lieutenant Peter [6614] 15–16, 21, 29, 32, 42, 65, 91, 92–3, 94, 95, 97–9

Walker, Captain Henry Faure [6611] 16–17, 19, 21–3, 24, 26, 33, 36, 47, 49, 67
Walters, Yeoman of Signals Wilfred [7022] 181, 193, 199, 229, 251
Watson, Bugler Edward [7194] 121–3, 124, 141
Wells, Lance Corporal John [12370] 189, 211, 219–20, 228, 294
West, Private George [10726] 148, 149, 150
White, Captain Gilbert [6275] 42, 43, 58–9, 74, 76, 101–2, 118, 130, 173, 285–6
Williams, Sergeant John [11939] 6, 7, 8, 10, 11, 19, 20, 23, 24, 25, 26, 28, 30, 32, 33, 34, 59, 165, 166, 167
Wilson, Leon [20137] 297–8
Wilson-Haffenden, Major Donald [6394] 11, 17, 20, 203, 234, 286–7

Younger, 2nd Lieutenant Allan Elton [6361] 99–101, 133–4, 137, 162–3, 209, 211

Index

Entries in **bold** type indicate photographs

Aa, River 106

Aalst 46

Abbeville bridgehead 257

Achicourt 95

Adam, General 186

Admiralty 239

air war 36, 37, 41, 42, 43–4, 45, 46

  Dornier bomber 225

  Dunkirk, Luftwaffe attacks upon
evacuation at 179, 180, 181, 182,
185, 186, 187–8, 189, 190, 191, 192,
193, 194, 195, 198, 201, 202, 206,
207, 208, **210**, 213, 214, 215, 217,
219, 222, 224–8, 229, 230, 231, 233,
242, 245, 246, 249, 250, 257, 260,
268, 269, 270, 271, 273, 274, 275,
286–7

  Dunkirk, RAF air cover for evacuation
at 224–5, **226**, 227

  Dunkirk, ships sunk by Luftwaffe
during evacuation at 180, 182, 187,
193, 198, 201, 207, **210**, 214, 219,
222, 227, 230, 231, 250, 257, 260,
269, 271

  French Air Force 101

  Hurricane 46, 225, 270

  Junkers 87 (Stuka) dive-bomber 57, 72,
73–4, 93, 94, 98, 120, 131, 136, 146,
166, 185, 190, 195, 198, 201, 202,
214, 222, 228, 242, 245

  Luftwaffe *see* Luftwaffe

  Messerschmitt 43, 46, 73, 190, 192,
224, 225, 227

  RAF *see* RAF

  refugees, Luftwaffe attack unarmed 43,
45, 53, 72, 73

  retreat to Dunkirk, Luftwaffe attack
Allied **56**, 57, 72, 73–4, 91, 93, 94,
95, 110, 117, 120, 130, 131, 136, 137,
138, 146, 166

  Spitfire 225, 227

Albany 219

alcohol, British Army use of 25–6, 85–6,
109, 111, 121–2, 137, 165, 194–5, 196,
200, 267

Alexander, General 234

Alexander, Ken 199

Allies *see under individual nation and army
name*

Amiens 20, 57

Ardennes 4, 41, 57, 153

Armentières 114, 131, **132**

Arras 57, 91, 92, 93, 95, 99, 101

artillery 7–8, 10, 11, 15, 24, 27, 29–30,
34, 43, 46, 49, 61, 63, 64, 81, 95, 101,
106, **116**, 119, 124–5, 126, 128, 133,
134, 136–7, 139, 140, 147–9, 150–3,
165, 169–70, 188, 189, 192, 194, 196,
198, 200, 205, 208, 211, 217–18, 234,
240, 243, 245–6, 285, 290–1, 297–8

Baldry, Bill 201, 202

battledress 6, 10, 19, 34, 83, 135, 201–2,
205

BBC 118, 258

Beauvais 267

Belgian Army:

  Dunkirk evacuation of 199

quality of 34, 47, 58–9, 199
retreating 37, 58–9
surrender of 135, 180
Belgium 4, 110
  Allied retreat through vii, 51, 53, **56**,
    57, 58–61, **62**, 63–8, 70–2
  fifth columnists in 86, 87–8
  fighting in 37, 42, 43, **44**, 45–51, **52**,
    53, **56**, 57, 58–61, **62**, 63–8, 70–2
  Germany invades 4
  people, Allied soldiers relations with
    43, **44**, 45, 46–7, 60–1, 62, 67–8,
    98–9
  refugees 43, 45, 48, 53, **89**
  surrender 135, 180
Bell, Bill 247
Bergues 117, 131; 133, 134, **160**, 165, 170
billeting 10, 12, 21–3, 26, **31**
Blanchard, General 117
blitzkrieg vii, 36
Bock, General von 4
Boulogne 102, 152
Bray–Dunes 179, 233, 234
Bren gun **40**, 45, 50, 78, 79, 94, 95, 113,
  135, 146, 169, 206, 215, 228, 275
Bresle, River 258
Brest 257, 275
bridges, blowing up 48, 53, **62**, 76, 77,
  78, 88, 105–6, 267, 297
British Army units:
  1st Division, HQ 11, 16, 17, 20, 203,
    234, 286–7
  1st Fife and Forfar Yeomanry 28
  7th Guards Brigade 205
    HQ 16–17, 19, 21–3, 24, 26, 33, 36,
      47, 49, 67
  15/19th Hussars 48
  51st (Highland) Division 257, 258,
    267
  Bedfordshire and Hertfordshire
    Regiment, 2nd Battalion 90, 111,
    113, 125, 135, 139–40, 174, 175, 205,
    206–7, 209, 215, 246–7
  Berkshire Regiment 125
  Border Regiment 18, **103**, **112**, 190,
    233
    1st Battalion 71–2, 78, 190, 219, 245

4th Battalion **112**
  5th Battalion 6–7, 24, 25, 27, 73,
    87–8, 107–9, 128, 175, 287, 298, 299
British Expeditionary Force (BEF) *see*
  British Expeditionary Force (BEF)
Cameron Highlanders 258, 259–60
Cheshire Regiment, 2nd Battalion 47,
  48–9, 126, 175, 215, 221–2
Coldstream Guards, 1st Battalion 47
Durham Light Infantry 95
  2nd Battalion 6, 10, 17, 25–6, 47, 224
  6th Battalion 6, 7, 8, 10, 11, 19, 20,
    23, 24, 25, 26, 28, 30, 32, 33, 34, 59,
    92, 131, 133, 165, 166, 167, 208
  8th Battalion 91, 93–5, 97, 133, 163,
    221, 222, 228, 284
  9th Battalion 64, 72, 91, 111, 130,
    131, 135–6, 181, 195, 233, 247, 249,
    288, 289
  10th Battalion 165
East Lancashire Regiment, 1st
  Battalion 36, 134, 135, 140, 145, 165,
  166, 167, 169, 170–2, 212, 287–8
East Riding Yeomanry 211
East Surrey Regiment 77, 135
  1st Battalion 12, 20, 60–1, 63–4,
    85–6, 125, 166, 219
  1/6th Battalion 42, 43, 58–9, 74, 76,
    101–2, 118, 130, 173, 285–6
  2/6th Battalion 275–7
East Yorkshire Yeomanry 200, 284–5
Grenadier Guards 49, 51
  3rd Battalion 206
Hampshire Regiment, 2nd Battalion
  198–9
Irish Guards 102
King's Royal Hussars, The15th/19th
  70
King's Royal Rifle Corps, 2nd
  Battalion 32, 118–21, 122, 123–4
Lincolnshire Regiment, 2nd Battalion
  33
Northamptonshire Regiment, 5th
  Battalion 67–8, 70, 87, 88, 90–1, 107,
  108, 111, 113, 200, 201, 217, 290
Nottinghamshire and Derbyshire
  Regiment, 2nd Battalion 77–8

Operations Section, General Staff
  Officer, Grade 3 59–60, 131, 185–6
Pioneers 30, 32, 166
Queen Victoria's Rifles 1st Battalion
  121–3, 124, 141
Queen's Royal West Kent Regiment
  166, 167
Rifle Brigade 60, 128, 129, 174–5, 236,
  295–6
Royal Army Medical Corps 206, 217
  5 General Hospital 110
  12th Field Ambulance 124–5, 137,
    139, 163, 189, 250
  141st Field Ambulance 26–7, 64,
    101, 109, 110–11
  159 Field Ambulance 110
Royal Army Ordnance Corps 71–2, 78,
  233
  3rd Army Field Workshop 102, 104,
    169–70, 186–8, 190, 201, 245
Royal Army Service Corps 155–7,
  234
  2nd Bulk Petrol Transport Company
    126, 162, 180, 189, 195, 200, 218,
    249, 286, 296–7, 298, 299
  5th Motor Ambulance Convoy 68,
    72, 88, 129, 289
Royal Artillery
  2nd Regiment, 6th Battery 7–8, 10,
    11, 24, 27, 29–30, 34
  27th Field Regiment 234, 245–6
  51st Heavy Artillery, Signal Section
    196, 200, 208, 243
  52nd Anti-Tank Regiment, 208
    Battery 147–9, 150–3
  61st Medium Regiment 43, 46
  65th Field Regiment 126, 128, 136–7,
    188, 189, 192, 194, 196, 198, 205,
    217–18, 290–1
  229 Heavy Artillery Regiment 137,
    240, 285, 297–8
Royal Corps of Military Police 139,
  213
  102 Provost Company 222
Royal Engineers 53, 212
  No 1 General Base Depot 118,
    173–4, 262–8, 272–3
  7th Field Company 220–1, 243, 245,
    294
  9 Field Company 16, 25, 45, 49, 61,
    101, 162, 163, 165, 212, 222, 240,
    242
  23 Field Company 188, 203
  61 Chemical Warfare Company
    99–101, 133–4, 137, 162–3, 209, 211
  135 Excavator Company 4, 6, 208,
    251
  210 Field Company 42, 76, 140, 161,
    163, 194, 200–2, 292
  218 Army Troops Company 6, 7, 8,
    19, 21, 29, 30, 32, 35, 71, 72, 76, 78,
    86
  253 Field Company 15, 37, 41–2, 46,
    59, 60, 114, 180–1, 187, 188, 190,
    192, 196, 239, 284
  Artisans Works Company 4, 6, 7, 10,
    194–5
  Field Park Company 58, 64–5, 76, 77,
    203, 205–6, 219
Royal Fusiliers 31
  2nd Battalion 43, 51, 53, 86, 90, 91,
    113, 114, 233
Royal Marines 256
Royal Norfolk Regiment, 2nd
  Battalion 12–13, 15, 34, 35, 37, 43,
  45, 45–7, 48, 53, 61, 63, 65–6, 67, 68,
  71, 73–4, 78, 79, 81–5, 145, 153–5,
  258–9, 260, 285, 297
Royal Sussex Regiment 131
  4th Battalion 10, 140–1
Royal Tank Regiment 96
  3rd Battalion 102, 104–7, 194
  4th Battalion 15–16, 21, 29, 32, 42,
    65, 91, 92–3, 94, 95, 97–9, 285
  5th Battalion 129–30, 273–5
  7th Battalion 93
Royal Ulster Rifles, 2nd Battalion 48,
  49–51, 60, 66–7, 139, 162, 190, 199,
  203, 234, 236, 284
Royal Warwickshire Regiment, 2nd
  Battalion 145, 146–7, 148, 149–50,
  151, 152, 153
South Staffordshire Regiment, 6th
  Battalion 189, 211, 219–20, 228, 294

Welsh Guards 101, 102
 1st Battalion 99
 2nd Battalion 102
Women's Auxiliary Air Force 297
British Expeditionary Force (BEF):
 I Corps 57
 II Corps 57, 101
 Belgian people, relationship with
  43, **44**, 45, 46–7, 60–1, 62, 67–8,
  98–9
 Belgium, fighting in 37, 42, 43, **44**,
  45–51, **52**, 53, **56**, 57, 58–61, **62**,
  63–8, 70–2
 Belgium, retreat through vii, 51, 53,
  56, 57, 58–61, **62**, 63–8, 70–2
 billeting 10, 12, 21–3, 26, **31**
 defeat/failure/shame viii, 3, 124,
  135, 136, 233, 283, 286, 288, 289,
  297
 departure for and arrival in France
  6–11, **9**
 diet/rations 10, 45, 66, 68, 85–6, 109,
  128, 137, 141, 245, 246, 249, 275,
  285, 286, 287, 290, 294
 exhaustion within 130, 131, 141, 161,
  163, 173, 175, 194, 196, **197**, 212,
  219, 239, 240, 251, 275, 286, 287,
  289, 292, 293, 295
 France, retreat through 72–114
 French people, relationship with 11,
  24, 25, 26–30, 33, 125
 heroes, returning troops greeted in
  Britain as viii, 43, 239, 283, 284, 288,
  291, 299
 joining up 4, 6
 leisure time 25–30, 125
 mail, censorship of 32
 march to war 37, 41–53
 massacres of troops by SS 145–57
 medical support services 26–7, 64, 83,
  84–5, 101, 109, 110–11, 124–5, 137,
  139, 152, 163, 170, 189, 196, 217,
  218, 219, 220, 229, 242–3, 250, 277,
  287, 288–9, 290, 291, 295
 morale 7, 8, 19, 20, 58, 65, 71, 90–1,
  93, 94, 154, 167, 221, 228, 239,
  246–7, 285, 290, 297, 299

 psychology of soldiers/shell shock 63,
  74, 94, 153, 167, 190, 199, 200, 201,
  212, 215, 247, 289, 291, 294, 298, 299
 remaining troops in France after
  Dunkirk 257
 repatriation of wounded soldiers 153,
  156
 reservists 11, 33, 53, 61, 65, 73, 82
 return home 239–53
 second evacuation of 257–8
 second force sent to France **256**, 257
 training 6, 17–18, 19, 33, 45, 49, 51,
  63, 71–2, 123, 288, 297
 see also British Army units
Brooke, Sir Alan 257
brothels, British soldiers visit 26–8, 32
Brown, George 296
Brussels 47, 48, 59, 60–1, 63, 64, 67–8,
 70, 72
Buchy 265, 267
Burton, Captain 183

Calais 104, 105, 117, 118–24, 126, 156,
 179, 212, 225, 243
canoes, use of 180, 202, 228
Cassel 146
casualties/wounded soldiers vii, 81,
 82–5, 94, 95, 130, 131, 161, 162, **168**,
 173, 174, 175, 180, 189, 199, 206,
 208, 211, 217, 218, 219, 220, 222,
 225, 229, 233, 234, **235**, 242–3,
 257–8, 276, 288, 297
Cazenove, Colonel 47
Cervia 215
Chamberlain, Neville 3, 46
Cherbourg 257
Churchill, Winston vii, 3, **5**, 46, 117,
 124, 180, 257, 258–9, 283
cockleboats 182, 293
communications 53, 105, 205–6, 263
Compiègne 267
conscientious objectors 30
counter-attacks, Allied 57, 58, 91–3
Crested Eagle, The 231, 233

Dainville 92
Davis, 2nd Lieutenant Hugh 134

Defender 293

Denmark 3

destroyers viii, 102, 125, 166, 173, 179, 180, 186, **191**, 192, 194, 199, 202, 207, 208, 209, 211, 214, 221, 222, 228, 229, 230, 233, 234, 240, 242, 243, 245, 246, 247, 250, 268, 270, 285

diet/rations 45, 66, 68, 85–6, 109, 128, 137, 141, 245, 246, 249, 275, 285, 286, 287, 290, 294

Dill, Field Marshal 102

dogs 83, 134, 213, 240, **241**

Dornier bomber 225f

Douai area 25, 42

Dover 236, 238, 240, 243, 247–8, 250, **253**, 284, 285–6, 290, **300**

Dunkirk:

air attacks upon evacuation at 179, 180, 181, 182, 185, 186, 187–8, 189, 190, 191, 192, 193, 194, 195, 198, 201, 202, 206, 207, 208, **210**, 213, 214, 215, 217, 219, 222, 224–8, 229, 230, 231, 233, 242, 245, 246, 249, 250, 257, 260, 268, 269, 270, 271, 273, 274, 275, 286–7

arrival of Allies at 165, 175–6, 180–1

defensive perimeter 58, 117, 133, 161, 221

docks 179, 186, 194, 218, 234

embarkation of rescue fleet at 185–6, 187, 188, 189, 190, 192, 193, 194, 198–9

evacuation from 177–236

fires in 165, 179, 181, **184**, 187, 228

food and water shortages 195, 196

harbour **184**, 186–7, 219, 249, 263

lorry pier 203, **204**

mines 231, 249, 250, 262

miracle of 251–2

mole 179, 185–6, 207, 208, 209, **210**, 211, 212, 215, **216**, 217, 218, 222, 228, 233, 234, 246, 293

night operations 229

panic/chaos/lack of discipline 145, 186, 192, 193, 194, 199, 200–2, 211, 233, 246, 269

queues 188, 189, 190, 192, 194, 200, 209, 222

rescue fleet 181–3, **184**, 185, 186, **191**, 192, 193, 198, 207, 208, 209, **223**

retreat to 51, 53–114, 117–41, **112**, **116**, **127**, **132**, **138**, **160**, 161–75, **172**

ships sunk at 180, 182, 187, 193, 198, 201, 207, **210**, 214, 219, 222, 227, 230, 231, 250, 257, 260, 269, 271

suicides 201

summary justice vii, 200–1, 202, 211

'Dunkirk spirit' 228, 283

Dyle, River 4, 37, 41, 44, 46, 47, 49, 58

Dynamo, Operation 3, 118, 179, 257, 283

organisation of 179

Route X 179

Route Y 179, 250

Route Z 179

see also Dunkirk

Eben-Emael fortress 4

E-boat 250

Endeavour 293

Enghein **75**

Escaut, River 57, 59, 74, 76, 78, 79, 85, 101

executions 87–8, 143–57

exhaustion 130, 131, 141, 161, 163, 173, 175, 194, 196, **197**, 212, 219, 239, 240, 251, 275, 286, 287, 289, 292, 293, 295

fifth column activities 10, 15, 74–5, 77–8, 86, 88, 90, 171

Fleet Air Arm 212, 228, 250

Forêt de Marchiennes 45

Forge les Eaux 265

Fort de Sainghain **14**

Fortune, General 259

France:

British retreat through 72–114

civilians, British soldiers' relations with 24, 25, 26–30, 33

fifth columnists 86
Resistance 278
surrender 257, 258–9
Fransu 97
French Air Force 101
French Army 8, 61, 65, 86, 97, 102, 105, 106, 119, 136, 137, 162–3, 189, 196, 209, 211, 215, 228, 233, 234, 240, 242, 247, 265, 275, 298, **300**
1st Army 117
arrival of soldiers in England 285, **241**, **300**
discipline, equipment and training 33, 34, 65
Dunkirk evacuation of 194, 209, 211, 212, 215, 228, 231, 233, 234, 241, 242, 247
morale 33, 59–60, 65
surrender 258–9
Fresnay-sur-Sarthe 11, 23
Furnes 117, 173

Gamelin, General **5**
gas attacks 49, 122
Gaulle, Charles de 258, 285
German Army:
Belgium, fighting in 37, 42, 43, **44**, 45–51, **52**, 53, **56**, 57, 58–61, **62**, 63–8, 70–2
discipline 260
enters Paris 256
halts Panzer advance 18 miles from Dunkirk 58, 161
impersonation of British soldiers and nuns 74–5, 77–8, 88, 90
massacres of unarmed Allied prisoners 143–57
Phoney War, Allied attitudes towards during 13, 19
professionalism 141, 155
reserves 141
ruthless nature of 43, 45, 53, 71, 72, 73, 143–57
see also German Army units *and* Luftwaffe
German Army units:
1st Battalion SS Totenkopf ('Death's Head') Division, 2nd Infantry Regiment 145, 155–7
Army Group A 57
Army Group B 4, 57, 58, 161
glider troops 4
Panzer Divisions 4, 41, 57, 58, 92, 104, 105, 108, 109, 161, 262, 278–9
SS 145, 146–57, 260
SS Liebstandarte Adolf Hitler Regiment 145
girlfriends, French 29–30, 125
Givenchy 97
Goering, Hermann 58
Gort Line 4, 15–37, **18**
Gort, Lord 4, **5**, 21, 113, 117
character 59–60
counter-attacks, plans 57, 58, 91
decision to evacuate 58, 113, 117
Gravelines 105, 106, 245
Guderian, General Heinz 41
Guines 104

Hagan, John 154
Halifax, Lord 117
Hall, Private 150
Halluin 20
Harvester, HMS 183, 193, 229, 239
Havelock 270, 272
Hazebrouck 102, 128, 296
Hebe 201
heroes, returning Allied troops greeted in Britain as viii, 43, 239, 283, 284, 288, 291, 299
Hesdin 263
Hitler, Adolf vii, 3, 4, 6, 57, 58, 117, 180
Holland 4, 41
hospital ships 180, 217, 218, 231–2
humour in battle vii, 78, 153
Hurricane 46, 225, 270

Icarus, HMS 213, 214, 245
Imperial War Museum vii
Ironside, General **5**
Isle of Man paddle steamer vii, 234, 236, **248**

Jasper, HMS 243, 249
Johnson, Jimmy 169
joining up 4, 6
Junkers 87 (Stuka) dive-bomber 57, 72, 73–4, 93, 94, 98, 120, 131, 136, 146, 166, 185, 190, 195, 198, 201, 202, 214, 222, 228, 242, 245

Keith, HMS 183, 207, 213–14, 215, 242–3, 250
Kelly, Tommy 287–8
Kerkhove Bridge 77
Knöchlein, Hauptsturmführer Fritz 145

L'Étoile 98
La Bassée canal 97, 153
La Panne 174, 175, 179, 185, 186, 203, 205–6, 236
La Tombe 47
Lambton, Major 165
Lancastria 257–8, 268–70, **271**, 272
Le Mans 10
Le Paradis 145, 153–7
Le Tréport 21, 29
leaflet drops 90–1
leisure time 25–8
Les Moeres 133
Letitia 293
Leuze 43
Lightoller, Commander 183, 185, 230, 292
Ligne de Contact 13
Lille 17, 20, 26–7, 72, 73, 125
'little ships' 179, **191**
London Fire Brigade 231, 251–2
Louvain **40**, 60, 61, **62**, 66
Luftwaffe 43, 45, 57, 58, 74, **103**, 137, 222, 224, 269, 270, 283
  Dornier bomber 225
  Dunkirk, attacks upon evacuation at 179, 180, 181, 182, 185, 186, 187–8, 189, 190, 191, 192, 193, 194, 195, 198, 201, 202, 206, 207, 208, **210**, 213, 214, 215, 217, 219, 222, 224–8, 229, 230, 231, 233, 242, 245, 246, 249, 250, 257, 260, 268, 269, 270, 271, 273, 274, 275, 286–7

Junkers 87 (Stuka) dive-bomber 57, 72, 73–4, 93, 94, 98, 120, 131, 136, 146, 166, 185, 190, 195, 198, 201, 202, 214, 222, 228, 242, 245
Messerschmitt 43, 46, 73, 190, 192, 224, 225, 227
refugees, attacks unarmed 43, 45, 53, 72, 73
retreat to Dunkirk, attacks Allied **56**, 57, 72, 73–4, 91, 93, 94, 95, 110, 117, 120, 130, 131, 136, 137, **138**, 146, 166
Luxembourg 4
Lynn-Allen, Captain 146, 149
Lys, River 101–2

Maginot Line 4, 11, 12–15, **14**, 29
mail, censorship of 32
Malo-les-Bains 179
Manstein, General Erich von 4
maps:
  Dunkirk **178**
  North France and Belgium **2**
Marck 105, 125, 126, 225
Marcoing 124, 139
Margate 211, 245, 294
Marque, River 16–17
massacres 143–57
  Le Paradis 153–7
  Wormhout 146–53
Massey 251
medical support services 26–7, 64, 83, 84–5, 101, 109, 110–11, 124–5, 137, 139, 152, 163, 170, 189, 196, 217, 218, 219, 220, 229, 242–3, 250, 277, 287, 288–9, 290, 291, 295
Menin Gate 102
Messerschmitt 43, 46, 73, 190, 192, 224, 225, 227
Meuse, River 4, 41
Mohnke, Hauptsturmführer Wilhelm 145, 153
mole, Dunkirk 179, 185–6, 207, 208, 209, **210**, 211, 212, 215, **216**, 217, 218, 222, 228, 233, 234, 246, 293
Mongomery, General 23
Mont des Cats 133–4

Montgomery, General 23, 50
Moore, Sergeant 150
Moore, Sir John 113
morale 8, 19, 20, 58, 65, 71, 90–1, 93, 94, 154, 167, 221, 228, 239, 246–7, 285, 290, 297, 299
mortars 64, 81, 82, 95, 106, 107, 133, 146, 154, 161, 162, 169
Mussolini, Benito 117
Mustang Mark III **226**

Nantes 29, 30, 278
Nazi-Soviet Pact 65
Nieuport 117
Norway 3, 7, 36
nuns, Germans dressed as 74, 76, 90

O'Callaghan, Bill 155, 156, 157
occupation of France, German 277, 278–9
Oranse 268, 272
Oudenaarde 64, 74

Paddy 136, 137, 140, 169, 196, 217, 218, 290–1
Padfield, Captain 148
Parks, George 161
Pétain, Marshal 4
Petit Maginot Line 15, 16
Petit Vimy 91
Poix 264
Pont-Remy 99
Pooley, Bert 156–7
Poperinghe 133, 136, 137, 139
Prague 233
Princessa, SS 189, 211, 228, 294
prisoners:
  British 13, 15, 70, 74–5, 123–4, 133, 140–1, 143–57, 169, 170–1, 260, **261**, 265–6, 292
  German **103**, 205, 265, 288–9
Provin 111
psychology of soldiers/shell shock 63, 74, 94, 153, 167, 190, 199, 200, 201, 212, 215, 247, 289, 291, 294, 298, 299

RAF (Royal Air Force) 7, 101, 223, 273
  1 Squadron 73
  13 (Army Co-operation) Squadron 43, 46
  17 Squadron 73, 224, 225
  54 Squadron 225, 227
  87 Squadron 73, 91–2
  92 Squadron 224, 227
  98 Squadron 268–70, 272, 273
  229 Squadron 224–5
  605 Squadron 227
  616 Squadron 227
  defence of Dunkirk evacuation 224–5, **226**, 227
  Fighter Command 224, 283
  Forward Air Ammunition Park 294
Ramsay, Vice Admiral Bertram 118, 179, 186
Ramsgate 286
Red Cross, British 84, 180, 285, 287, 288–9, 290, 291, 295, 299
refugees 43, 45, 48, 51, 53, 72, 73, **89**, 98, 100–1, 129–30, 273, 276
Reliance 293
repatriation of wounded soldiers 153, 156
Renaix 76, 77
Renown 182, 293
rescue fleet 181–3, **184**, 185, 186, **191**, 192, 193, 198, 207, 208, 209, **223**
reservists 11, 33, 53, 61, 65, 73, 82
Resistance, French 278
Resolute 293
Rommel, General Erwin 92, 259
Rosenael 262, 263
Ross, HMS 193, 199, 229, 251
Roubaix 22
Rouen 99, 265, 266–7, 268
rowing boats 192, 198–9
Royal Daffodil 211, 284
Royal Navy viii, 102, 180, 183, 194, 198, 199, 206, 207, 208, 211, 212, 213, 229, 230, 242–3, 249, 250, 251, 252, 257–8, 260, 292–3
Runstedt, General von 58
Ryder, Major 154, 155

Saint Amand 65
Sandown, HMS **238**
Scimitar, HMS 208, 243
Sedan 41, 59
Senlis 267, 268
shame, British soldier's reaction to
    withdrawal from France 135, 136, 163,
    165, 166, 233, 288
Shannon 181–2, 192, 230–1, 242, 249,
    293
Sharpshooter, HMS 182–3, 185, 193, 230
Shearwater, HMS 242
Shropshire 277
Siegfried Line 11, 19, 250
Simpson, Colonel 165
snipers 50, 51, 60, 107–9, 123, 134
Soignes, Forest of 42
Somme 97–8, 161, 257, 258, 263
Soviet Union 65
Spitfire 225, 227
St Malo 257
St Nazaire 257, 268, 272
St Valéry-en-Caux 257, 258, 259, 260,
    261
Steenvorde 133
summary justice, British vii, 200–1, 202,
    211
Sundowner 183, 185, 208, 230, 292

surrender of Allied troops 117, 119,
    123–4, 129, 135, 145, 146, 154, 155,
    169, 180, 260, 262, 276

Tankerton Towers 182, 209, 251
Tennant, Captain William 179
Tom Tit 182, 209, 251
Tournai 76
training, British troops 6, 17–18, 19, 33,
    45, 49, 51, 63, 71–2, 123, 288, 297

trawlers 180, 182, 207, **210**
Trianon 21

'uncle target' 50–1
uniforms *see* battledress

Vanquisher, HMS **216**
Veckring 15
vehicles, abandoning/destroying 133,
    135, 161, 163, **172**, 180, 193, **235**,
    260
Venomous, HMS **191**, 193, 207, 213,
    229, 230, 240
Veules-les-Roses 260
Victoria Cross 50, 82
Vimy 97, 111
Vivacious, HMS **210**

Wahagnies 59
Wakeful 250
Walrus 95
Waterloo 43
Wattrelos 42
weapons *see under individual name of
    weapon*
Wehrmacht 3, 41, 151
Whitehall, HMS 202
Williams, Peter 105
Windsor, HMS 212, 231, 233, 240,
    252
Woesten 133
Wormhout 145, 146–53
Woumen 110
Wytschaete 125

Young, Porky 125
Ypres 102
Yser, River 107